zoontologies

zoontologies

the question of the animal

Cary Wolfe, Editor

 University of Minnesota Press   Minneapolis / London

An earlier version of "Sloughing the Human," by Steve Baker, appeared in *Performance Research* 5, no. 2 (2000): 70–81; reprinted with permission from Taylor & Francis Ltd., http://www.tandf.co.uk. Portions of "Animal Body, Inhuman Face," by Alphonso Lingis, originally appeared in *Discourse* 20, no. 3 (fall 1998): 194–203; reprinted by permission of Wayne State University Press. "At a Slaughterhouse, Some Things Never Die," by Charlie LeDuff, first appeared in the *New York Times* (June 16, 2000) as part of a series on race in America; reprinted with permission of The New York Times Agency for Rights and Permissions.

Every effort was made to obtain permission to reproduce copyrighted material in this book. If any proper acknowledgment has not been made, we encourage copyright holders to notify us.

Published by the University of Minnesota Press
111 Third Avenue South, Suite 290
Minneapolis, MN 55401-2520
http://www.upress.umn.edu

Library of Congress Cataloging-in-Publication Data

Zoontologies : the question of the animal / Cary Wolfe, editor.
     p.   cm.
Includes bibliographical references and index.
    ISBN 0-8166-4105-6 (HC : alk. paper) — ISBN 0-8166-4106-4 (PB : alk. paper)
1. Animals (Philosophy) I. Wolfe, Cary.
   B105.A55 Z66 2003
   179'.3—dc21

                                        2002011805

Printed in the United States of America on acid-free paper

The University of Minnesota is an equal-opportunity educator and employer.

12 11 10 09 08 07 06 05 04 03   10 9 8 7 6 5 4 3 2 1

For Allison

About them frisking played
All the beasts of the earth . . .

Contents

Introduction

Cary Wolfe

This collection sets its sights on what is perhaps the central problematic for contemporary culture and theory, particularly if *theory* is understood as centrally engaged in addressing a social, technological, and cultural context that is now in some inescapable sense posthuman, if not quite posthumanist. Many of the leading theorists of the past three decades have devoted considerable attention to the question of the animal under a variety of figures or themes: Julia Kristeva in *Powers of Horror* and *Strangers to Ourselves* (the abject, ethnicity); Jacques Derrida in a host of texts from *Of Spirit* to *Glas, The Post Card,* and essays such as "Eating Well" and "Force of Law" (the sacrificial symbolic economies of "carnophallogocentrism"); Gilles Deleuze and Félix Guattari in *A Thousand Plateaus, Kafka: The Question of a Minor Literature,* and elsewhere (becoming-animal, the critique of Freud and of psychoanalysis); Jacques Lacan and Slavoj Žižek in any number of texts ranging from Lacan's seminars and *Écrits* to Žižek's *Enjoy Your Symptom!* and *Looking Awry* (the Thing, the Real, monstrosity); Stanley Cavell's *The Claim of Reason* ("skeptical terror of the other"); Georges Bataille in *Theory of Religion* and *Visions of Excess* and René Girard in *Violence and the Sacred* (animal sacrifice, the socius and the sacred); bell hooks in *Black Looks,* Michael Taussig in *Mimesis and Alterity,* and Étienne Balibar in his collection with Immanuel Wallerstein, *Race, Nation, and Class* (the relation of animality to exoticism, racism, and imperialism); Donna Haraway in works ranging from *Primate Visions* through *Simians, Cyborgs, and Women* to the recent *ModestWitness@SecondMillenniumFemaleManMeetsOncoMouse* (animality as a figure for "situated knowledges" and the embodiment of subjectivity, so crucial to contemporary feminist philosophy of science in Haraway and in others such as Katherine Hayles and Evelyn Fox Keller).

This list could easily be extended, of course, but my point here is that all of this work remains widely scattered among disparate and often hard-to-locate discussions episodically embedded in a wide range of texts. For example, Jacques Derrida's investigation of the sacrificial symbolic economies of "carno-phallogocentrism" has always been, for him, an absolutely central concern, but it is scattered over literally thousands of pages and more than a score of texts. But here, we have access to an incisive, focused articulation of how Derrida approaches the question of the animal in his critique of Jacques Lacan, "And Say the Animal Responded?"[1] Or again, Gilles Deleuze and Félix Guattari's discussion of "becoming-animal" remains awash in the nearly thousand pages of *A Thousand Plateaus* and, in a different vein, their studies of Kafka, Spinoza, and much else besides, so it is enormously useful to have available here the supple exploration and condensation of their work in essays by Alphonso Lingis on the dynamics of trans-species embodiment and Paul Patton on Monty Roberts, the man behind the "horse whisperer" phenomenon that has spawned a novel, a big-budget feature film, and other spin-offs.

What such popular culture phenomena indicate—quite reliably, as it turns out—is that the pressing relevance of the question of the animal has been generated in contemporary culture more outside the humanities than within. Indeed, although the place of the animal as the repressed Other of the subject, identity, logos, and the concept reaches back in Western culture at least to the Old Testament (and, in a different register, to the Platonic tradition), what is different about our own moment is that two primary factors have combined to enable an archaeology and mapping of this problematic that was unavailable for contemporaries of Freud, Sartre, or Nietzsche, even though the question of the animal in their texts called for a reading that can only be completed—or, more strictly speaking, only begun—now.

The first of these two factors is the crisis of humanism itself over the past three decades in critical theory, brought on, in no small part, first by structuralism and then poststructuralism and its interrogation of the figure of the human as the constitutive (rather than technically, materially, and discursively constituted) stuff of history and the social. Here, very schematically, one might cite as decisive Claude Lévi-Strauss's critique of Sartre's neo-Hegelian reliance on the category of consciousness in the face of what Sartre called the practico-inert, and, after that, Derrida's even more radical insistence on *différance* as unmasterable exteriority in his critique of Lévi-Strauss's own structuralism in "Structure, Sign, and Play in the Discourse of the Human Sciences." In a different theoretical register, one might equally point toward Louis Althusser's relentless dismantling of Marxist humanism and, beyond that, the work of Althusser's student, Michel Foucault, who began his ascendancy against Althusser's own philosophical idealism, made manifest in the latter's privileging of the economic and of Marxist "science" over and against what Foucault would later famously anatomize as the "discourses" and "techniques" of modernity mapped in *The Archaeology of Knowledge* and *Discipline and Punish.* To these seminal reroutings of contemporary theory away from the constitutive figure of the human in several different directions—or, more properly speaking, toward an exposure of the human's own impossibility—one must also add the new transdisciplinary theoretical paradigms that have poured into the human sciences over the past few decades (cybernetics and systems theory, chaos theory, and the like), paradigms that have had little use and little need for the figure of the human as either foundation or explanatory principle. (One might note here too what is perhaps the most subterranean story of all in contemporary theory: the steady influence of the "hard" on the "human" sciences. One thinks here of Foucault's interest in Canguilhem and Jacob, Lacan's in cybernetics, Lyotard's in chaos theory, and so on.)

The second factor, of course, is the fact toward which I have already gestured, however briefly: the radically changed place of the animal itself in areas outside the humanities. Indeed, the humanities are, in my view, now struggling to catch up with a radical revaluation of the status of nonhuman animals that has taken place in society at large. A veritable explosion of work in areas such as cognitive ethology and field ecology has called into question our ability to use the old saws of anthropocentrism (language, tool use, the inheritance of cultural behaviors, and so on) to separate ourselves once and for all from animals, as experiments in language and cognition with great apes and marine mammals, and field studies of extremely complex social and cultural behaviors in wild animals such as apes, wolves, and elephants, have more or less permanently eroded the tidy divisions between human and nonhuman. And this, in turn, has led to a broad reopening of the question of the ethical status of animals in relation to the human—an event whose importance is named but not really captured by the term *animal rights.* Indeed, as I have tried to show elsewhere, one of the central ironies of animal rights philosophy—an irony that points directly to the pressing need for this collection—is that its philosophical frame remains an essentially humanist one in its most important philosophers (utilitarianism in Peter Singer, neo-Kantianism in Tom Regan), thus effacing the very difference of the animal other that animal rights sought to respect in the first place.[2] In this, of course, animal rights philosophy is not alone in its readiness to resort to a liberal humanism it would seem to undermine in its attempt to extend the sphere of ethical and political consideration—a problematic that links the question of the animal other rather directly to other investigations in contemporary cultural studies that focus on questions of identity and subjectivity.

What was promising in the liberal philosophical tradition for the prospect of thinking the question of the animal was its emptying of the category of the subject, its insistence that subjectivity—and with it freedom—no longer depended on possession of any single identifiable attribute, such as membership in a certain race or gender. And from there it was but one short step for animal rights philosophy to insist that species too should be set aside, that membership in a given species should have no bearing on thinking the subject of freedom and rights. But the problem, of course, is that while the category of the subject was *formally* empty in the liberal tradition, it remained *materially* full of asymmetries and inequalities in the social sphere, so that theorizing the subject as "nothing in particular" could easily look like just another sign of the very privilege and mobility enjoyed by those who were quite locatable indeed on the social ladder—namely, at the top.

It is in response to what we might call this self-serving abstraction of the subject of freedom that much of the work in what is now known, for better or worse, as cultural studies and identity politics arose to reassert the social and material "location" (to use Homi Bhabha's term) or "standpoint" (to use an older vocabulary still) of the subject. The problem with *this* mode of critique is that it often reinscribes the very humanism it appears to unsettle, so that the subject, while newly "marked" by critique, is marked by means of a very familiar repertoire, one that constitutes its own repression—or what Derrida in "Eating Well" will characterize as a "sacrifice"—of the question of the animal and, more broadly still, of the nonhuman. Or, as Lyotard puts it, what such a maneuver "hurries" and "crushes" is everything he means by the terms "heterogeneity, dissensus, event, thing": "the unharmonizable." And, in this light, the point of thinking with renewed rigor the question of the animal is to disarticulate the problem of a properly postmodern pluralism from the concept of the human with which progressive political and ethical agendas have traditionally been associated—and to do so, moreover, *precisely by taking seriously* pluralism's call for attention to embodiment, to the specific materiality and multiplicity of the subject—not so much for the pragmatic reason of addressing more adequately our imbrication in the webworks of what Emerson called the "Not-Me" (the environment, from the bacterial to the ecosystemic, our various technical and electronic prosthesis, and so on), but rather for the theoretical reason that the "human," we now know, is not now, and never was, itself.[3]

What I hope to provide in this volume is not so much a comprehensive collection that somehow exhaustively maps the question of the animal and of species difference in all its various dimensions—an impossible task within any confines—but rather a set of coordinates for exploring further the very different ways in which that problem has been approached in contemporary theory and culture. Readers will be struck—and pleased, I hope—by the range they will find here, which runs from the academic and scholarly end of the spectrum (Jacques Derrida's contribution, for instance, or Judith Roof's) to the experimental philosophical writing of Alphonso Lingis and the investigative journalism of Charlie LeDuff. Some of the essays here—Derrida, Roof, Patton—work "vertically," one might say, taking a particular text, problem, or thinker and excavating it in detail. The other half of the volume, roughly—Heise, Baker, Lingis, LeDuff—is composed of essays that work more "horizontally" to survey a broad field of interactions and practices involving not only animals and how we treat them and use them in our contemporary cultural practices, but also our *own* "animality" and how we react and respond to it, sometimes violently and disturbingly, sometimes touchingly and illuminatingly.

The anxieties and strategies that attend those questions in science, art, and popular culture form the focus of the contributions here by Judith Roof, Steve Baker, and Ursula Heise, respectively. Roof's essay takes it for granted—as well it should—that no figure is more central to making these anxieties and strategies a permanent part of our everyday intellectual life than Sigmund Freud. As is well known, Freud's career, from beginning to end, is concerned with exploring, but also securing, the borderland between human and nonhuman animals, and it is scarcely possible to think about what the animal means to us in the modern and postmodern period without working through Freud's theories of drive and desire and the anthropological work on sacrifice and sexuality of *Totem and Taboo* and *Civilization and Its Discontents*. Roof takes us to a more out-of-the-way corner of Freud's work, however: his intense, and indeed fetishistic, interest in the protist and its twin concept, the germ-plasm, as "an instrumental interspecies example of the wider truth of his psychodynamic formulations," ones that serve as "primal, deathless reference points for Freud's thinking about life processes." Roof finds that such gestures and the angst that attends them in Freud—our need to reference our biological and animal origins as "proof" of our theories of human sexuality, only to then throw the ontological privilege of the human itself into question by that very linkage—are alive and well in contemporary conversations about what the genetic code means to our own self-understanding. As she argues, belief in DNA would seem to require as well a belief in the commonality of all life, but at the same time "faith in DNA also provides the illusion of a mastery of all life located, via knowledge of DNA, in science and in the human. That this surreptitious mastery requires a fetish suggests both the immense scope of this unity and the strength of pro-human prejudice."

As Ursula Heise points out, such prejudice has traditionally been associated with the technical and the technological, over and against the natural world. The contemporary phenomenon of engineered life-forms, however—of the sort found in films such as *Blade Runner,* in the *SimLife* series of computer games, the Tamagotchi cyber-pet craze, and elsewhere—complicates the question considerably, in a world in which the distinction between nature and its other is already conceptually and practically eroded. Heise focuses her discussion in light of the alarming contemporary phenomenon of animal species extinction, which, she argues, "crucially shapes the way in which the artificial animal forms are approached and evaluated." For her, the questions raised and addressed by such forms are "how much nature we can do without, to what extent simulations of nature can replace the 'natural,' and what role animals, both natural and artificial, play in our self-definition as humans." Rather than seeing such engineered life-forms as an ever-more depressing incursion of technology into a vanishing, pristine natural world, she draws our attention instead to their ethical possibilities, in which "the advocacy of the cyborg animal can be viewed as at least in part a call to abandon speciesist prejudice and to accept alternative life-forms as beings with an existence and rights of their own."

A popular and powerful concept in contemporary cultural theory—
"hybridity"—is certainly afoot here, and it has been imaged, sometimes
disturbingly, sometimes comically, in a surprising array of contemporary
art. No one knows more about such things than Steve Baker, whose book
The Postmodern Animal explores on a larger canvas many of the issues he
discusses here in "Sloughing the Human." Working out of a theoretical
orientation indebted to Derrida and to Deleuze and Guattari, Baker in-
vestigates how the fretful relations between human and animal play out
in what he calls the "taking on of animality" in contemporary art. It will
come as no surprise to readers of Derrida—whose essay "*Geschlecht* II:
Heidegger's Hand" is the seminal text here—that *hands*, associated de-
finitively in Heidegger with the humanity of Man and his capacity for
thought, have been a crucial symbolic nexus of the traffic across the
human–animal divide in artwork from Joseph Beuys to contemporary
video artist Edwina Ashton. Whether the hand can change hands, we
might say—what it means for the hand to be handed over from human
to animal—raises complex questions, as Derrida's reading of Heidegger
suggests, of ethical responsibility, of what it means to give and take, and
with whom or what such a relation may obtain. This relation between
self and other, like and same, may be rewritten in representational terms
as a question of *mimesis,* which has often been regarded in contemporary
philosophy, as in Deleuze and Guattari, with suspicion, as the enemy
rather than agent of a relationship of *becoming* between humanity and
animality (about which more in a moment). What Baker finds, however,
is that mimesis of the animal in contemporary art—as in the well-known
work of William Wegman—tends to be "both outlandish and preposterously transparent," making "no claims to the 'nature' of the imitated animal," and acting out instead "playful exchanges between the human and
the animal, or between one animal and another, which may allude to
borders and distinctions but which are not impeded by them."

Here, it is crucial to pay attention to the distinction between the visual and textual representation to which Baker draws our attention, and to
ask ourselves what modes of thinking the animal other are possible in
what Derrida has called the "spatial arts" that may too readily be foreclosed in the domain of language. This is so, as I argue in my own contribution, because in the philosophical tradition questions of the relationship between humans, animals, and the problem of ethics have turned
decisively on the problem of cognition and, even more specifically in the
modern and postmodern period, on the capacity for language. It would
be overly simple, but not wrong, to say that the basic formula here has

been: no language, no subjectivity. This equation has in turn traditionally laid to rest, more or less, the question of our ethical obligation to creatures who, because they lack language, lack the ability to "respond" (to use the term Derrida will scrutinize in Jacques Lacan's writings on the animal) in that two-way exchange (so the story goes) that is crucial to the ethical relationship—about which more in a moment. In the absence of language, we are told, animals remain locked within a universe of more or less automated "reactions" (to use the Cartesian formulation), a set of pre-programmed and instinctive routines and subroutines, so that they are really more like machines than people, more like objects than subjects.

That is not to say that there are not some extremely sophisticated forms of this position. Indeed, a good portion of my essay is concerned with just how sophisticated and compelling those arguments can be, beginning with the lineage of ordinary language philosophy that runs from Ludwig Wittgenstein (perhaps the central figure in what Richard Rorty has famously called the "linguistic turn" in twentieth-century philosophy) through the Harvard philosopher Stanley Cavell to poet, essayist, and animal trainer Vicki Hearne. Here, as I try to show, the issue is not so much an unsophisticated theory of language that is used to separate human and animal; indeed, Hearne's work on how we communicate with animals and inhabit a shared world with them by building a common vocabulary in the training relationship is as supple and complex as any work I know of on this problem. Instead—and this is amplified in Paul Patton's searching discussion of the training relationship—it is the disconnection between what such work seems to teach us about the complexity of animal phenomenology and subjectivity, and the ethical implications opened by that new knowledge, that appear, strangely enough, to be severely attenuated at best.

We find the same sort of lacuna in a very different type of philosopher, the late French poststructuralist philosopher Jean-François Lyotard, who is most well known, surely, for his study *The Postmodern Condition*. Lyotard was always intensely interested in questions of justice, ethics, and law, and he attempted in many places to articulate these concerns in terms of a resolutely posthumanist theory of language and discourse (as is developed with remarkable rigor, for example, in *The Differend*), which sought to explain the power of discourse not to obey the human but to constitute it. It is all the more remarkable, then, that Lyotard's concept of ethics stops at the water's edge of species difference. This is less surprising, however, when we remember that these questions are mediated decisively by Lyotard's relation to Kant. For Lyotard, the genius of the Kantian notion of ethics is that it attempts to theorize the necessity of the ethical relation without specifying its contents—without supplying, to put it crudely, a formula for what constitutes ethical conduct in all cases. The problem, however, is that the *subject* of the ethical relationship presumed in Kant—the "addressee" of the call to ethics, to use the technical term Lyotard focuses on—continues to be a quite identifiably and constitutively human one: the "community of reasonable beings" that excludes animals.

This Kantian blockage is brought into even sharper focus in the work of one of the most unique and increasingly influential figures in contemporary thought, Emmanuel Levinas, whose theorization of the ethical relation Lyotard references in detail. Levinas is regarded by many as perhaps the most important ethical philosopher of the postmodern moment, and what is so original and challenging about his notion of ethics, as Zygmunt Bauman has characterized it, is that it is not based on a model of "fair exchange and reciprocity of benefits" (as in John Rawls's influential social-contract model, which is important to both Cavell and Hearne), but rather on what Levinas has called a "total responsibility" to the Other "without waiting for reciprocity."[4] The opening this potentially provides for bringing the question of the animal other into the ethical equation would seem clear enough, but the problem is that it is immediately foreclosed, once again, by an essentially Kantian problematic: by the fact that the subject of ethics, here as in Lyotard, is by definition human—only the human, to use Levinas's figure, has a face. The good news, and the bad news, then, of Levinas's ethics is—to use a well-known characterization—that it is a "humanisme de l'Autre homme," a humanism of the Other *man*.

No one has made this limitation in Levinas clearer than Jacques Derrida, in texts such as "Eating Well" and "At this very moment in this work here I am." Indeed, for triangulating the relations of ethics, language, and the question of the animal, few comparisons could be more illuminating. Derrida's work in this area has reached a new and sustained pitch of intensity over the past several years in what amounts to a book's worth of material on the question of the animal in Descartes, Kant, Heidegger, Levinas, and Lacan, first delivered over eight hours as a series of lectures in 1997 at a conference in France devoted to his work titled "L'animal autobiographique"—a portion of which, on Lacan, we are fortunate enough to have appear in print here for the first time.

What Derrida's body of work on the animal makes clear is that at this juncture in the discussion—the juncture marked by Lyotard's and Levinas's quite distinct failures—the conversation can move in a few different directions. One can take the traditional equation of subjectivity and language at its word and then question the claim that only the human possesses language (which many contemporary language studies with animals seem to do more and more convincingly), which in turn reopens the entire problem of ethical obligation, but in more or less traditional terms. Or, rather than extending the ability of "languaging" outward, beyond the human sphere, one can instead move in the opposite direction and erode that notion of language from the inside out to show that if animals never quite possessed it, neither do we, with the result that language, rather than simplifying the question of ethics by securing the boundary between the human and the rest of creation, instead now reopens it—permanently, as it were—by embedding us in a world to which the human *is subject*. This, of course, is Derrida's strategy; as he puts it in these pages, "were we even to suppose—something I am not ready to concede—that the 'animal' were incapable of covering its tracks, by what right could one concede that power to *the human,* to the 'subject of the signifier'?" (emphasis added).

A third direction is suggested by substituting Michel Foucault's term *discourse* for the more limited term *language*: namely, to question at its root the assumption that the problem of language (and beyond that, cognition) is fundamental to questions of ethics *at all*. On this view—and it is one shared to varying degrees by Foucault, Deleuze and Guattari, and other less textually oriented strands of poststructuralist theory— language is but a specific modality or technology of a larger set of dynamics and relations that have to do with taking a polymorphous, heterogeneous world of relations and (by means of power, techniques, disciplines, diagrams, models, and the like) making them manageable and putting them to use. Over and against some popular misunderstandings of Foucault's theorization of power's omnipresence, however, this does not mean that power and ethics are opposites. Indeed, as Paul Patton—himself a dedicated horseman of many years as well as translator of Deleuze's *Difference and Repetition* and scholar of poststructuralist philosophy—argues here, the training of horses, whether in the traditional "cowboy" methods of domination or the gentler ways of "horse whisperer" Monty Roberts, is indeed an exercise of power, a form of what Foucault calls "government." But this is "by no means incompatible with ethical relations and obligations toward other beings" of whatever species, Patton argues, be they human or animal. Indeed, part of what is valuable about the work of Hearne, Roberts, and others—and about the experience of actually training an animal—is that it helps to make clear the *requirements* and *obligations* of those hierarchical relations of power we do enter into (with animals, with children, with each other) and draws our attention to how those requirements are always specific to the beings involved, in the light of which, he argues, the presumption of a one-size-fits-all notion of "equality in all contexts" is "not only misleading but dangerous." Moreover, the training relationship draws our attention to the fact that the modes of communication involved in building and sustaining relations with each other, out of which the ethical relationship grows, need not be verbal or linguistic at all, but instead involve a myriad of other forms of connection.

Just how myriad—and how ethically charged—those forms can be is the subject of Alphonso Lingis's remarkable essay "Animal Body, Inhuman Face," which sets out from the coordinates mapped in poststructuralist philosophy by Deleuze and Guattari. Here, the ethical thrust is toward opening the human to the heterogeneity and multiplicity within which it has always been embedded. As Brian Massumi, translator of *A Thousand Plateaus,* has put it, the desire of identity and unity, of transcendence, "is always to take a *both/and* and make it an *either/or,* to reduce the complexity of pragmatic ethical choice to the black or white of Good or Bad."[5] In Deleuze and Guattari, however, the fundamental ethical relationship seems to be one that recognizes and generates different modes of becoming (rather than being) and constantly works to destabilize identity and unity. Such a view would seem to call for a very different *practice* of philosophy as a form of writing—one that is less about making arguments and articulating propositions to be met with a yes or a no, and more about generating connections and proliferating lines of inquiry in what Deleuze and Guattari have called a "rhizomatic" network of thinking (against the "arboreal" practice of traditional philosophy).

And that is exactly what we find on display in Lingis's essay, which explores how the multiplicity of the animal world is unleashed in our own sexuality, our own bodies. In sex, he writes, "Our sense of ourselves, our self-respect shaped in fulfilling a function in the machinic and social environment, our dignity maintained in multiple confrontations, collaborations, and demands, dissolve; the ego loses its focus as center of evaluations, decisions, and initiatives. Our impulses, our passions, are returned to animal irresponsibility." As Massumi puts it—in a passage of major resonance for Lingis's contribution—"Bodies that fall prey to transcendence are reduced to what seems to persist across their alterations. Their very corporeality is stripped from them, in favor of a supposed substrate—

soul, subjectivity, personality, identity—which in fact is no foundation at all, but an end effect, the infolding of a forcibly regularized outside" (112). The primary figure for that regularization in Lingis is, of course, the face, whose "arbitration operates by binary oppositions, dichotomies, bipolarities. No. Yes." The face—or what Deleuze and Guattari call "faciality"[6]—can cover the whole body, indeed the whole world; it is a grid, a diagram, a binary machine, and is in its very nature despotic; it takes the human animal and makes it Man; it takes the lover and makes her Citizen; it takes the animal and makes it "bestial." And in this understanding, language, the Signifier, is a technology that can just as readily stifle ethical relations as ensure them.

This insistence on the difference between the ontological and the linguistic or textual raises in turn a question that animates this collection as a whole: the relationship between what I have elsewhere called the *discourse* of animality—the use of that constellation of signifiers to structure how we address others of *whatever* sort (not just nonhuman animals)—and the living and breathing creatures who fall outside the taxonomy of Homo sapiens.[7] There are two distinct points here. As for the first, one might well observe that it is crucial to pay critical attention to the discourse of animality quite irrespective of the issue of how non-human animals are treated. This is so, as a number of scholars have observed, because the discourse of animality has historically served as a crucial strategy in the oppression of *humans* by other humans—a strategy whose legitimacy and force depend, however, on the prior taking for granted of the traditional ontological distinction, and consequent ethical divide, between human and nonhuman animals. As Étienne Balibar has observed, for example, "every theoretical racism draws upon *anthropological universals*," underneath which we find "the persistent presence of the same 'question': that of *the difference between humanity and animality*" that is at work in "the systematic 'bestialization' of individuals and racialized human groups."[8] The second point I wish to make here is not so much a corollary to Balibar's observation as it is a countervailing addendum: that even though the *discourse* of animality and species difference may theoretically be applied to an other of whatever type, the consequences of that discourse, in *institutional* terms, fall overwhelmingly on nonhuman animals, in our taken-for-granted practices of using and exploiting them.

It is on the site of those consequences—for animals and for humans—that Charlie LeDuff's riveting piece for the *New York Times*, "At a Slaughterhouse, Some Things Never Die," may be located. Set in a Smithfield Foods pork packing plant in rural North Carolina, LeDuff's article—which was published as the sixth installment in a series titled "How Race Is Lived in America"—shows how the relations of hierarchy, domination, and exploitation between humans and animals are uncannily and systematically reproduced in relations of class, race, and ethnicity among humans themselves.[9] "They treat you like an animal" in the plant, one worker complains of the brutalizing, backbreaking work, and a well-worn saying about the slaughterhouse is "They don't kill pigs here, they kill people." Here, racial hierarchy takes the place of species hierarchy, with whites at the top, in managerial or mechanical positions, American Indians below that (mostly of the Lumbee tribe, who are historically a significant population in this part of eastern North Carolina), and then the dirty, bloody jobs of the kill floor and disassembly line reserved mostly for blacks and Mexicans. "The place reeks of sweat and scared animal, steam and blood," LeDuff writes, and in this inferno of animal terror and human struggle, the closer one has to be to the killing and the blood, the more one's own workday becomes a site of violence, which is visited upon the animals themselves, as LeDuff graphically describes it, with chilling efficiency and automation.

Relations between the races—both in the plant and out—are almost totally segregated, uniformly suspicious, and often hostile, as blacks and Mexicans, particularly, see each other as the competition that keeps wages and working conditions from ever improving. Long-standing racial tension between whites and blacks replays itself here in a different key; as an older black worker warns, "There's a day coming soon when the Mexicans are going to catch hell from the blacks, the way the blacks caught it from the whites." Only now, competition between blacks and Mexicans takes place within a global economy in which the Mexican workers cannot "push back" because many of them are illegal immigrants, working the "picnic line" on the factory floor for eight or nine dollars an hour to pay off the "coyotes" who smuggled them into the country. And underneath it all, of course, at the bottom of the ladder of exploitation and abuse, are the animals themselves—19 million of them slaughtered every year by Smithfield Foods alone to feed America's seemingly bottomless hunger for meat. Here, we find a graphic illustration of the material consequences of the culture of "carno-phallogocentrism," and we come away with a graphic sense of just how hyphenated, how conjoined, those consequences are for human and nonhuman animals alike.

Notes

1. Derrida's coinage of the term *carno-phallogocentrism* takes place in the interview "'Eating Well' or the Calculation of the Subject," in *Who Comes after the Subject?*, ed. Eduardo Cadava, Peter Connor, and Jean-Luc Nancy (New York: Routledge, 1991).

2. See my "Old Orders for New: Ecology, Animal Rights, and the Poverty of Humanism," *diacritics* 28:2 (summer 1998): 21–40.

3. Slavoj Žižek, in his critique of liberal democracy, articulates this linkage even more pointedly (though not entirely unproblematically). In *Looking Awry: An Introduction to Jacques Lacan through Popular Culture* (Cambridge: MIT Press, 1991), Žižek writes, "The subject of democracy is thus a pure singularity, emptied of all content, freed from all substantial ties," but "the problem with this subject does not lie where neoconservatism sees it." It is not that "this abstraction proper to democracy dissolves all concrete substantial ties," but rather that "*it can never dissolve them.*" The subject of democracy is thus "smeared with a certain 'pathological' stain" (to use Kant's term) (164–65). In *Tarrying with the Negative: Kant, Hegel, and the Critique of Ideology* (Durham, N.C.: Duke University Press, 1993), Žižek elaborates the linkage between the "abstract" subject of liberalism and the unfortunate term *political correctness* even more specifically by arguing that in "the unending effort to unearth traces of sexism and racism in oneself," in fact, "the PC type is not ready to renounce what really matters: 'I'm prepared to sacrifice everything *but that*'—but what? The very gesture of self-sacrifice." Thus, "In the very act of emptying the white-male-heterosexual position of all positive content, the PC attitude retains it as a universal form of subjectivity" (213–14).

4. Zygmunt Bauman, *Postmodern Ethics* (Oxford: Basil Blackwell, 1993), 220, 85.

5. Brian Massumi, *A User's Guide to Capitalism and Schizophrenia: Deviations from Deleuze and Guattari* (Cambridge: MIT Press, 1992), 112. Subsequent references are given in the text.

6. On "faciality" in Deleuze and Guattari, see Massumi's very helpful collation in ibid., 172–73 n. 54.

7. See my forthcoming *Animal Rites: American Culture, the Discourse of Species, and Posthumanism* (Chicago: University of Chicago Press) and my "Faux Post-Humanism, or, Animal Rights, Neocolonialism, and Michael Crichton's *Congo*," *Arizona Quarterly* 55:2 (summer 1999): 115–53.

8. Étienne Balibar, "Racism and Nationalism," in Étienne Balibar and Immanuel Wallerstein, *Race, Nation, Class: Ambiguous Identities*, trans. of Balibar by Chris Turner (London: Verso, 1991), 56.

9. The deleterious practices of factory farming of hogs in North Carolina have been the subject of intense journalistic scrutiny. See, for example, David Cecelski and Mary Lee Kerr's article "Hog Wild" in *Southern Exposure* (fall 1992), and the five-part series on the subject published in the *Raleigh News and Observer,* February 19–26, 1995, reprinted March 19, 1995. A powerful and disturbing portrait of slaughterhouses and their effects on humans as well as animals is provided by artist Sue Coe in her book *Dead Meat* (New York: Four Walls Eight Windows Press, 1995), which contains an excellent introduction on the business and culture of meat eating by Alexander Cockburn.

In the Shadow of Wittgenstein's Lion: Language, Ethics, and the Question of the Animal

Cary Wolfe

Forms of Language, Forms of Life: Wittgenstein, Cavell, and Hearne

In 1958, toward the end of his *Philosophical Investigations*, Ludwig Wittgenstein set down a one-sentence observation that might very well serve as an epigraph to the debates that have taken place over the past century on animals, language, and subjectivity. "If a lion could talk," Wittgenstein wrote, "we could not understand him."[1] This beguiling statement has often been misunderstood—I am not even sure that I understand it myself—and it is complicated by Wittgenstein's contention elsewhere that "To imagine a language is to imagine a form of life."[2] What can it mean to imagine a language we cannot understand, spoken by a being who cannot speak—*especially* in light of his reminder that "The kind of certainty is the kind of language-game" (*Wittgenstein Reader,* 213)? And, earlier still: "If I were to talk to myself out loud in a language not understood by those present my thoughts would be hidden from them" (211). "It is, however, important as regards this observation that one human being can be a complete enigma to another. We learn this when we come into a strange country with entirely strange traditions; and, what is more, even given a mastery of the country's language. We do not *understand* the people. (And not because of not knowing what they are saying to themselves.)" (212).

1

It is the caginess, if you will, of the muteness of Wittgenstein's lion that rightly catches the attention of Vicki Hearne in her book *Animal Happiness*. Hearne—a poet, renowned horse trainer and dog trainer, and serious student of the philosophical lineage that runs from Wittgenstein through Stanley Cavell—calls Wittgenstein's statement "the most interesting mistake about animals that I have ever come across," because "lions do talk to some people"—namely, lion trainers—"and are understood" (a claim about language that we will have occasion to revisit).[3] What interests her is how Wittgenstein's statement seems—but only seems—to body forth an all too familiar contrast between the confidently transparent intersubjective human community, on the one hand, and the mute, bedarkened beast, on the other. It is this contrast, and this humanism, however, that Wittgenstein is out to trouble, for, as Hearne notes, "The lovely thing about Wittgenstein's lion is that Wittgenstein does not leap to say that his lion is languageless, only that he is not talking"—a remark that is "a profundity rarely achieved, because of all it leaves room for" (*Animal Happiness*, 169). "The reticence of this lion," she continues, "is not the reticence of absence, absence of consciousness, say, or knowledge, but rather of tremendous presence," of "all consciousness that is beyond ours" (170).

What Hearne puts her finger on here—what she finds attractive in the style or posture of Wittgenstein's "mistake"—is the importance of how we face, face up to, the fact of a "consciousness . . . beyond ours"; more specifically, what value is attached to the contention that animals "do not talk, that no bit of their consciousness is informed by the bustle and mediations of the written, the symbolic" (171). For Hearne, what makes Wittgenstein's intervention valuable is that this darkness or muteness of the animal other is shown to be more a problem for *us* than for the animal. "The human mind is nervous without its writing, feels emptiness without writing," she reminds us. "So when we imagine the inner or outer life of a creature without that bustle, we imagine what we would be like without it—that is, we imagine ourselves emptied of understanding" (ibid.). Thus, Wittgenstein's lion "in his restraint remains there to remind us that knowledge . . . comes sometimes to an abrupt end, not vaguely 'somewhere,' like explanations, but immediately"—a fact dramatized for Hearne when the understanding between lion and lion trainer goes wrong. Wittgenstein's lion, "regarded with proper respect and awe, gives us unmediated knowledge of our ignorance" (173).

"Not vaguely 'somewhere,' like explanations," is anything but a throwaway phrase in this instance, for it takes us to the very heart of Wittgenstein's transvaluation of philosophical skepticism, one best elaborated by Stanley Cavell. For Cavell, our tendency to see the reticence of Wittgenstein's lion as a lack of subjectivity is symptomatic of nothing so much as "our skep-tical terror about the independent existence of other minds"—a terror that is, in a certain sense, about our failure to be god, to be "No One in Particular with a View from Nowhere," as Hearne puts it (*Adam's Task*, 233, 229). And this terror, in turn, drives the fantasy that, through philoso-phy, we somehow might be. As Hearne writes of "thinkers who like to say that a cat cannot be said to be 'really' playing with a ball because a cat does not seem to know our grammar of what 'playing with' and 'ball' are" (a position, incidentally, that is sometimes attributed to Wittgenstein):

> This more or less positivist position requires a fundamental assump-tion that "meaning" is a homogeneous, quantifiable thing, and that the universe is dualistic in that there are only two states of meaning in it—significant and insignificant, and further that "significant" means only "significant to me.". . . Such positivism of meaning looks often enough like an injunction against the pathetic fallacy, but seems to me to be quite the opposite. (Ibid., 238)

In Hearne and Cavell's reading, skeptical terror generates certain philo-sophical concepts of language and its relation to consciousness and subjec-tivity that it is Wittgenstein's business to subvert—and subvert in a rather peculiar way. As Cavell puts it, what prevents our understanding of animals—take Wittgenstein's lion as only the most hyperbolic example—"is not too much skepticism but too little" (quoted in ibid., 114). For Cavell, the philosophical false start that Wittgenstein wants to reroute is "the [skeptic's] idea that the problem of the other is the problem of *knowing* the other," when in fact one of the most valuable things about our encounter with the supposedly "mute" animal is that it "sooner makes us wonder what *we* conceive knowledge to be" (quoted in ibid.; emphasis added). If we follow Wittgenstein's lead, Cavell argues, "One is not encouraged . . . to go on searching for a something—if not a mechanism, or an image, then a meaning, a signified, an interpretant—that explains how calls reach what they call, how the connection is made," but rather "to determine what keeps such a search going (without, as it were, moving). Wittgenstein's an-swer, as I read it, has something to do with what I understand as skepti-cism, and what I might call skeptical attempts to defeat skepticism." For Cavell, Wittgenstein not only "shows us that we maintain unsatisfiable pic-tures of how things must happen"; he also forces us to think through "why we are, who we are that we are, possessed of this picture."[4]

Wittgenstein's specific intervention, then—his "skeptical attempts to defeat skepticism"—is to turn philosophical skepticism back on itself, back on the human. Hence, the project of what is often remarked as Wittgenstein's conventionalism is in no small part "to make us dissatisfied with the idea of universals as explanations of language."[5] Philosophy may always seem to want to situate itself outside the noise and contingency of language games, "but it depends on the same fact of language as do the other lives within it": that "it cannot dictate what is said *now*, can no more assure the sense of what is said, its depth, its helpfulness, its accuracy, its wit, than it can insure its truth to the world" (*Claim*, 189). As Hearne puts it in an essay on the famous language experiments with Washoe the chimpanzee, "the issue of what Washoe is doing, what condition of language we are dealing with, is not an intellectual problem, a puzzle." If Washoe uses language and remains dangerous despite that (which she most certainly does), "then I may be thrown into confusion . . . and may want to deny Washoe's personhood and her language rather than acknowledge the limits of language—which can look like a terrifying procedure" (*Adam's Task*, 39).

This means, in Cavell's words, that "We begin to feel, or ought to, terrified that maybe language (and understanding, and knowledge) rests upon very shaky foundations—a thin net over an abyss" (*Claim*, 178). And it is also an apt description of what Wittgenstein has in mind when he says, famously, that to imagine a language is to imagine a "form of life." As Hearne puts it, "one can hang out with people who speak no English and learn something of which objects are meant by which words. What is much harder to know, what you have to be deeply, genuinely bilingual to know, is what the object or posture itself means. I may know that *shlumah-ney* means what I call 'candle,' but not whether candles are sacred to my 'informants,' and not such things as whether to ask permission to use the candle to read in bed at night" (*Animal Happiness*, 170). For Cavell, "It is such shades of sense, intimations of meaning, which allow certain kinds of subtlety or delicacy of communication: the communication is intimate, but fragile. Persons who cannot use words, or gestures, in these ways with you may yet be in your world, but perhaps not of your flesh" (*Claim*, 189).

At this point in the argument, the Wittgensteinian lineage would seem to be promising indeed for our ability to reconjugate the relations between language, species, and the question of the subject, not least because Wittgenstein's conventionalism would appear to more or less permanently unsettle the ontological difference between human and animal, a difference expressed, as it were, in the philosophical tradition by the capacity for language: first, by holding that that ontological difference is itself constituted by a language that cannot ground and master a world of contingency via "universals"; and second, by showing how language does not provide an answer to the question "What's the difference between human and animal?" but rather keeps that question live and open by insisting that the differences between participants in specific language games and those "not of their flesh" may be as profound as those usually taken to obtain between the human *as such* and the animal *as such*—as if there were, any longer, any such thing *as such*.

What Wittgenstein's account makes possible, in other words, is what we might call a conventionalist understanding of the shared dynamics of a world building that need not, in principle, be tied to species distinctions *at all*. On this account, not *the* world but simply *a* world emerges from building a shared form of life through participation in a language game. And indeed, this is the direction in which Hearne has taken Wittgenstein's cue in her writings on how the shared language of animal training makes possible a common world between beings with vastly different phenomenologies. For Hearne, "training creates the kind of knowledge all talking does, or ought to do—knowledge of the loop of intention and openness that talk is, knowledge of and in language" (*Adam's Task*, 85). And if "the sketchiness of the tokens of this language game" might look to a scientist like "the wildest sort of anthropomorphizing"— as when a trainer says a certain dog has a mischievous sense of humor— what has to be remembered is that "a reason for trying to get a feel for a dog-human language game is that it sharpens one's awareness of *the sketchiness of the tokens of English*" (ibid., 71–72; emphasis added). "With horses as with dogs," she continues, "the handler must learn to believe, to 'read' a language s/he hasn't sufficient neurological apparatus to test or judge, because the handler must become comprehensible to the horse, and to be understood is to be open to understanding, much more than it is to have shared mental phenomena. It is as odd as Wittgenstein suggested it is to suppose that intersubjectivity depends on shared mental phenomena" (106). What it depends on instead is the "flow of intention, meaning, believing," the "varied flexions of looped thoughts," which is why "The behaviorist's dog will not only seem stupid, she will be stupid. If we follow Wittgenstein in assuming the importance of assessing the public nature of language, then we don't need to lock a baby up and feed it by machine in order to discover that conceptualization is pretty much a function of relationships and acknowledgement, a public affair" (58).

And yet, in both Hearne and Cavell, what I will characterize, much too quickly here, as a kind of humanism, a palpable nostalgia for the human, returns through the back door to severely circumscribe the ethical force of the shared world building with animals that seems at first glance promised by their appropriation of Wittgenstein, leaving the animal ethically if not phenomenologically bedarkened and the human insufficiently interrogated by the encounter. The clunkiest symptom of this, perhaps, is the social-contract theory of rights that Hearne borrows, at least in part, from Cavell (who in turn borrows it largely from John Rawls).[6] To put it very schematically, the contractarian view holds that

> morality consists of a set of rules that individuals voluntarily agree to abide by, as we do when we sign a contract. . . . Those who understand and accept the terms of the contract are covered directly; they have rights created and recognized by, and protected in, the contract. And these contractors can also have protection spelled out for others who, though they lack the ability to understand morality and so cannot sign the contract themselves, are loved or cherished by those who can. . . . As for animals, since they cannot understand the contracts, they obviously cannot sign; and since they cannot sign, they have no rights. . . . [T]hose animals that enough people care about (companion animals, whales, baby seals, the American bald eagle) though they lack rights themselves, will be protected because of the sentimental interests of people. I have, then, according to contractarianism, no duty directly to your dog or any other animal, not even the duty not to cause them pain or suffering; my duty not to hurt them is a duty I have to those people who care about what happens to them.[7]

This is the view, derived from Kant, that is expounded by Hearne, nearly to the letter, in an essay originally published under the title "What's Wrong with Animal Rights?" In order to be in a rights relation with another, she argues, "the following minimum conditions must hold": "I must know the person," "The person must know me," "The grammar of the reciprocal possessive must apply," and "Both of us must have the ability to conceive the *right* in question itself" (*Animal Happiness*, 209). For Hearne, "if I do not own you, own up to you, then I do not acknowledge you, I repudiate you. You cannot have interests or rights in relationship to me unless we own each other" (206).

Not surprisingly, this leads Hearne into all sorts of tortured formulations that would seem to forget everything that she has spent the better part of her career teaching us about nonhuman others and the worlds we may inhabit with them: "The kind of possession I have in mind is not like slavery. It does not bind one party while freeing the other. . . . [I]f I abuse my dog on the grounds that she is my dog, then I do not, at the moment at least, in fact own the dog, am not owning up to what goes into owning a dog, do not understand my own words when I say I own the dog and can therefore do as I please with her" (208). Or again, writing of her famous Airedale, "Drummer can speak to his owner, but he cannot speak either to or of the state. Therefore the state cannot grant rights to Drummer, cannot be *his* state. Hence it is not an incidental or accidental but a central fact that in practice the only way a dog's rights are protected, against neighbors or the state, is *by way of an appeal to the owner's property rights in the dog*" (212). Of course, this is tantamount to simply wishing that all owners will be "good" ones. And if they are not—if an owner decides to set his dog on fire, instead of its equivalent under the law (as property), a chair or table—then does this not beg the question that the whole *point* of granting rights to the animal would be to *directly* recognize and protect it (as we do with the guardianship of the child) against such an owner who decides to forget or abrogate, for whatever reason, what "ownership means"?

In addition to the usual objections associated with the contractarian view of ethics, which I will list briefly in a moment, matters are not helped any in *Cavell*'s case by his (admittedly) iconoclastic reading of Wittgenstein's concept of "forms of life." In contrast to what he calls the dominant "ethnological" or "horizontal" reading of this moment in Wittgenstein, Cavell emphasizes the "biological or vertical sense," which "recalls differences between the human and so-called 'lower' or 'higher' forms of life, between, say, poking at your food, perhaps with a fork, and pawing at it, or pecking at it." Here—and we will return to this figure in our discussion of Jacques Derrida's reading of Heidegger—"the romance of the hand and its apposable thumb comes into play, and of the upright posture and of the eyes set for heaven; but also the specific strength and scale of the human body and of the human senses and of the human voice."[8] Cavell's aim is to take issue with those who see Wittgenstein's conventionalism as an automatic refutation of skepticism, a reading in which "the very existence of, say, the sacrament of marriage, or of the history of private property, or of the ceremony of shaking hands, or I guess ultimately the existence of language, constitutes proof of the existence of others" (*This New,* 42)—a position that would be consonant with the "hard" conventionalist reading of a Richard Rorty or a Stanley Fish. Instead, Cavell's emphasis not on "*forms* of life, but forms of *life*" intends to "mark the limit and give the conditions of the use of criteria as applied to others" (ibid., 42–43), with the larger aim of contesting the "sense of political or social conservatism" that for many readers attends Wittgenstein's *Philosophical Investigations* (44). The idea here, from Cavell's vantage, is that by positing a figure of the human form of *life* not reducible to the immanence ("forms") of language games, Wittgenstein provides a yardstick, or at least a background, against which those language games (private property, for instance) may be judged as desirable or wanting.[9] What Cavell calls "the practice of the ordinary"—being responsible to the everyday details of a specific "form of life"—"may be thought of as the overcoming of iteration or replication or imitation by repetition, of counting by recounting, of calling by recalling. It is the familiar invaded by another familiar" (*This New*, 47).

And yet the problem is that this moment—and it is for Cavell the moment of ethics—is accompanied by a strong return to the very humanism that his phenomenological speculations had promised to move us beyond. If we take seriously the ethnological or conventionalist sense of Wittgenstein's "forms of life," as Cavell realizes we must, then we are faced very quickly with this ethical dilemma: the balkanization of language games promises to circumscribe ever more tightly those who share my world—those who are, to use Cavell's phrase, "of my flesh." The verticality of language games that Wittgenstein insists on strengthens the shared ethical call of those *within* the game, but only at the expense of weakening the ethical call in relation to those who speak in other tongues (hence Cavell's worries about Wittgenstein's conventionalist conservatism).

It is as if to arrest this runaway mitosis of the linguistic and ethical field that both Hearne and Cavell reintroduce a certain figure of the human familiar to us from the liberal tradition. In Hearne, for example, the language of animal training provides a shared language game, and hence shared world, between trainer and animal; but, ethically speaking, that symmetry of relation, as she describes it, is belied by the radical *asymmetry* that obtains when the ethical relation of rights is properly expressed, as she argues, in the institution of property ownership. And it is not at all clear, of course, that we have any ethical duty whatsoever to those animals with whom we have not articulated a shared form of life through training or other means. Hearne's contractarian notion of rights only reinforces the asymmetrical privilege of the ethnocentric "we," whereas the whole point of rights would seem to be that it affords protection of the other *exactly in recognition of* the dangers of an ethnocentric self-privileging that seems to have forgotten the fragility and "sketchiness" of its *own* concepts, its *own* forms of life, in the confidence with which it restricts the sphere of ethical consideration.

In Cavell, things play out rather differently, specifically in his rendering of the human "form of life" over against "the so-called 'lower'" forms. In *The Claim of Reason*, the slippage from human to human*ist* and the ethical foreclosure that attends it is especially pronounced. Investigating the biological or "vertical" sense of "forms of life" as "the background against which our criteria do their work; even, make sense," Cavell quotes Wittgenstein: "only of a living human being and what resembles (behaves like) a living human being can one say: it has sensations; it sees; is blind; hears; is deaf; is conscious or unconscious" (83). Cavell takes this and other similar moments in Wittgenstein to mean that it is not any conventionalist criterion but our biological form of life that leads us to such attributions, so that "To withhold, or hedge, our concepts of psychological states from a given creature"—exactly the position taken by Thomas Nagel in his well-known essay "What Is It Like to Be a Bat?"—"is specifically to withhold *the source of my idea* that living beings are things that feel; it is to withhold myself, to reject my response to anything as a living being; to blank so much as my idea of anything as *having a body*" (ibid.; first emphasis added). When we do so,

> There is nothing to read from that body, nothing the body is *of*; it does not go beyond itself, it expresses nothing. . . . It does not matter to me now whether there turn out to be wheels and springs inside, or stuffing, or some subtler or messier mechanism. . . . What this 'body' lacks is *privacy*. . . . Only *I* could reach that privacy, by accepting it as a home of my concepts of the human soul. When I withdraw that acceptance, the criteria are dead. . . . And what happens to me when I withhold my acceptance of privacy—anyway, of otherness—as the home of my concepts of the human soul and find my criteria to be dead, mere words, word-shells: I said a while ago in passing that I withhold myself. What I withhold myself from is my attunement with others—with all others, not merely with the one I was to know. (Ibid., 84–85)

Now, many things could be said about this fascinating passage. One might, for example, ask why the sentences on "wheels and springs" do not beg the question that is often raised so forcefully in science fiction—in the film *Blade Runner*, say—about why there *should* be any necessary relation between the phenomenological and ethical issues that attend what we usually denote by the term *human* and the particular physical mechanism of its realization. Or one might point to how phrases such as "nothing the body is *of*" reintroduce the danger of what Daniel Dennett has called the "Cartesian theatre" of a mind (or ego, cogito, or, here, "soul"), which threatens to evaporate into "No one in particular with a view from nowhere."[10] Or one might argue, as I have elsewhere, that a passage such as this makes clear why the supposed "weakness" of philosophical conventionalism is precisely its strength;[11] that is, instead of openness to the other depending on a representationalist adequation between otherwise "dead" criteria and the genus of being whose "true" nature allows us to say that those criteria are being properly deployed—in which case we are forced to ask, How much "of our flesh" is flesh enough?—relevant criteria should instead apply consistently and dispassionately across the board, pragmatically, not because certain entities are a priori certain *types of beings.* In this light, the problem is that there is in the foregoing passage nothing to stop the difference between "wheels and springs" and "some subtler or messier mechanism" from readily rescripting itself not only as the difference between human and android (to stay with the *Blade Runner* example), but also, for our purposes here, as the difference between human and animal.

My larger point, however, is that this "living being" turns out to be a fairly familiar sort of creature after all (as is suggested most pointedly, perhaps, by the discourse of "privacy" that wends its way through the previous passage, reaching back to Hearne's ethical foreclosure via the discourse of private property). And hence it belies Cavell's opening of the human to the animal other by rewriting the differences in *degree* in "patterns we share with other life forms" (*This New,* 48) as differences in *kind*—a maneuver made possible by grounding those otherwise conventional differences in their proper "biological" "sources." In Cavell, in other words, the opening of the human to the shared world of the animal other via the "sketchiness" of our own form of life—a sketchiness revealed in the encounter with philosophical skepticism—is in the end foreclosed by the fact that the animal other matters only insofar as it mirrors, in a diminished way, the *human* form that is the "source" of recognizing animals as bodies that have sensations, feel pain, and so on. And here, Cavell's liberal humanism links him rather unexpectedly, I think, with the animal rights philosophy of Peter Singer and Tom Regan, for whom our responsibility to the animal other is grounded, as I have argued elsewhere, in the fact that it exhibits in diminished form qualities, potentialities, or abilities that exist in their fullest realization in human beings.[12]

To put it in more strictly philosophical terms, there is a way—as Richard

Rorty would no doubt be the first to argue—in which all of this is already hardwired into Cavell's primary philosophical commitment to the importance of the problem of skepticism. Skepticism takes seriously, if you will, the loss of the world, its exile, as the price paid for knowledge after Kant. As Cavell writes of the Kantian "settlement" with skepticism in *In Quest of the Ordinary,* "To settle with skepticism . . . to assure us that we do know the existence of the world, or rather, that what we understand as knowledge is *of* the world, the price Kant asks us to pay is to cede any claim to know the thing in itself, to grant that human knowledge is not of things as they are in themselves. You don't—do you?—have to be a romantic to feel sometimes about that settlement: Thanks for nothing."[13] It is a "romantic" bridling against this Kantian settlement that, for Cavell, links Wittgenstein to Heidegger—*and,* as I will suggest later, opens Cavell to Derrida's critique of Heideggerian humanism. For Cavell, Wittgenstein's notion of criterion "is as if a pivot between the necessity of the relation among human beings Wittgenstein calls 'agreement in form of life' and the necessity in the relation between grammar and world," and it is this "recuperation or recoupment or redemption of the thing (in itself)," exiled as the *Ding an sich* by Kant's "settlement," that links Heidegger's late philosophy with Wittgenstein as "a function of their moving in structurally similar recoils away from Kant's settlement with the thing in itself, a recoil toward linking two 'directions' of language—that outward, toward objects, and that inward, toward culture and the individual" (*This New,* 49–51). For Cavell, in other words, both Wittgenstein and Heidegger remain committed, though granted in a very complicated way, to a fundamental alignment between the grammar of objects, of things in the world, and the grammar of language games and the forms of life they generate; more than that, it is the biological or vertical "form of life" of the human that is both the "source" of our attributions to the world and the "background"—the back*ground,* to put a finer point on it—against which they must be judged.

What the Victim Can (Not) Say: Lyotard (with Levinas)

However supple and nuanced the meditations on language, phenomenology, and species difference in the Wittgenstein/Cavell/Hearne line—and I have tried to show that they are nuanced indeed—the countervailing force of a deeply ingrained humanism in their work should propel us, I think, to contrast their views with those of poststructuralist philosophy, because the latter is widely held to be nothing if not post- or at least antihumanist. I have in mind here, specifically, the work of Jean-François

Lyotard and Jacques Derrida: Lyotard, because of the tight coupling in his work of the formal analysis of language games to questions of law and ethics, and the philosophical imperative of what he calls "the inhuman"; and Derrida, because no contemporary theorist has carried out a more searching, if episodic, investigation of the question of the animal—an investigation that turns, in no small part, on an ongoing reading of Heidegger that we will soon want to contrast with Cavell's.

For Lyotard, the question of the animal is embedded within the larger context of the relationship between postmodernity and what he has called "the inhuman." As is well known, in *The Postmodern Condition* Lyotard borrows the Wittgensteinian concept of the "language game" to theorize the social and formal conditions of possibility for what he presents as a distinctly postmodern type of pluralism made possible by the delegitimation of the "grand metanarratives" of modernity.[14] For Lyotard, the effect of seizing upon Wittgenstein's invention is not only to radicalize his Kantian insistence on the differences between different discourses (the descriptive and the prescriptive, for example), and not just to thereby "attack the legitimacy of the discourse of science" (because on this view science now "has no special calling to supervise the game of praxis"). It is also to reveal "an important current of postmodernity"—indeed, from a Lyotardian vantage, perhaps *the* most important current: "The social subject itself seems to dissolve in this dissemination of language games. The social bond is linguistic, but is not woven with a single thread" (*Postmodern Condition,* 40). If, on this view, modernity consists of "a shattering of belief" and a "discovery of the 'lack of reality' of reality" (ibid., 77), then what matters now is the posture one adopts toward this discovery of the postmodern at the heart of the modern:

> If it is true that modernity takes place in the withdrawal of the real . . . it is possible, within this relation, to distinguish two modes. . . . The emphasis can be placed on the powerlessness of the faculty of presentation, on the nostalgia for presence felt by the human subject, on the obscure and futile will which inhabits him in spite of everything. The emphasis can be placed, rather, on the power of the faculty to conceive, on its "inhumanity" so to speak . . . on the increase of being and the jubilation which result from the invention of new rules of the game, be it pictorial, artistic, or any other. (Ibid., 79–80)

What the breakdown of the metanarratives of modernity properly calls for, then, is an opening of all language games to constant "invention" and "dissensus" rather than a Habermasian *con*sensus which "does violence to the heterogeneity of language games" (ibid., xxv, 65–66, 72–73); an opening to "new presentations" in the arts and literature and, in the sciences, what he calls "paralogy"—a mode of scientific questioning that is not reducible to the "performativity principle" of technoscience under capital, but rather takes seriously such phenomena as chaos, paradox, and the like, and in so doing spurs itself toward the invention of new rules, "producing not the known but the unknown" (61).

It is against the performativity model of knowledge and legitimation and its expression in the "inhuman" juggernaut of technoscience wedded to capital (in which, as Lyotard only half-jokes, "whoever is the wealthiest has the best chance of being right") that Lyotard imagines a *second* sort of "inhuman" as its antagonist. "What if human beings, in humanism's sense," he writes, "were in the process of, constrained into, becoming inhuman? . . . [W]hat if what is 'proper' to humankind were to be inhabited by the inhuman," a "familiar and unknown guest which is agitating it, sending it delirious but also making it think?"[15] There are, in fact, two different *positive* senses of the inhuman at work here. The first hinges on Lyotard's retheorization of the subject as the "subject of phrases," "dispersed in clouds of narrative language elements" and components of language games, each with "pragmatic valences specific to its kind," each giving "rise to institutions in patches—local determinism" (*Postmodern Condition,* xxiv). This radically antianthropocentric concept of the subject reaches its apotheosis in *The Differend,* where Lyotard argues that "Phrase regimes coincide neither with 'faculties of the soul' nor with 'cognitive faculties.' . . . You don't play around with language. And in this sense, there are no language games. There are stakes tied to genres of discourse." It is this discursive model of the subject that Lyotard sets squarely against the "anthropocentrism" that "in general presupposes *a* language, a language naturally at peace with itself, 'communicational' [in a Habermasian sense], and perturbed for instance only by the wills, passions, and intentions of humans."[16]

The question squarely before us, of course, is whether this reconceptualization of the subject enables us to fundamentally rethink the relations of language, ethics, and the question of the animal. In fact, Lyotard raises this question, if only in passing, in *The Differend*—a text that would seem especially promising in this connection in its resolute antianthropocentrism:

> French *Aïe,* Italian *Eh,* American *Whoops* are phrases. A wink, a shrugging of the shoulder, a taping [sic] of the foot, a fleeting blush, or an attack of

tachycardia can be phrases.—And the wagging of a dog's tail, the perked ears of a cat?—And a tiny speck to the West rising upon the horizon of the sea?—A silence? . . .—Silence as a phrase. The expectant wait of the *Is it happening?* as silence. Feelings as a phrase for what cannot now be phrased. (70)

Here, Lyotard would seem to extend the sense of "language games" in his earlier work, via a rather capacious concept of the "phrase," in directions not unlike those developed by Hearne in her work on trans-species communication.

And this possibility would seem only further strengthened by the introduction to the essays collected in *The Inhuman,* where Lyotard offers a gloss on the inhuman in a second, even stronger sense that is worth quoting at length:

What shall we call human in humans, the initial misery of their child-hood, or their capacity to acquire a "second" nature which, thanks to language, makes them fit to share in communal life, adult consciousness and reason? That the second depends on and presupposes the first is agreed by everyone. The question is only that of knowing whether this dialectic, whatever name we grace it with, leaves no remainder.

If this were the case, it would be inexplicable for the adult himself or herself not only that s/he has to struggle constantly to assure his or her conformity to institutions . . . but that the power of criticizing them, the pain of supporting them and the temptation to escape them persist in some of his or her activities. . . . There too, it is a matter of traces of inde-termination, a childhood, persisting up to the age of adulthood.

It is a consequence of these banal observations that one can take pride in the title of humanity, for exactly opposite reasons. Shorn of speech, in-capable of standing upright, hesitating over the objects of interest, not able to calculate its advantages, not sensitive to common reason, the child is eminently human because its distress heralds and promises things pos-sible. Its initial delay in humanity, which makes it the hostage to the adult community, is also what manifests to this community the lack of humani-ty it is suffering from, and which calls on it to become more human. (3–4)

It is not enough that "our contemporaries find it adequate to remind us that what is proper to humankind is its absence of defining property, its nothingness, or its transcendence, to display the sign 'no vacancy,'" for what such a posture "hurries, and crushes, is what after the fact I find I have always tried, under diverse headings—work, figural, heterogeneity, dissensus, event, thing—to reserve: the unharmonizable" (4). The child, then, inhabits the inhuman in the same way that the postmodern inhabits the modern, and what makes this analogy initially seem so useful for theorizing the animal other is that it posits a permanently incipient multiplicity and self-difference at the very core of subjectivity as such, and in doing so promises to help us extend contemporary transvaluations of the structural homology between child and animal available to us at least since Freud.[17]

Lyotard's work thus seems at first glance to mark an advance beyond Cavell's on the question of the animal. For both—and for both within a Kantian frame of sorts—the animal marks an outside or limit that is of a piece with the Kantian Thing, in the face of which knowledge comes to an end. And in and by that end, the ends of the humanist model of subjectivity are interrogated. Unlike Cavell's skepticism, however, Lyotard does not regard this "withdrawal of reality" nostalgically, as a "loss" of reality, but rather finds in it a generative possibility for pluralism. More pointedly, and in more strictly philosophical terms, Lyotard does not retain nostalgia, as Cavell's skeptical frame does, for some representational alignment, however sophisticated, between the grammar of language games and the grammar of the world of objects—a nostalgia that becomes problematic, as we have seen, in Cavell's reading of the "biological" sense of Wittgenstein's "form of life."

In Lyotard, however, this potential opening for theorizing the standing of the animal other is foreclosed, in the end, by the very Kantianism he shares with Cavell. As he explains early in *The Differend*—in a passage we should hear in concert with the earlier quotation on the dog's tail, the cat's perked ears, and "silence as a phrase":

> The differend is the unstable state and instant of language wherein something which must be able to be put into phrases cannot yet be. This state includes silence, which is a negative phrase, but it also calls upon phrases which are in principle possible. This state is signaled by what one ordinarily calls a feeling.... In the differend, something "asks" to be put into phrases, and suffers from the wrong of not being able to be put into phrases right away. This is when the human beings who thought they could use language as an instrument of communication learn through the feeling of pain which accompanies silence (and of pleasure which accompanies the invention of a new idiom), that they are summoned by language, ... that what remains to be phrased exceeds what they can presently phrase, and that they must be allowed to institute idioms which do not yet exist. (13)

What bars the animal from this otherwise potentially welcoming theorization is the direct linkage in Lyotard between the "feeling" of something that "asks" to be phrased and the Kantian notions of the presentable and the sublime that Lyotard develops in a number of texts. As he had already explained in *The Postmodern Condition,* the "strong and equivocal emotion" of the sublime sentiment is indicative of the "conflict between the faculties of a subject, the faculty to conceive something and the faculty to 'present' something" (77); and it takes place "when the imagination fails to present an object which might, if only in principle, come to match a concept. We have the Idea of the world (the totality, of what is) but we do not have the capacity to show an example of it"—such Ideas are "unpresentable" (78). It is the sublime sentiment, born of this conflict, that creates differends and is the spur for new phrases, new discursive rules and inventions.

That the Kantian problematic of the sublime provides the overarching context for the earlier passage I quoted on "feeling," "silence," and animal kinesics in relation to phrases is even clearer in *The Differend.* And the problem is that once these "silences" and "emotions" are framed in Kantian terms, a certain order of subject is presupposed that automatically prevents the animal from occupying any of the discursive positions necessary for the ethical force of the differend to apply. The "silence" and "feeling" of the mute or unspoken are not available to the animal, because animals do not possess the capacity to phrase; thus, their silence and feeling, even if they can be said to exist, cannot express a differend; it is not a withholding, and thus it does not express the ethical imperative of dissensus and the differend. As Lyotard writes in *Just Gaming* of the ethical call, the position of the addressee is privileged: "First, one acts from the obligation that comes from the simple fact that I am being spoken to, that you are speaking to me, and then, and only then, can one try to understand what has been received. In other words, the obligation operator comes first and then one sees what one is obligated to."[18] In this sense, as he explains, ethics has no positive content. "There is no content to the law," Lyotard writes. "And if there is no content, it is precisely because freedom is not determinant. Freedom is regulatory; it appears in the statement of the law only as that which must be respected; but one must always reflect in order to know if in repaying a loan or in refusing to give away a friend, etc., one is actually acting, *in every single instance,* in such a way as to maintain the Idea of a society of free beings" (*Just Gaming,* 85). The famous "so that" (*so daß*) of Kant's categorical imperative "does not say: 'If you want to be this, then do that,'" but rather "marks

the properly reflective use of judgment. It says: Do whatever, not on condition that, but *in such a way as* that which you do, the maxim of what
you do, can always be valid as, etc. We are not dealing here with a determinant synthesis but with an Idea of human society" (ibid.).

Here, the linkage between a particular notion of the subject and a spe-
cific sense of ethics is very close to what we find in the work of Emmanuel
Levinas—a connection that seems to have reached its high-water mark in
Lyotard's work during the period of the conversations with Jean-Loup
Thébaud collected under the title *Just Gaming*.[19] There, Lyotard explains
that it is "the absolute privileging of the pole of the addressee" in Levinas
that "marks the place where something is prescribed to me, that is, where
I am obligated before any freedom" (37). What this means is that the ethical "you must," the obligation attendant upon the addressee, the prescriptive as such, cannot be "derived" from reason (or, in Kantian terms,
from the descriptive). And so it is folly—and in Lyotard's terms, in fact, a
form of terrorism—to try to offer reasons for the origin or content of
ethical obligation. "The 'you must,'" Lyotard writes, "is an obligation that
ultimately is not even directly experienced"; it "is something that exceeds
all experience" (45–46).[20]

The question, then, is whether this Levinasian sense of the ethical
makes it possible to think anew the question of the nonhuman animal.
John Llewelyn, in a concise and exacting essay titled "Am I Obsessed by
Bobby? (Humanism of the Other Animal)," has tackled this question
head-on. Bobby (as the more dedicated readers of Levinas will know) is
the name of a dog about whom Levinas writes in an essay from 1975, in
which, as Llewelyn puts it, he "all but proposes an analogy between the
unspeakable human Holocaust and the unspoken animal one."[21] Bobby,
who strayed into the prison camp where Levinas and his fellow Jewish
prisoners had themselves "become accustomed to being treated as less
than human" (235), evinced, as dogs will do, friendship and loyalty to the
prisoners, greeting them at the end of each day with bright eyes and wagging tail without regard for their "inhuman" condition. But the problem
for Levinas, according to Llewelyn, is that "Bobby lacks the brains to universalize his maxim. He is too stupid, *trop bête*. Bobby is without *logos*
and that is why he is without ethics . . . since the ethics of Emmanuel
Levinas is analogous to the ethics of Immanuel Kant." As Kant writes,
"Since in all our experience we are acquainted with no being which
might be capable of obligation (active or passive) except man, man therefore can have no duty to any being other than man" (quoted in ibid.,
236). As Llewelyn is at pains to point out, it is not that the question

famously raised by Jeremy Bentham with regard to animals—can they suffer?—is irrelevant for Kant.[22] If, in Kant's view, we seek our own happiness as a "natural end," and "since that natural end includes man's well-being as an animal, the maxim 'Treat nonhuman animals as if they have no capacity for suffering' is not one that can be consistently conceived as a law of nature," because "Such a conception is inconsistent with what one knows about animals from one's own experience of being one" (241).

At the same time, however, Kant "remains adamant that we can have direct duties only to beings that have *Wille* understood as pure practical reason" (ibid.). And for Levinas, according to Llewelyn, things are even more stringent than in Kant. First, it is crucial to Levinas "whether in the eyes of the animal we can discern a recognition, however obscure, of his own mortality . . . whether, in Levinas' sense of the word, the animal has a face" (240), because only if he or she does can the ethical call of "the first word addressed to me by the Other"—"Thou shalt not murder/kill"—apply to my relation with a nonhuman other. And here, for Levinas, the answer is quite unambiguously "no" (243). Second, for Levinas, "I can have direct responsibilities only toward beings that can speak"; both Levinas and Kant (like Hearne) "require an obligating being to be able to make a claim in so many words. No claim goes without saying, even if the saying is the silent saying of the discourse of the face"—a formulation that ratifies, as it were, Lyotard's Kantian reading of "feelings," "silence," and the "withholding" of the phrase that in the end excludes the animal in *The Differend*. In an echo of Cavell's meditation on "the romance of the hand and its apposable thumb," "the upright posture," and "the eyes set for heaven," we find in Levinas that "The Other has only to look at me. Indeed, what is expressed in his face may be expressed by his hand or the nape of his neck" (241)—the full resonance of which we will explore in a moment in Derrida's reading of "Heidegger's Hand." And although for Levinas this "very *droiture* of the face-to-face, its uprightness or rectitude, is the expression of the other's *droit* over me," that relationship can never include Bobby or any animal who, deprived of *Wille*, reason, and language, remains, for all ethical purposes, faceless (242).

Similarly, in Lyotard, one does not know what the ethical call calls for, but one certainly knows *for whom* it calls:

> There is a willing. What this will wants, we do not know. We feel it in the form of an obligation, but this obligation is empty, in a way. So if it can be given a content in the specific occasion, this content can only be circumscribed by an Idea. The Idea is . . . "the whole of reasonable beings" or the preservation of the possibility of the prescriptive game. But this whole of

reasonable beings, I do not know if the will wants it or what it wants with it. I will never know it. (*Just Gaming*, 70)[23]

Lyotard's answer to the question he poses in *The Differend*—"And the wagging of a dog's tail, the perked ears of a cat?"—will come as no surprise, then, when he writes earlier in the book that the animal, because it does not have the means to bear witness, is "a paradigm of the victim" (28) who suffers wrongs but cannot claim damages:

> Some feel more grief over damages inflicted upon an animal than over those inflicted upon a human. This is because the animal is deprived of the possibility of bearing witness according to the human rules for establishing damages, and as a consequence, every damage is like a wrong and turns it into a victim *ipso facto*.—But, if it does not at all have the means to bear witness, then there are not even damages, or at least you cannot establish them. . . . That is why the animal is a paradigm of the victim. (Ibid.)

Thus, we are returned in Lyotard's work, via Kant, to an essential (if extremely sophisticated) humanism regarding the ethical and the animal: first, in the taken-for-granted muteness of the animal which, crucially, can never be a "withholding" that, via the "feelings" that generate differends, is ethically productive of or included in the postmodern pluralism that Lyotard wants to promote; and second, in the theorization of the ethical community of "reasonable beings" whose standing is grounded in the capacity for language, whether formalized subsequently via the social contract to which only humans are party, or by the reinstatement of the Kantian divide between direct duty to humans and indirect duty to animals. For Lyotard as for Cavell, it is on the specific site of the ethical standing of the animal other that we get the clearest picture of a humanism that is otherwise sometimes hard to see. For both, the animal is that Kantian outside that reveals our traditional pictures of the ontological fullness of the human to have been fantasies all along, built on the sands of disavowal of our own contingency, our own materiality, our own "spoken-ness." But once that work is done, the animal is returned to its exile, its facelessness, as the human now retains a privileged relationship—indeed, a constitutive one—not to its own success but to its hard-won failure, from which the animal remains excluded. In the end, for Lyotard, we may not be us, but at least we retain the certainty that the animal remains the animal.

"The Animal, What a Word!": Derrida (with Levinas)

Given the shortcomings of the Lyotardian frame, I would like to turn now to the work of Jacques Derrida, who writes in *Of Spirit: Heidegger and the Question* that the "discourse of animality remains for me a very old anxiety, a still lively suspicion."[24] This is certainly true, but it seems to have reached a new pitch of intensity and, one is tempted to say, passion or *com*passion in Derrida's recent work delivered as eight and a half hours of lectures at Cerisy-la-Salle in 1997 at a conference devoted to Derrida's work, titled "L'Animal autobiographique."[25] In the opening section, titled "The Animal That Therefore I Am (More to Follow)," he lists upward of twenty texts in which the question of the animal has arisen throughout his career—and nowhere more densely, perhaps, than in his reading of Martin Heidegger.

In "*Geschlecht* II: Heidegger's Hand," Derrida makes a statement that must seem, to any reader—*especially*, perhaps, to those who think of themselves as Derrideans—a sweeping one indeed, when he says of Heidegger's writing on the hand that "Here in effect occurs a sentence that at bottom seems to me Heidegger's most significant, symptomatic, and seriously dogmatic," one that risks "compromising the whole force and necessity of the discourse." The sentence he has in mind from Heidegger is this: "Apes, *for example*, have organs that can grasp, but they have no hand."[26] What can Heidegger mean here, particularly in that such a statement remains, as Derrida notes, willfully ignorant of the whole body of "zoological knowledge" to the contrary (173)?[27] What Heidegger has in mind, it turns out, is a figure of the hand whose being is determined not by biological or utilitarian function—"does not let itself be determined as a bodily organ of gripping" (172)—but rather one that can serve as a figure for thought, and a particular mode of thought at that. It is this that distinguishes the *Geschlecht* of humanity from the rest of creation. "If there is a thought of the hand or a hand of thought, as Heidegger gives us to think," Derrida writes, "it is not of the order of conceptual grasping. Rather this thought of the hand belongs to the essence of the *gift*, of a giving that would give, if this is possible, without taking hold of anything" (173). We find here a contrast—an "abyss," in fact, as Derrida will argue—between the grasping or "prehension" associated with the "prehensile" organs of the ape (*Of Spirit*, 11) and the hand of man, which "is far from these in an infinite way *(unendlich)* through the abyss of its being. . . . This abyss is speech and thought. 'Only a being who can speak, that is, think,'" Heidegger writes, "'can have the hand and be handy *(in der Handhabung)* in achieving works of handicraft'" (quoted in "*Geschlecht* II," 174). Even more specifically, "Only when man speaks does he think—not the other way around, as metaphysics still believes. Every motion of the hand in every one of its works carries itself *(sich trägt)* through the element of thinking, every bearing of the hand bears itself *(gebärdet sich)* in that element. All the work of the hand is rooted in thinking. Therefore, thinking *(das Denken)* itself is man's simplest, and for that reason hardest, *Hand-Werk*" (quoted in ibid., 175).

We should be reminded here of a similar moment in Cavell's reading of Heidegger that takes the statement "Thinking is a handicraft" not only to mean that the hand and the "fantasy of the apposable thumb" figures thought as a distinctly human relation to the world, but also, more pointedly, that it reminds us of Heidegger's "interpretation of Western conceptualizing as a kind of sublimized violence," a sort of "clutching" or "grasping" through what we might call "prehensile" conceptualization whose apotheosis is "the world dominion of technology" (*Conditions Handsome,* 38, 41).[28] In opposition to all of this Cavell finds Heidegger's emphasis on thought as "reception," as a kind of welcoming, elaborated by Heidegger in passages that insist on "the derivation of the word thinking from a root for thanking," as if "giving thanks for the gift of thinking" (38–39).

It should not surprise us at this juncture that Derrida's critique of this cluster of figures in Heidegger is surely more pointed than Cavell's, because Cavell, as we have seen, remains in some important sense a part of that humanist tradition to which Heidegger belongs. To put it another way, Cavell's taking seriously of the problem of skepticism is simultaneously taking seriously the nondeconstructibility of the opposition between giving and taking. But "the nerve of the argument," Derrida writes, "seems to me reducible to the assured opposition of *giving* and *taking*: man's hand *gives and gives itself, gives* and *is given,* like thought . . . whereas the organ of the ape or of man as a simple animal, indeed as *animal rationale,* can only *take hold of, grasp, lay hands on the thing.* The organ can *only* take hold of and manipulate the thing insofar as, in any case, it does not have to deal with the thing *as such,* does not let the thing be what it is in its essence" ("*Geschlecht* II," 175). But, of course—and here is the difference with Cavell—"Nothing is less assured," as Derrida has argued in any number of texts, "than the distinction between *giving* and *taking*" (176).

Heidegger's hand is only an especially charged figure for what Derrida in *Of Spirit* will critique in Heidegger as "the profoundest metaphysical humanism," where he subjects to rigorous deconstruction Heidegger's tortured theses in *Fundamental Concepts of Metaphysics* that (1) "The stone is without world," but (2) "The animal is poor in world," unlike (3) Man, who is "world-forming" or world-building (48). As Derrida remarks, what at first looks like a difference only in *degree* between the "poverty" of the animal and the plenitude of the human in relation to having a world is paradoxically maintained by Heidegger as a difference in *kind,* a "difference in essence" (48–49). The central problem here is one of "two values incompatible in their 'logic': that of lack and that of alterity" (49); in the interests of determining the "we" of *Dasein,* of Being, "The lack of world for the animal is not a pure nothingness"—as it would be for the stone—"but it must not be referred, on a scale of homogeneous degrees, to a plenitude, or to a non-lack in a heterogeneous order, for example that of man" (ibid.). The animal for Heidegger, therefore, paradoxically "has a world in the mode of not-having" (50); it "can have a world because it has access to entities, but it is deprived of a world because it does not have access to entities *as such* and in their Being" (51). And this is so, in turn, because the animal does not have language. As Derrida emphasizes, "This inability to name is not primarily or simply linguistic; it derives from the properly *phenomenological* impossibility of speaking the phenomenon whose phenomenality as such, or whose very *as such,* does not appear to the animal and does not unveil the Being of the entity" (53). For Heidegger, then, "There is no animal *Dasein,* since *Dasein* is characterized by access to the 'as such' of the entity and to the correlative possibility of questioning" (56–57). The animal has no hand or, to put it in the Levinasian terms we have already touched on, the animal has no face; it cannot be an Other.

A formal symptom of this discourse of the animal in Heidegger that brings "the consequences of a serious mortgaging to weigh upon the whole of his thought" (57) is that it is presented in the dogmatic form of a *thesis*—a reductive genre that Derrida clearly bridles against in principle. The form of thesis presupposes "that there is one thing, one domain, one homogeneous type of entity, which is called animality *in general,* for which any example would do the job" (ibid.). The monstrosity of the thesis is its dogmatism, and it partakes of the same logic that drives the "monstrosity" of Heidegger's hand, which becomes for Derrida a figure for Heidegger's flight from *différance* generally, but specifically as it is disseminated through the sites of species difference and sexual difference— a double point that will help make especially clear Derrida's differences with Levinas. "*The* hand of *the* man, of man *as such,*" Derrida writes; "Heidegger does not only think of the hand as a very singular thing that would rightfully belong only to man, he always thinks the hand *in the singular,* as if man did not have two hands but, this monster, one single hand" (182).

It is the rejection of "animality in general," and of singularity and identity *in general,* that is amplified considerably in Derrida's recent lecture "The Animal That Therefore I Am (More to Follow)." The "animal, what a word!" he exclaims (392). "[W]ithin the strict enclosure of this definite article ('the Animal' and not 'animals') . . . are *all the living things* that man does not recognize as his fellows, his neighbors or his brothers. And that is so in spite of the infinite space that separates the lizard from the dog, the protozoon from the dolphin, the shark from the lamb, the parrot from the chimpanzee" (402). For Derrida, this "immense multiplicity of other living things . . . cannot in any way be homogenized, except by means of violence and willful ignorance"; it "is not simply a sin against rigorous thinking, vigilance, lucidity or empirical authority," he continues, "it is also a crime. Not a crime against animality precisely, but a crime of the first order against the animals, against animals. Do we agree to presume that every murder, every transgression of the commandment 'Thou shalt not kill' concerns only man?" (416). Here Derrida offers a strong reprise of his diagnosis of the "carno-phallogocentrism" of the Western philosophical tradition in the interview "Eating Well." In both texts, the Word, *logos,* does violence to the heterogeneous multiplicity of the living world by reconstituting it under the sign of identity, the *as such* and *in general*—not "animals" but "*the* animal." And as such, it enacts what Derrida calls the "sacrificial structure" that opens a space for the "non-criminal putting to death" of the animal—a sacrifice that (so the story of Western philosophy goes) allows the transcendence of the human, of what Heidegger calls "spirit," by the killing off and disavowal of the animal, the bodily, the materially heterogeneous, the contingent—in short, of *différance.*[29]

And yet Derrida's recent work moves beyond "Eating Well," or perhaps fleshes out its full implications (if you will allow the expression), in a couple of important ways—ways that will, moreover, sharpen our sense of his complex relationship with Levinas on the question of ethics; for, in the Cerisy lecture, Derrida is struggling to say, I believe, that the question of the animal is, *"at this very moment"* (to borrow from the title of his well-known essay on Levinas), not just any difference among others; it is, we might say, the most different difference, and therefore the most instructive—*particularly* if we pay attention, as he does here, to how it has been consistently repressed even by contemporary thinkers as otherwise profound as Levinas and Lacan. To pay proper attention to these questions, "It would not be a matter of 'giving speech back' to animals," Derrida writes, "but perhaps of acceding to a thinking, however fabulous and chimerical it might be, that thinks the absence of the name and of the word otherwise, as something other than a privation" ("The Animal

That Therefore I Am," 416)—to enact, as it were, a radical transvaluation of the "reticence" of Wittgenstein's lion. But how to do this?

In a move that is bound to be surprising, Derrida returns to the central question famously raised by Jeremy Bentham in response to Descartes: the question with animals is not can they talk, or can they reason, but can they *suffer.* "Once its protocol is established," Derrida writes, "the form of this question changes everything" (396), because "From Aristotle to Descartes, from Descartes, especially, to Heidegger, Levinas and Lacan," posing the question of the animal in terms of either thought or language "determines so many others concerning *power* or *capability [pouvoirs]*, and *attributes [avoirs]*: being able, having the power to give, to die, to bury one's dead, to dress, to work, to invent a technique" (395). What makes Bentham's reframing of the question so powerful is that now, "The question is disturbed by a certain *passivity.* It bears witness, manifesting already, as question, the response that testifies to sufferance, a passion, a not-being-able." "What of the vulnerability felt on the basis of this inability?" he continues; "What is this non-power at the heart of power? . . . What right should be accorded it? To what extent does it concern us?" (396). It concerns us very directly, in fact—as we know from both Heidegger and Levinas—for "Mortality resides there, as the most radical means of thinking the finitude that we share with animals, the mortality that belongs to the very finitude of life, to the experience of compassion, to the possibility of sharing the possibility of this non-power, the possibility of this impossibility, the anguish of this vulnerability and the vulnerability of this anguish" (ibid.).[30]

It is here, at this precise juncture, that Derrida's complex relationship with Levinas on the question of ethics—and, for that matter, with Lyotard—comes most sharply into focus. On the one hand, they share a certain sense of ethics. As Richard Beardsworth explains in *Derrida and the Political,* the relationship between ethics, the other, and time is central to the critique of Heidegger in both Derrida and Levinas. For both, "Time is not only irrecoverable; being irrecoverable, time is ethics."[31] Even more to the point for the "passivity" and "vulnerability" of the animal other invoked by Derrida is the fact that Heidegger *appropriates* the limit of death "rather than returning it to *the other* of time. The existential of 'being-towards-death' is consequently a 'being-able' *(pouvoir-être),* not the impossibility of all power." For Levinas and Derrida, on the other hand,

the 'impossibility' of death for the ego confirms that the experience of finitude is one of radical passivity. That the 'I' cannot experience its 'own' death means, firstly, that death is an immanence *without* horizon, and secondly, that time is that which exceeds my death, that time is the generation which precedes and follows me. . . . Death is not a limit or horizon which, recognized, allows the ego to assume the 'there' [as in Heidegger's 'being-towards-death']; it is something that never arrives in the ego's time, a 'not-yet' which confirms the priority of time over the ego, marking, accordingly, the precedence of the other over the ego. (Beardsworth, *Derrida and the Political*, 130–31)

What this means, then, is that "death *im*possibilizes existence," and does so both for me *and* for the other—because death is no more "for" the other than it is for me—so that "the alterity of death rather than signalling the other signals the *alterity* of the other, the other, if one wishes, as the recurrence of time" (132).

For Levinas and for Derrida, this has crucial implications for their view of ethics, for it suggests that the subject is always "too late" in relation to the other qua the absolute past, even as it is in that relation that the ethical fundamentally resides. At the root of ethical responsibility, then, is, paradoxically, its impossibility. But it is in this impossibility that the possibility of justice resides—a justice not reducible to the immanence of any particular socially or historically inscribed doctrine of law. As Derrida explains in "Force of Law: The 'Mystical Foundation of Authority,'"

A decision that did not go through the ordeal of the undecidable would not be a free decision, it would only be the programmable application of unfolding of a calculable process. It might be legal; it would not be just. . . . Here we 'touch' without touching this extraordinary paradox: the inaccessible transcendence of the law before which and prior to which 'man' stands fast only appears infinitely transcendent and thus theological to the extent that, so near him, it depends only on him, on the performative act by which he institutes it. (Quoted in ibid., 44–45)

And it is here, of course, that the sense of ethics in Levinas and Derrida is diametrically opposed to what we find in a utilitarian such as Peter Singer, the leading figure in animal rights philosophy. For Singer, ethics means, precisely, the application of a "calculable process"—namely, the utilitarian calculus that would tally up the "interests" of the particular beings in question in a given situation, regardless of their species, and would determine what counts as a just act according to which action maximizes the greatest good for the greatest number.[32] In doing so, however, Singer's utilitarian ethics would violate everything that the possibility of justice depends on in Derrida. First, it would run aground on Kant's separation of prescriptive and descriptive discourses, because "If one knew how to be moral, if one knew how to be free, then morality and freedom would be objects of science" (ibid., 52)—and we all know that there is no science of ethics. Second, and more seriously—Derrida is quite forceful on this point—it reduces ethics to the very antithesis of ethics by reducing the aporia of judgment in which the possibility of justice resides to the mechanical unfolding of a positivist calculation. This is what Derrida has in mind, I think, when he writes,

> I have thus never believed in some homogeneous continuity between what calls *itself* man and what *he* calls the animal. I am not about to begin to do so now. That would be worse than sleepwalking, it would simply be too asinine *[bête]*. To suppose such a stupid memory lapse or to take to task such a naïve misapprehension of this abyssal rupture would mean, more seriously still, venturing to say almost anything at all for the cause. . . . When that cause or interest begins to profit from what it simplistically suspects to be a biological continuism, whose sinister connotations we are well aware of, or more generally to profit from what is suspected as a geneticism that one might wish to associate with this scatterbrained accusation of continuism, the undertaking in any case becomes . . . aberrant. ("The Animal That Therefore I Am," 398)

From Derrida's point of view, then, the irony of Singer's utilitarian calculus, *even if* in the service of "the cause" of the animal, is that it would be "asinine," not only because of its "geneticism" and "continuism" (manifested in its concept of "interests"), but also because it would be, ironically enough, the sort of mechanical behavior (the utilitarian calculus) that Descartes associated with the animal and the "bestial."[33]

This does not mean, of course, that Derrida does not take very seriously the ethical question of nonhuman animals or, for that matter, all of the issues associated with the term *animal rights*. Indeed, it is this, as much as anything, that separates him from Levinas. Here, we could do no better than to return to Derrida's own discussion of Levinas's attractions and limits in "Eating Well." For Levinas, subjectivity "is constituted first of all as the subjectivity of the *hostage*"; the subject is held hostage by the other, in responsibility to the other, in the imperative "Thou shalt not kill." But in Levinas, as in the Judeo-Christian tradition generally, this is not understood as a "Thou shalt not put to death the living in general" (112–13). But why not? Because, as Derrida shows, "Levinas's thematization of the other 'as' other presupposes the 'as'-structure of Heideggerian ontology" (Beardsworth, *Derrida and the Political*, 134); it holds, that is, that the other can appear *as such*—not as an ontological positivity, as in Heidegger, but rather as a form of *privileged negativity* (what Levinas often calls "passivity," "anarchy," or "vulnerability") that is *always* the form of the ethical *as such*. For Derrida, on the other hand, one must keep the "there" of ethics, the site of the other, "as complex as possible, as a 'play' of time and law, one which refuses the exemplary localization of thought" of the sort that we find, for instance, in Levinas's contention that the "authentically human" is the "being-Jewish in every man" (ibid., 124). Conversely, for Derrida, "for the other to be other it must already be less than other" because the alterity of the other is always already caught in what "Eating Well" calls the "sacrificial economy" of carno-phallogocentrism; and hence, "one cannot 'welcome the other as other'"; in consequence of which, as Beardsworth notes, "alterity can only be the loss of the other in its self-presentation, that is, the 'trace' of the other" (134). What Levinas surrenders, then, is "a differentiated articulation *between* the other and the same," the effect of which "is the loss in turn of the *incalculable* nature of the relation between the other and its others (the community at large)" (125).[34]

For Derrida, then—to return to "Eating Well"—the surest sign of this recontainment of the alterity of the other in Levinas is that the ethical status of the "community at large" is purchased at the expense of the sacrifice of all forms of difference that are not human—most pointedly, of course, of the animal—whereas for Derrida, the animal *in the plural* is precisely what keeps open the ethical moment of the self via its passivity, because the animal's *death, its mortality, is not sacrificed.* "Discourses as original as those of Heidegger and Levinas, disrupt, of course, a certain traditional humanism," Derrida argues in "Eating Well." "In spite of the differences separating them, they nonetheless remain profound humanisms *to the extent that they do not sacrifice sacrifice.* The subject (in Levinas's sense) and the *Dasein* are 'men' in a world where sacrifice is possible and where it is not forbidden to make an attempt on life in general, but only on the life of man" (113). For Derrida, on the other hand, the animal "has its point of view regarding me. The point of view of the absolute other, and nothing will have ever done more to make me think through this absolute alterity of the neighbor than these moments when I see myself seen naked under the gaze of a cat" ("The Animal That Therefore I Am," 380).

And when Derrida says "man" we should, I think, hear him quite pointedly, for the problem with animal difference is strictly analogous to the recontainment of *sexual* difference in both Heidegger and Levinas.[35] As for the latter, Derrida explains that from Levinas's point of view, it is not woman or femininity per se but rather sexual difference as such that is ethically secondary, the point being that "the possibility of ethics could be saved, if one takes ethics to mean that relationship to the other as other which accounts for no other determination or sexual characteristic in particular. What kind of an ethics would there be if belonging to one sex or another became its law or privilege?" And yet, Derrida continues, it is not clear that Levinas is not here restoring "a classical interpretation" that "gives a masculine sexual marking to what is presented either as a neutral originariness or, at least, as prior and superior to all sexual markings . . . by placing (differentiated) sexuality beneath humanity which sustains itself at the level of Spirit" ("Choreographies," 450–51; see also "At this very moment, 40–44). And that "humanity" sustains *itself,* as we have already seen, by means of the "carnivorous" sacrificial structure that orders the relationship between the world "of spirit" and the animal; hence the full force of Derrida's comment late in the Cerisy lecture that, in the philosophical tradition, he has never "noticed a protestation *of principle* . . . against the general singular of an animal whose sexuality is as a matter of principle left undifferentiated—or neutralized, not to say castrated" ("The Animal That Therefore I Am," 408).

If Derrida's differences with Levinas on the question of ethics, writing, and the animal are perhaps clear by now, it worth briefly highlighting his differences with Lyotard as well. All three share the sense of ethics voiced in Lyotard's *Just Gaming*: that "Any attempt to state the law . . . to place oneself in the position of enunciator of the universal prescription is obviously infatuation itself and absolute injustice" (99). But Derrida would draw our attention to the ethical implications for "'the crossing of borders' between man and animal" ("The Animal That Therefore I Am," 372) that reside in their respective theories of language. Here, what we might call Lyotard's radical formalism would appear to be problematic, for, as Samuel Weber notes, in Lyotard "the concern with 'preserving the purity' and singularity 'of each game' by reinforcing its isolation from the others gives rise to exactly what was intended to be avoided: 'the domination of one game by another, namely, 'the domination of the prescriptive,'" in the form of: *thou shalt not let one language game impinge upon the singularity of another*" (*Just Gaming*, 104). And so, if in Lyotard the Kantian "outside," marked by the difference between the conceivable and the presentable, is what permanently keeps open the ethical necessity of dissensus and invention, the price that Lyotard pays for this way of formulating the problem is that the language games themselves become in an important sense pure and self-identical, and hence the boundaries between them become in principle absolutely uncrossable. Thus, the field of "general agonistics" of which any language game partakes (*Postmodern Condition*, 10) is, as Weber rightly points out, not so agonistic (or so general) after all, for it is restricted by the countervailing force of Lyotard's concept of the language game, which can be in struggle neither internally (because it is a singularity determined by a finite set of rules) nor externally (because the incommensurability of all games is to be protected at all costs) (*Just Gaming*, 104).

For Derrida, on the other hand, the outside is always already inside; in Lyotardian terms, the verticality of the language game is always already constitutively eroded by the horizontality of the field of inscription and signification—of *différance* and the trace, of writing—of which it is part. And hence, the ethical subject of the Kantian "Idea" in Lyotard's scheme— the subject of the "community of reasonable beings"—is always already constitutively derailed by the *un*reason, the *a*logological force of the *écriture* upon whose disavowal the Law constructs itself in a process that Derrida calls "the law of Law." For Kant, we should remember, "the moral law is transcendent because it transcends the sensible conditions of time and space"; but for Derrida, the *différance* of law, the law of Law, consists in the fact that "If the law is, on the one hand, unaccountable"—and this is where Derrida's relationship with Levinas is triangulated via different relations to Kant—"on the other hand it is *nowhere* but *in* its inscriptions in history, whilst not being reducible *to* these inscriptions either" (Beardsworth, *Derrida and the Political*, 29). Thus, the Kantian gives way to the Nietzschean realization, as Weber puts it, that "Otherness, then, is not to be sought *between* games that are supposed to be essentially self-identical, but *within* the game as such" (*Just Gaming*, 106). Or, as Geoff Bennington characterizes it, in more strictly Derridean terms, for Derrida "language is not essentially human . . . ; the refusal to think of language as in some way a separate domain over against the world . . . implies the consequence of an essential inhumanity of language."[36]

This difference between Lyotard's sense of language and Derrida's has very direct implications for thinking the problematic of the animal in relation to ethics. As Vicki Kirby points out, if one

> reads the substance of materiality, corporeality, and radical alterity together, and places them outside or beyond representation, the absolute cut of this division actually severs the possibility of an ethical relation

with the Other. . . . [E]thical responsibility to the Other therefore becomes an act of conscious humility and benevolent obligation to an Other who is not me, an Other whose difference is so foreign that it cannot be known. Yet a Derridean reading would surely discover that the breach in the identity and being of the sovereign subject, and in the very notion of cognition itself, is not merely nostalgic loss nor anticipated threat or promise. It is a constitutive breaching, a recalling and differentiating within the subject, that hails it into presence. As impossible as it may seem, the ethical relation to radical alterity is to an other that is, also, me. (*Telling Flesh*, 95)

This is precisely what Derrida has in mind, I think, when he contends in "Eating Well" that

The idea according to which man is the only speaking being, in its tradi-tional form or in its Heideggerian form, seems to me at once undisplace-able and highly problematic. Of course, if one defines language in such a way that it is reserved for what we call man, what is there to say? But if one reinscribes language in a network of possibilities that do not merely en-compass it but mark it irreducibly from the inside, everything changes. I am thinking in particular of the mark in general, of the trace, of iterabili-ty, of *différance*. These possibilities or necessities, without which there would be no language, *are themselves not only human*. . . . And what I am proposing here should allow us to take into account scientific knowledge about the complexity of "animal languages," genetic coding, all forms of marking within which so-called human language, as original as it might be, does not allow us to "cut" once and for all where we would in general like to cut. (116–17)

It is not simply a matter, however, of contesting humanism's tradi-tional notion of language and reconceiving it in terms of the technicity and inhuman dynamics of *différance*; for once *that* stratagem of human-ism has been met, there remains the privileged *relation to that relation* that more contemporary, sophisticated forms of humanism of the sort we find in Lacan and Levinas have reserved for themselves. As Derrida ex-plains in "The Animal That Therefore I Am," philosophers from Aristotle to Lacan, Kant, Heidegger, and Levinas all "say the same thing: the animal is without language. Or more precisely unable to respond, to respond with a response that could be precisely and rigorously distinguished from a reaction" (400). To "respond" rather than merely "react," one must be capable of "erasing," and "even those who, from Descartes to Lacan, have

conceded to the said animal some aptitude for signs and for communication, have always denied it the power to *respond*—to *pretend,* to *lie,* to
cover its tracks or *erase* its own traces"—hence the fallback position of
humanism (as in Lacan) that it is the difference between communication
and metacommunication, signifying and signifying *about* signifying, the
ability *to lie by telling the truth,* as Lacan puts it, that surely distinguishes
the human from the animal. But, as Derrida notes, even if we concede
that this is a more compelling distinction between human and animal
than simply language use as such, it is nonetheless deeply problematic in
one fundamental sense: "The fact that a trace can always be erased, and
forever, in no way means—and this is a critical difference—that someone, man *or* animal, *can of his own accord* erase his traces" (401).

The specific moment in Derrida's intervention is crucial. It helps to
make clear how it is that Derrida is interested in the historical and institutional specificity—not "merely," as it were, the ontological problematics—
of the question of the animal. Here, Richard Beardsworth's objection in
Derrida and the Political about Derrida's ethical formalism is worth lin-
gering over for a moment. Beardsworth calls on Derrida to engage more
directly the question of the trace and technicity as it relates to contemporary technoscience, because the latter constitutes an unprecedented
speeding up of the relationship between the human and the technical that
"risks reducing the *différance* of time, or the aporia of time"—whose very
excess constitutes the "promise" of the impossible "we" to come to which
any form of political organization is ethically responsible (146)—"to an
experience of time that *forgets* time" (148). But what we find in Derrida's
later work—and above all for Beardsworth in *Of Spirit*—is an under-
estimation of "the speed with which the human is losing its experience *of*
time," with the result that the "promise" of ethics and politics ends up
"*appearing* too formal, freezing Derrida's deconstructions . . . which turn
the relation between the human and the technical into a 'logic' of supplementarity without history" (154). Thus, for Beardsworth, "There are,
consequently, 'two' instances of 'radical alterity' here which need articulation, and whose relation demands to be developed: the radical alterity of
the promise and the radical alterity of the other prior to the ego of which
one modality (and increasingly so in the coming years) is the technical
other" (155).

But *only one modality,* I would hasten to add. Indeed, it seems likely to
me—though there is no way, strictly speaking, to prove the point—that
Beardsworth's call for "the promise to appear *through* the relation between
the human and the nonhuman" (156) gets rerouted in much of Derrida's

later work (especially in *Of Spirit*) via the question of the animal. Beardsworth asks, "with attention to the radical alterity of time, do Derrida's earlier analyses of originary technicity become eclipsed? If not . . . then *how* does one develop the relations between the promise and originary technicity?" (153). The answer, it seems to me, is via the question of the animal, *precisely* with the intention of developing a concept of the promise that is not once again automatically exclusive of nonhuman others; for Derrida would surely ask of Beardsworth whether *his* concept of the radical alterity of time in this instance is not symptomatic of the humanism with which Derrida takes issue in "The Animal That Therefore I Am" in his meditations on the shared passivity, anguish, and vulnerability of the human *and* the animal in relation to death. In his later work, Derrida's strategy, I would suggest, is exactly the reverse of what Beardsworth calls for: attention to the question of the qualitative transformation of time not by way of attention to the speed of technoscience, but to what one might call the "slowness" of the animal other. Here, time, rather than being "for" the human—*even in* the form of its inhumanity in technicity, to which the human nevertheless maintains a privileged relationship—instead consists of a radical asynchronicity: horizontally, in evolutionary qualities and tendencies that persist across species lines (the facts of our mammalian being, of "involuntary" physiological traits and gestural repertoires, the experience of disease and, most important, the death that fatefully links the world of human and animal); and vertically, in the differences between species in their power over time, their ability to compress it, if you will, for adaptive advantage by making use of different technicities (including, of course, the technicity of the body as the first tool, but also of the brain and the tool proper, with its apotheosis in technoscience).

In these terms, one might think of the speed of time that Beardsworth (following Bernard Stiegler) associates with the specific phenomenon of technoscience as part of a larger evolutionary process of chronicities and periodicities in which all animals participate, sharing a passivity in a larger, radically ahuman economy of time's scarcity and alterity. All animals strive to increase their control over ever longer periods of future time in the interests of anticipating and adapting to changes in their environment. The differences between species may thus be described in terms of the ability to process increased temporal complexity and the constant introduction of novel periodicities into the environment, as organisms constantly adjust to each other's increasingly well-honed periodicities by introducing ever more efficient ones of their own, leading to a supersaturation of chronicities that in turn generates a scarcity of *time* that drives evolutionary process.[37] From this vantage—to return to the relationship between time and technicity—what Derrida's work on the animal would stress is the *inhuman* rather than the *human* relation *to the inhumanity of time and technicity itself.* This is what Derrida means, I believe—in a formulation germane to Beardsworth's own historicism—when he writes: "As for history, historicity, even historicality, those motifs belong precisely . . . to *this* auto-definition, *this* auto-apprehension, *this* auto-situation of man or of the human *Dasein* with respect to what is living and with respect to animal life; they belong to this auto-biography of man that I wish to call into question today" (393).

This does not mean, however, that Derrida is not attuned to the historical specificity of our relation to animals. Indeed, "The Animal That Therefore I Am" is even more striking than "Eating Well" in the forthrightness with which it meets this question. There, he argues that "for about two centuries" we have been involved at "an alarming rate of acceleration" in a transformation of our experience of animals (36), in which our

> traditional forms of treatment of the animal have been turned upside down by the joint developments of zoological, ethological, biological and genetic *forms of knowledge* and the always inseparable *techniques* of intervention . . . by means of farming and regimentalization at a demographic level unknown in the past, by means of genetic experimentation, the industrialization of what can be called the production for consumption of animal meat, artificial insemination on a massive scale, more and more audacious manipulations of the genome, the reduction of the animal not only to production and overactive reproduction (hormones, crossbreeding, cloning, etc.) of meat for consumption but also of all sorts of other end products, and all that in the service of a certain being and the so-called human well-being of man. (394)

For Derrida, no one can "seriously deny the disavowal that this involves . . . in order to organize on a global scale the forgetting or misunderstanding of this violence that some would compare to the worst cases of genocide" (39). But this genocide takes on a particular, historically specific form. As Derrida puts it in one of the more striking passages in all of his work on animals,

> it is occurring through the organization and exploitation of an artificial, infernal, virtually interminable survival, in conditions that previous generations would have judged monstrous, outside of every supposed norm

of a life proper to animals that are thus exterminated by means of their continued existence or even their overpopulation. As if, for example, instead of throwing people into ovens or gas chambers, (let's say Nazi) doctors and geneticists had decided to organize the overproduction and overgeneration of Jews, gypsies and homosexuals by means of artificial insemination, so that, being more numerous and better fed, they could be destined in always increasing numbers for the same hell, that of the imposition of genetic experimentation, or extermination by gas or by fire. In the same abattoirs. (394–95)

It is in response to this historically specific transformation of our relations with animals that "voices are raised—minority, weak, marginal voices, little assured of their discourse, of their right to discourse and of the enactment of their discourse within the law, as a declaration of rights—in order to protest, in order to appeal . . . to what is still presented in such a problematic way as *animal rights*." Indeed, from the vantage of Derrida's recent work, the value of animal rights, however problematic its formulation may be, is that it "involves a new experience of this compassion," has opened anew "the immense question of pathos," of "suffering, pity and compassion," and "the place that has to be accorded to the interpretation of this compassion, to the sharing of this suffering among the living, to the law, ethics, and politics that must be brought to bear upon this experience of compassion" (395).

Disarticulating Language, Subject, and Species: Maturana and Varela (with Bateson)

A signal advantage of Derrida's formulation of the "trace beyond the human" is that it allows us not only to "move from the 'ends of man,' that is the confines of man, to the 'crossing of borders' between man and animal" ("The Animal That Therefore I Am," 372), but also to make an interdisciplinary crossing between philosophy and the sciences with the aim of crafting a posthumanist theory of the relations between subjectivity, species, and signification in the broadest sense. As Eva Knodt has pointed out, the exploration of the possible convergences between the "two cultures" of science and the humanities "remains blocked as long as difference is modeled upon linguistic difference, and linguistic self-referentiality is considered the paradigm for self-referentiality generally."[38] Here, of course, a good deal depends on how one understands Derrida's notions of writing and textuality, but, in any case, we would need to distinguish, I think, between what Knodt calls the "pan-textualist assumptions" of

Derrida's formulations and those of a Lyotard, not just on the question of language, but also on the question of science—and the relation of both to the larger, trans-species question of communication.[39]

Here, my aim will be to give some substance to Derrida's own very general suggestions that such disciplinary crossings be pursued, as he reminds us when he protests Heidegger's dogmatic humanism toward the animal in the face of a growing and highly differentiated "zoological knowledge" ("*Geschlecht* II," 173). But when we move the discussion into this register of the signifying behaviors of (at least some) animals, we need to remind ourselves, as Derrida is quick to point out, that it is not simply a question of "giving language back to the animal," but rather of showing how the difference in *kind* between human and animal that humanism constitutes on the site of language may instead be thought as difference in *degree* on a continuum of signifying processes disseminated in field of materiality, technicity, and contingency, of which "human" "language" is but a specific (albeit highly refined) instance. In other words, to recall Derrida's admonition "the animal, what a word!" is to remember that while the question of signifying behaviors may seem relevant only for some animals in particular (namely, those, such as the great apes, in whom linguistic behaviors have been observed), the larger point is that this reopening of the question of language has enormous implications for the *category* of the animal in general—the animal in the "singular," as Derrida puts it—and how it has traditionally been hypostatized over and against the category of the human—again in the singular.

I have no intention, of course, of surveying what has become the immense field within ethology of animal language studies.[40] And though I will turn very briefly to these issues at the end of this essay, I will largely be ignoring complex questions of institutional disciplinarity in the relations between science and philosophy, questions that would no doubt require their own very different investigation. Similarly, I will be postponing until another occasion a detailed comparison of the theories of meaning in poststructuralism and contemporary systems theory—the latter of which has received its most sophisticated elaboration in the work not of Maturana and Varela, but of Niklas Luhmann. For now, however, I want to examine the theoretical frame for understanding the relations of species and "linguistic domains" provided by the work of Humberto Maturana and Francisco Varela. For them, the baseline physiological structure that an animal must possess to provide the physical basis for the emergence of "third-order structural couplings" and, within that, "linguistic domains" is sufficient cephalization—that is, a certain concentration and density of neural tissue. As they put it, "the function of the nervous system diversifies tremendously with an increase in the variety of neuronal interactions, which entails growth in the cephalic portion. . . . [T]his increase in cephalic mass carries with it enormous possibilities for structural plasticity of the organism. This is fundamental for the capacity to learn."[41]

For Maturana and Varela, learning and what we usually call "experience" is precisely the result of "structural changes" within the nervous system, and specifically within the synapses and their "local characteristics" (167). Unlike mechanical cybernetic systems, even those that are capable of elementary forms of reflexivity and self-monitoring (artificial intelligence systems, for example), biological systems are self-developing forms that creatively reproduce themselves by embodying the processes of adaptive changes that allow the organism to maintain its own autonomy or "operational closure." For Maturana and Varela—and this is the theoretical innovation for which they are best known—all living organisms are therefore "autopoietic" unities; that is, they are "continually self-producing" according to their own internal rules and requirements, which means that they are in a crucial sense *closed* and self-referential in terms of what constitutes their *specific* mode of existence, even as they are *open* to the environment on the level of their material structure. As they explain it,

> autopoietic unities specify biological phenomenology as the phenomenology proper to those unities with features distinct from physical phenomenology. This is so, not because autopoietic unities go against any aspect of physical phenomenology—since their molecular components must fulfill all physical laws—but because the phenomena they generate in functioning as autopoietic unities depends on their organization and the way this organization comes about, and not on the physical nature of their components (which only determine their space of existence). (*Tree*, 51)

The nervous system, for example, "does not operate according to either of the two extremes: it is neither representational nor solipsistic. It is not solipsistic, because as part of the nervous system's organism, it participates in the interactions of the nervous system with its environment. These interactions continuously trigger in it the structural changes that modulate its dynamics of states. . . . Nor is it representational, for in each interaction it is the nervous system's structural state that specifies what perturbations are possible and what changes trigger them" (169).

This is the view widely held in neurobiology and cognitive science, where most scholars now agree—to take perhaps the most often-cited example, color vision—that "our world of colored objects is literally independent of the wavelength composition of the light coming from any scene we look at. . . . Rather, we must concentrate on understanding that the experience of a color corresponds to a specific pattern of states of activity in the nervous system which its structure determines" (ibid., 21–22). For Maturana and Varela, then, the environment does not present stimuli to the organism, replete with specifications and directions for appropriate response in an input/output model. As they put it, "the changes that result from the interaction between the living being and its environment are brought about by the disturbing agent but *determined by the structure of the disturbed system*" (96; emphasis added). What this means is that "the nervous system does not 'pick up information' from the environment, as we often hear. On the contrary, it brings forth a world by specifying what patterns of the environment are perturbations and what changes trigger them in the organism" (169). It is this break with the representational model that distinguishes the work of Maturana and Varela from most of even the most sophisticated work on self-organizing systems in the sciences—a fact whose full epistemological implications I will return to later in this essay.

In animals with sufficient cephalization and plasticity, it is possible for "interactions *between* organisms to acquire in the course of their ontogeny a *recurrent* nature" (180), and only with reference to that specific ontogeny, in its various degrees of contingency and uniqueness, can we understand the animal's behavior. When these interactions become recurrent, organisms develop a *"new phenomenological domain"* (ibid.): *"third-order structural couplings"* (181) or "social life for short" (189). As Maturana and Varela put it, what is common to third-order unities is that "whenever they arise—if only to last for a short time—they generate a particular internal phenomenology, namely, one in which *the individual ontogenies of all the participating organisms occur fundamentally as part of the network of co-ontogenies that they bring about in constituting third-order unities*" (193).[42] In these instances, the evolutionary problem immediately becomes how, given such variation, the autopoiesis of the social structure will be maintained. The answer, in a word, is *communication* (196, 198–99)—and communication in the specific antirepresentationalist sense we have already touched upon.

To understand the relationship between the broader phenomenon of communication and the more specific matter of language as such, it might be useful to contrast the communication of relatively nonplastic social animals, the social insects, with those of more plastic animals, such as wolves or humans. In the case of the insects, communication can take place by a small number of direct chemical signals (trophallaxis) because the behavior to be regulated is not susceptible to great ontogenic variation. When the reverse is true, however—when ontogenic variation must be not just tolerated but in fact made productive for the autopoiesis of the social structure—then the animal must develop "acquired communicative behaviors" that depend on the animal's individual ontogeny as part of a third-order unity. When this happens, the animal is engaged in the production of a "linguistic domain," behaviors that "constitute the basis for language, but . . . are not yet identical with it" (207).[43] Even though human beings are not the only animals that generate linguistic domains, "what is peculiar to them is that, in their linguistic coordination of actions, they give rise to a new phenomenal domain, viz. the *domain of language*. . . . In the flow of recurrent social interactions, language appears when the operations in a linguistic domain result in coordinations of actions about actions that pertain to the linguistic domain *itself*" (209–10). "In other words," they conclude, "we are in language or, better, we 'language,' only when through a reflexive action we make a linguistic distinction of a linguistic distinction" (210).

Now, this view of the specificity of language as *metalinguistic*—as the ability to make linguistic distinctions about linguistic distinctions—may at first glance seem similar to some of the familiar strategies of humanism that we have already examined (the Lacanian view critiqued by Derrida, for example). Here, however, Maturana and Varela emphasize that the relationship between linguistic domains, the emergence of language per se, and species is dynamic and fluid, one of degree and not of kind. It is not an ontological distinction, in other words, even if it is a phenomenological one. As they are quick to point out, "cogent evidence" now shows that other animals (most famously, great apes) are "capable of interacting with us in rich and even recursive linguistic domains" (212) and, more than that, it seems that in many of these instances animals are indeed capable of "making linguistic distinctions of linguistic distinctions"—that is, of languaging.[44] For them, language is "a permanent biologic possibility in the natural drift of living beings" (ibid.). The point, of course, is not to determine whether or not animals can "make all the linguistic distinctions that we human beings make" (215), but rather to rigorously theorize the *disarticulation* between the category of language and the category of species, for only if we do so can the relationship between human, animal, and language be theorized in *both* its similarity and its difference.[45]

We can gain an even more finely grained sense of how systems theory thinks this relationship by turning to the work of Gregory Bateson. As he points out in his analysis of "play" among mammals, this phenomenon "could only occur if the participant organisms were capable of some degree of metacommunication, *i.e.*, of exchanging signals which would carry the message 'this is play.'"[46] "The playful nip denotes the bite," he continues, "but it does not denote what would be denoted by the bite"—namely, aggression or fight (181). What we find here, as in other behaviors among animals, such as "threat," "histrionic behavior," and "deceit," is what Bateson calls "the primitive occurrence of map-territory differentiation," which "may have been an important step in the evolution of communication." As he explains, "Denotative communication as it occurs at the human level is only possible *after* the evolution of a complex set of metalinguistic (but not verbalized) rules which govern how words and sentences shall be related to objects and events. It is therefore appropriate to look for the evolution of such metalinguistic and/or metacommunicative rules at a prehuman and preverbal level" (180).

As Bateson points out, however, it is not as if such instances are simply transcended by the advent of specifically human modes of verbal interaction, for "such combinations as histrionic play, bluff, playful threat," and so on "form together a single total complex of phenomena" that we find not only in various childhood patterns of behavior, but also in adult forms such as gambling, risk taking, spectatorship, initiation and hazing, and a broad range of ritualistic activities—all of which are examples of "a more complex form of play: the game which is constructed not upon the premise 'This is play' but rather around the question 'Is this play?'" In all of these, we find more elaborate forms of the map-territory relation at work in mammalian play generally, where "Paradox is doubly present in the signals which are exchanged. . . . Not only do the playing animals not quite mean what they are saying but, also, they are usually communicating about something which does not exist" (182). The playful baring of the fangs between two wolves, for example, signifies the bite that does not exist; but the bite that does not exist itself signifies a *relationship*—in this case of dominance or subordination—whose "referent," if you will, is itself the third-order unity of the pack structure, within which the signification is meaningful.

Indeed, as Bateson argues, mammalian communication in general is "primarily about the rules and the contingencies of relationship." For example, the familiar movements a cat makes in "asking" you for food are, behaviorally speaking, essentially those that a kitten makes to a mother cat, and "if we were to translate the cat's message into words, it would not be correct to say that she is crying 'Milk!' Rather, she is saying something like 'Mama!' Or perhaps, still more correctly, we should say that she is asserting 'Dependency! Dependency!'" From here, "it is up to you to take a *deductive* step, guessing that it is milk that the cat wants. It is the necessity for this deductive step"—and this strikes me as a brilliant insight—"which marks the difference between preverbal mammalian communication and *both* the communication of bees and the languages of men" (367).

For Bateson, then, it may be that "the great new thing" in the evolution of human language is not "the discovery of abstraction or generalization, but the discovery of how to be specific about something other than relationship"—to be denotative about actions and objects, for example. But what is equally remarkable is how tied to the communication of preverbal mammals human communication continues to be (ibid.). Unlike the digital mode of communication typical of verbal languages, in which the formal features of signs are not driven "from behind" by the real magnitudes they signify—"The word 'big' is not bigger than the word 'little,'" to use Bateson's example—in the analogical form of kinesic and paralinguistic communication used by preverbal mammals, "the magnitude of the gesture, the loudness of the voice, the length of the pause, the tension of the muscle, and so forth—these magnitudes commonly correspond (directly or inversely) to magnitudes in the relationship that is the subject of discourse" (374), and they are signaled via "bodily movements," "involuntary tensions of voluntary muscles," "irregularities of respiration," and the like. "If you want to know what the bark of a dog 'means,' you look at his lips, the hair on the back of his neck, his tail, and so on" (370). It is true, as Bateson argues, that human languages have a few words for relationship functions, "words like 'love,' 'respect,' 'dependency,'" but "these words function poorly in the actual discussion of relationship between participants in the relationship. If you say to a girl, 'I love you,' she is likely to pay more attention to the accompanying kinesics and paralinguistics than to the words themselves" (374). In other words—and here we should be reminded of Cavell's discussion of "skeptical terror" of the other—she will look for the involuntary message your body is sending in spite of you, because "discourse about relationship is commonly accompanied by a mass of semivoluntary kinesic and autonomic signals which provide a more trustworthy comment on the verbal message" (137).[47]

Bateson's work on language, communication, and species helps to amplify and elaborate what Derrida has in mind, I think, in his formulation of the trace beyond the human, and this in two senses: first, in evolutionary terms, as the outcome of processes and dynamics not specifically or even particularly human that remain sedimented and at work in the domain of human language broadly conceived; and second, in terms of how language is traced by the material contingency of its enunciation in and through the body, in its "involuntary" kinesic and paralinguistic significations that communicate in and through in ways that the humanist subject of "intention" and "reflection" cannot master, ways that link us to a larger repertoire and history of signification not specifically human and yet intimately so. This view of language has important implications for our ability to theorize the continuities, while respecting the differences, between human and animal subjectivities in relation to the emergence of linguistic domains. As Bateson argues, the ability to distinguish between play and nonplay—the ability to make statements whose paradoxical status of the sort we find in play is a direct result of an organism's understanding and manipulation of a metacommunicative frame—is directly related to the emergence of something like subjectivity as a dynamic that is recursively tied to the evolution of increasingly complex communicative behaviors (185).[48] For Maturana and Varela as well,

> It is in language that the self, the I, arises as the social singularity defined by the operational intersection in the human body of the recursive linguistic distinctions in which it is distinguished. This tells us that in the network of linguistic interactions in which we move, *we maintain an ongoing descriptive recursion which we call the "I." It enables us to conserve our linguistic operational coherence and our adaptation in the domain of language.* (231)[49]

This processive, recursive, antirepresentational account of the relationship between material technicities, linguistic domains, and the emergence of subjectivities has the advantage of allowing us to address the specificity of our similarities and differences with other creatures—especially those creatures who are enough like us to complicate and challenge our discourses of subjectivity—but without getting caught in the blind alleys of "intention" or "consciousness" (or, what amounts to the same thing on methodological terrain in the sciences, "anthropomorphism") that have plagued attempts to understand in what specific sense we share a world with nonhuman animals. All of which is summed up nicely, I think, by philosopher and cognitive scientist Daniel Dennett, who writes that language "plays an enormous role in the structuring of a human mind, and the mind of a creature lacking language—and having really no need for language—should not be supposed to be structured in these ways. Does this mean that languageless creatures 'are not conscious at all' (as Descartes insisted)?"[50] No, because to put the question that way presupposes

> the assumption that consciousness is a special all-or-nothing property that sunders the universe into vastly different categories: the things that have it . . . and the things that lack it. Even in our own case, we cannot draw the line separating our conscious mental states from our unconscious mental states. . . . [W]hile the presence of language marks a particularly dramatic increase in imaginative range, versatility, and self-control . . . these powers do not have the *further* power of turning on some special inner light that would otherwise be off. (Ibid.)

This does not mean that the question of language is not ethically to the point—quite the contrary. Indeed, it is worth articulating the relationship between language and species as specifically as possible, not least because a persistent problem in contemporary theory has been theorizing the specificity or singularity of *particular* animals and the ethical implications of their particular attributes. In contemporary theory—I am thinking here especially of the important work by Gilles Deleuze and Félix Guattari—the power and importance of the animal is almost always its pull toward a *multiplicity* that operates to unseat the singularities and essentialisms of identity that were proper to the subject of humanism. But this is of little help in addressing the ethical differences between abusing a dog and abusing a scallop—differences that would seem, to many people, to be to the point, even if they are certainly not ethically the *only* point (in which case considerations of biodiversity and the like might come into play as well).

Revisiting Jeremy Bentham's critique of Descartes, as we saw Derrida do earlier, Dennett argues that although languaging and suffering "usually appear to be opposing benchmarks of moral standing," in fact it makes sense to argue that the greater an animal's capacities in the former regard, the greater its capacities in the latter, "since the capacity to suffer is a function of the capacity to have articulated, wide-ranging, highly discriminative desires, expectations, and other sophisticated mental states" (449)—which helps to explain the intuitive sense most of us have that the suffering of a horse or a dog is a weightier matter than that of a crawfish. "The greater the scope, the richer the detail, the more finely discriminative the desires, the worse it is when those desires are thwarted," he continues. "In compensation for having to endure all the suffering, the smart creatures get to have all the fun. You have to have a cognitive economy with a budget for exploration and self-stimulation to provide the space for the recursive stacks of derived desires that make fun possible. You have taken a first step"—and here we should recall Maturana and Varela's "linguistic distinction of a linguistic distinction"—"when your architecture permits you to appreciate the meaning of 'Stop it, I love it!' Shallow versions of this building power are manifest in some higher species, but it takes a luxuriant imagination, and leisure time—something most species cannot afford—to grow a broad spectrum of pleasures" (450).

And yet, Dennett, like Bateson, remains tied to an essentially representationalist frame, one that continues to believe in "objective" or "correct" interpretations of heterophenomenological observations. Aside from the epistemological problems that such a position has on its own terms—problems I have discussed elsewhere in some detail[51]—it is only when that frame is rigorously dismantled, I believe, that fruitful interdisciplinary interchange of the sort we can generate between Derrida and Maturana and Varela can begin. Indeed, as I want to argue now, to believe that organisms internalize the environment in the form of "representations" or even "information" is to have already committed the kind of Cartesian hubris diagnosed by Derrida in "The Animal That Therefore I Am," because this putatively "objective" or "realist" view of the world— the world of which organisms have more or less "accurate" representations depending on the sophistication of their filtering mechanisms—is, despite appearances, referenced to an idealism founded on the fantasy that human language (in this case, the language of science) is sovereign in its mastery of the multiplicity and contingency of the world. It is the fantasy, to put it in the hybrid terms I am using here, that there is such a thing as a nondeconstructible observation.

To return to Maturana and Varela's handling of this problem, the nervous system may operate by way of its own autopoietic closure, but "we as observers have access both to the nervous system and to the structure of its environment. We can thus describe the behavior of an organism as though it arose from the operation of its nervous system with representations of the environment or as an expression of some goal-oriented process. These descriptions, however, do not reflect the operation of the nervous system itself. They are good only for the purposes of communication among ourselves as observers" (*Tree*, 132). To say as much confronts us, however, with "a formidable snag" because "it seems that the only alternative to a view of the nervous system as operating with representations is to deny the surrounding reality" (133). The way out of this dilemma, they contend, is to understand the difference between first-order and second-order observation (to borrow Niklas Luhmann's terms). In first-order observation, we are dealing with the observation of objects and events—a territory, to use Bateson's metaphor—in terms of a given map or code based on a fundamental, constitutive distinction that organizes the code. In second-order observation, however, we are observing observations—and observing, moreover, how those observations are constructed atop an unobservable blindness to the wholly contingent nature of their constitutive distinction. (The legal system, for example cannot carry out its observations of legal versus illegal while at the same time recognizing the essential identity of both sides of the distinction, its essential tautology, its own self-instantiation ex nihilo: legal is legal.) Thus, as Dietrich Schwanitz puts it, "If observation is to be made observable, it is necessary to bring about a change of distinction, a displacement of the difference—in other words, a kind of deconstruction."[52] "As observers," Maturana and Varela explain,

> we can see a unity in *different* domains, depending on the distinctions we make. Thus, on the one hand, we can consider a system in that domain where its components operate, in the domain of its internal states and structural changes. . . . On the other hand, we can consider a unity that also interacts with its environment and describe its history of interactions with it. . . . Neither of these two possible descriptions is a problem per se: both are necessary to complete our understanding of a unity. It is the observer who correlates them from his outside perspective. . . . The problem begins when we unknowingly go from one realm to another and demand that the correspondences we establish between them (because we see these two realms simultaneously) be in fact a part of the operation of the unity. (135–36)

If this sounds circular, it is—and it is precisely this circularity that provides the bridge between the second-order systems theory of Maturana and Varela and the deconstruction of Derrida.[53] Writing of the "slightly dizzy sensation" that attends "the circularity entailed in using the instrument of analysis to analyze the instrument of analysis," Maturana and Varela suggest that *every act of knowing brings forth a world* because of the "inseparability between a particular way of being and how the world appears to us." For us, as languaging beings, this means that "Every reflection, including one on the foundation of human knowledge, invariably takes place in language, which is our distinctive way of being human and being humanly active" (26). Or, as Maturana puts it elsewhere in an especially exacting formulation:

Contrary to a common implicit or explicit belief, scientific explanations . . . constitutively do not and cannot operate as phenomenic reductions or give rise to them. This nonreductionist relation between the phenomenon to be explained and the mechanism that generates it is operationally the case because the actual result of a process, and the operations in the process that give rise to it in a generative relation, *intrinsically take place in independent and nonintersecting phenomenal domains*. This situation is the reverse of reductionism. . . . [This] permits us to see, particularly in the domain of biology, that there are phenomena like language, mind, or consciousness that require an interplay of bodies as a generative structure but do not take place in any of them. In this sense, science and the understanding of science lead us away from transcendental dualism.[54]

What Maturana and Varela offer, I think, is their own version of how, as in Derrida's account (to borrow Rodolphe Gasché's characterization), the conditions of possibility for discourse are at the same time conditions of impossibility.[55] More precisely, we can insist on these "independent and nonintersecting phenomenal domains" that thus, in *being nonintersecting*, defy the mastery of any Concept, Identity, or *logos*, but we can do so only by means of the phenomenal domain of language. For Maturana and Varela, however—and this, I think, captures the full force of Derrida's radicalization of the concept of the "trace beyond the human" for the present discussion—that phenomenal domain requires "an interplay of bodies as a generative structure" but does not take place in any one of them. As Maturana puts it in a formulation that, in light of Bateson's work on mammalian communication, has particular resonance for Derrida's insistence on the fundamentally ahuman character of language, its erosion by its other, by *all its others*: "as we human beings exist in language, our bodyhood is the system of nodes of operational intersection of all the operational coherences that we bring forth as observers in our explanation of our operation" ("Science and Daily Life," 49). Hence, "the bodyhood of those in language changes according to the flow of their languaging, and the flow of their languaging changes contingently to the changes of their bodyhood. Due to this recursive braiding of bodyhood changes and consensual coordinations of actions in language, everything that the observer does as a human being takes place at the level of his or her operational realization in his or her bodyhood in one and the same domain," even though different cognitive domains, such as the "practical" and the "theoretical," may "in the conversational domains in which they are distinguished as human activities" appear to be totally different (45).

Circularity in Maturana and Varela, then, leads us back to the contingency of the observer, and in two specific senses: first, an observer whose observations are constituted by the domain of language, but a domain of language that is not foundational because it is "only" the result of broader evolutionary processes not specifically, humanly, linguistic at all; and second, an observer who, because "recursively braided" to its bodyhood, is always already internally other and in a profound sense "animal." But where Derrida's emphasis on the deconstructibility of the observer's observation would fall on the paradoxical relationship between *logos* and the internal differential dynamics of language, for Maturana and Varela, the emphasis would fall instead on the paradoxical relationship between the observer's discursive self-reference and its biological heteroreference: vertically in the bodyhood of the observer, and horizontally in the observer's evolutionary emergence via inhuman dynamics and mechanisms—with the paradoxical result that only beings like this could have emerged to provide an explanation of how beings like this could have emerged to provide an explanation of how beings like this, and so on. For both, the hypostatized relation between "inside" and "outside" is thus made dynamic, a differential interplay that deontologizes as it reconstitutes.[56] In Derrida, however, the deconstructibility of *logos* propels us outward toward the materiality and contingency that Maturana and Varela will associate with environment and structure, whose demands and "triggers" constitute a very real problem for the autopoiesis of the organism. In this way, the analyses of Derrida and of Maturana and Varela move, in a sense, in opposite directions: Derrida's from the inside out, as it were, from the originary problem of the self-reproduction of *logos* to the contingency of the trace; and Maturana and Varela's from the outside in, from the originary problem of the overwhelming contingency and complexity of the environment to the autopoiesis of self-referential organization that, by reducing complexity, makes observation possible.[57]

It would be tempting, I suppose, to find in Derrida's "trace beyond the human" the opening of a radicalized concept of language to a kind of biologization—not just "materialization," which would be Derridean enough for most Derrideans, but more pointedly, in the later work, to *"the problem of the living"*; and, similarly, to find in the biology of Maturana and Varela a kind of linguisticization of biology, in their attention to the epistemological problem that language is "our starting point, our cognitive instrument, and our sticking point" (*Tree,* 26). But here, one last caveat from systems theory is in order, for what makes such a "conver-

gence" possible (if one wants to put it that way) is, paradoxically, not at-
tempting to step outside the limits of different disciplines and language
games, but rather pushing them internally to their own self-deconstructive
conclusions. In this light, what looks at first glance like the solipsistic insistence on self-reference and operational closure in systems theory
might be seen instead in the services of what Carolyn Merchant calls
a "reconstructive knowledge" based on "principles of interaction (not
dominance), change and process (rather than unchanging universal
principles), complexity (rather than simple assumptions)."[58]

In this light we can see systems theory, as Luhmann puts it, as "the
reconstruction of deconstruction."[59] For Luhmann—to put it very
schematically—we live in a "functionally differentiated" society, in which
we find a horizontal proliferation of language games and social systems,
none of which provides a totalizing perspective on the others, and all of
which are observations that are blind to their own constitutive distinctions. The fact of this self-referential closure of language games, however,
paradoxically drives them toward a kind of convergence, so that it is precisely *by* working vertically in different disciplines that Derrida and
Maturana and Varela end up complementing one another. As Luhmann
puts it in *Observations on Modernity,* what we find here is not "reciprocal
impulses that could explain the expansion of certain thought dispositions," but rather an "equifinal process" "that leads to a result from different starting points and that is dissolving traditional ontological metaphysics."[60] "With all the obvious differences that result from the different
functions and codings of these systems, remarkable similarities appear":

> The effect of the social relationship shows itself in the nonrandom conse-
> quences of the autonomy of function systems. They prove themselves to
> be similar despite all their differences (and in this specific sense, as mod-
> ern) because they have achieved operative segregation and autonomy.
> This is not possible except in the form of arrangements that require,
> among other things, an observation of the second order [as in Maturana
> and Varela's separation of phenomenal domains, or Derrida's logic of the
> supplement] as a systems-carrying normal operation. This explains the
> conspicuous finding that this society accepts contingencies like none
> other before it. (60–61)

It may also help to explain how we find the *biologists* Maturana and
Varela sounding a lot like the *philosopher* Derrida in *Autopoiesis and
Cognition,* where they contend that

The domain of discourse is a closed domain, and it is not possible to step outside of it through discourse. Because the domain of discourse is a closed domain it is possible to make the following ontological statement: *the logic of the* description *is the logic of the* describing *(living) system (and his cognitive domain)*.

This logic demands a substratum for the occurrence of the discourse. We cannot talk about this substratum in absolute terms, however, because we would have to describe it. . . . Thus, although this substratum is required for epistemological reasons, nothing can be said about it other than what is meant in the ontological statement above.[61]

"Nothing outside the text" indeed! Except, of course, everything.

Notes

1. Ludwig Wittgenstein, *The Wittgenstein Reader,* ed. Anthony Kenny (Oxford: Blackwell, 1994), 213. Subsequent references are given in the text.

2. Vicki Hearne, *Adam's Task: Calling Animals by Name* (New York: Random House, 1987), 4. Subsequent references are given in the text.

3. Vicki Hearne, *Animal Happiness* (New York: HarperCollins, 1994), 167. Subsequent references are given in the text.

4. Stanley Cavell, *Philosophical Passages: Wittgenstein, Emerson, Austin, Derrida* (Oxford: Blackwell, 1995), 151–52.

5. Stanley Cavell, *The Claim of Reason: Wittgenstein, Skepticism, Morality, and Tragedy* (Oxford: Oxford University Press, 1979), 187–88. Subsequent references are given in the text.

6. See Stanley Cavell, *Conditions Handsome and Unhandsome: The Constitution of Emersonian Perfectionism* (Chicago: University of Chicago Press, 1990), 1–33, 101–26. Subsequent references are given in the text.

7. Tom Regan, "The Case for Animal Rights," in *In Defense of Animals,* ed. Peter Singer (New York: Harper and Row, 1985), 16. See here especially Regan's detailed discussion of Rawls's contract theory and Kant's "indirect duty" view in *The Case for Animal Rights* (Berkeley: University of California Press, 1983), 163–94.

8. Stanley Cavell, *This New Yet Unapproachable America: Lectures after Emerson after Wittgenstein* (Albuquerque, N.Mex.: Living Batch Press, 1989), 41–42. Subsequent references are given in the text.

9. Here, Cavell's reading of the human form of life in Wittgenstein links up directly with his rendering of Emersonian "perfectionism." See his introduction to *Conditions Handsome and Unhandsome.*

10. See Daniel Dennett, *Consciousness Explained* (Boston: Little, Brown, 1991), esp. 431ff.

11. See my "Old Orders for New: Ecology, Animal Rights, and the Poverty of Humanism," *diacritics* 28:2 (summer 1998): 21–40.

12. See my "Faux Post-Humanism, or, Animal Rights, Neocolonialism, and Michael Crichton's *Congo*," *Arizona Quarterly* 55:2 (summer 1999): 115–53.

13. Stanley Cavell, *In Quest of the Ordinary: Lines of Skepticism and Romanticism* (Chicago: University of Chicago Press, 1988), 31.

14. What Wittgenstein means by the term "language game," Lyotard writes, "is that each of the various categories of utterance can be defined in terms of rules specifying their properties and the uses to which they can be put—in exactly the same way as the game of chess is defined by a set of rules determining the properties of each of the pieces, in other words, the proper way to move them" (Jean-François Lyotard, *The Postmodern Condition: A Report on Knowledge*, trans. Geoff Bennington and Brian Massumi, foreword by Fredric Jameson [Minneapolis: University of Minnesota Press, 1984], 10). Subsequent references are given in the text. As for the "grand metanarratives," Lyotard writes, "The sometimes violent divergences between political liberalism, economic liberalism, Marxism, anarchism, the radicalism of the Third Republic and socialism, count for little next to the abiding unanimity about the end to be attained. The promise of freedom is for everyone the horizon of progress and its legitimation. . . . [Yet] it was not a lack of progress but, on the contrary, development (technoscientific, artistic, economic, political) that created the possibility of total war, totalitarianisms, the growing gap between the wealth of the North and the impoverished South, unemployment and the 'new poor,' general deculturation and the crisis in education (in the transmission of knowledge), and the isolation of the artistic avant-gardes" (*The Postmodern Explained*, ed. Julian Pefanis and Morgan Thomas, trans. Julian Pefanis, Morgan Thomas, Don Barry, Bernadette Maher, and Virginia Spate, afterword by Wlad Godzich [Minneapolis: University of Minnesota Press, 1993], 82).

15. Jean-François Lyotard, *The Inhuman*, trans. Geoffrey Bennington and Rachel Bowlby (Stanford, Calif.: Stanford University Press, 1991), 2–3. Subsequent references are given in the text.

16. Jean-François Lyotard, *The Differend: Phrases in Dispute*, trans. Georges Van Den Abbeele, foreword by Wlad Godzich (Minneapolis: University of Minnesota Press, 1989), 137–38. Subsequent references are given in the text. As Lyotard notes, the idea that "nothingness" could be filled in or is simply epiphenomenal—even if we remain squarely within formalism or conventionalism, founders upon the aporia that Bertrand Russell attempts to arrest with the Theory of Logical Types (ibid., 138)—a topic I have taken up elsewhere on the work on Niklas Luhmann; see my *Critical Environments: Postmodern Theory and the Pragmatics of the "Outside"* (Minneapolis: University of Minnesota Press, 1998), 65–70, 117–28.

17. Here, we might consult, among many others, Diana Fuss in her editorial introduction to the collection *Human, All Too Human* (New York: Routledge, 1996), which points out that "The vigilance with which the demarcations between humans and animals, humans and things, and humans and children are watched over and safeguarded tells us much about the assailability of what they seek to preserve: an abstract notion of the human as unified, autonomous, and unmodified subject," whereas the "all too" of Nietzsche's famous formulation "All too human" "locates at the center of the human some unnamed surplus—-some residue, overabundance, or excess"—Lyotard's "remainder"—that is "embedded inside the human as its condition of possibility" (3–4).

18. Jean-François Lyotard and Jean-Loup Thébaud, *Just Gaming*, trans. Wlad Godzich, afterword by Samuel Weber (Minneapolis: University of Minnesota Press, 1985), 41–42. Subsequent references are given in the text.

19. And it connects rather directly, as Simon Critchley has noted, with Cavell's sense of the ethical import of skepticism: "In Stanley Cavell's terms, it is the very unknowability of the other, the irrefutability of skepticism, that initiates a relation to the other based on acknowledgement and respect. The other person stands in a relation to me that exceeds my cognitive powers, placing me in question and calling me to justify myself" ("Deconstruction and Pragmatism—Is Derrida a Private Ironist or a Public Liberal?" in *Deconstruction and Pragmatism*, ed. Chantal Mouffe [London: Routledge, 1996], 32).

20. In fairness, Lyotard is quick to specify his difference with Levinas late in *Just Gaming*, when he write that, in Levinas's view, "it is the transcendental character of the other in the prescriptive relation, in the pragmatics of prescription, that is, in the (barely) lived experience of obligation, that is truth itself. This 'truth' is not ontological truth, it is ethical. But it is a truth in Levinas' own terms. Whereas, for me, it cannot be the truth. . . . It is not a matter of privileging a language game above others," but rather of "the acceptance of the fact that one can play several games" (60–61). Now, this may remove Lyotard somewhat from the sort of objection readily raised against Levinas's position—indeed, it is raised by Lyotard himself in his "Levinas notice" in *The Differend* under the guise of "the commentator," who would object that "the less I understand you, he or she says to the Levinasian (or divine) text, the more I will obey you by that fact; for, if I want to understand you (in your turn) as a request, then I should not understand you as sense" (115). But that reservation toward Levinas does not remove Lyotard's sense of ethics from the paradoxical problem noted by several critics, including Samuel Weber in his Afterword to *Just Gaming*: if "It is necessary for a singular justice to impose its rule on all the other games, in order that they may retain their own singularity," then it is also "necessary to be able to distinguish between this violence, in some way legitimate and necessary, and 'terror,' de-

scribed as the attempt to reduce the multiplicity of the games or players through exclusion or domination. But how, then, can we conceive of such a justice, one that assures, 'by a prescriptive of universal value,' the *nonuniversality* of singular and incommensurable games?" (103).

21. John Llewelyn, "Am I Obsessed by Bobby? (Humanism of the Other Animal)," in *Rereading Levinas,* ed. Robert Bernasconi and Simon Critchley (Bloomington: Indiana University Press, 1991), 235. Subsequent references are given in the text.

22. And here he would seem to contest the reading of Kant given by Tom Regan in *The Case for Animal Rights.* On this point Llewelyn writes, "It is argued that Kant's concession that we have indirect duties to animals can be reduced to absurdity on the grounds that rationality is the only morally relevant characteristic that he can admit by which to distinguish animals from other nonhuman beings and that therefore, if we are to refrain from treating animals only as means because that is likely to lead us to treat fellow humans as means only, we should for the same reason refrain from treating only as means inanimate objects like hammers" (240).

23. Interestingly enough, Lyotard suggests in passing that he seems to want to maintain *in principle* the possibility of nonhuman animals as part of this community of reasonable beings, for, as he states in *The Differend,* "The community of practical, reasonable beings (obligees and legislators, since that is the hypothesis) includes just as well entities that would not be human. This community cannot be empirically tested. Concession: we can't really say if and how the object or referent intended by the Idea of this community is possible, but it is at least possible to conceptualize this community, it is not a 'being of reason,' or an empty concept: it is a community of persons. . . . On the scale of the single entity, it signifies autonomy. The community of practical, reasonable beings merely extends this principle of autonomy onto the scale of all possible entities, on the condition that they satisfy the definition of a practical, reasonable being, that is, of a person" (126). Theoretically, on this view, *if it could be shown* that some animals fulfill the definition of a practical, reasonable being in the Kantian sense, then they would presumably fall under the sphere of ethical consideration. But if that community "cannot be empirically tested," and because in Kant the bar of definition is pitched in such a way that it coincides more or less in fact with the subject qua human as that which can "universalize its maxim," then we are forced to say that Lyotard's Kantianism excludes the animal other, if not on principle, then certainly in effect. Hence, the distinction between species does not necessarily do any work in Lyotard's reading of Kantian ethics; but then, it does not need to. See also here Steve Baker's interesting discussion of Lyotard's contention, in *Signé Malraux* (Paris: Grasset, 1996), that cats exist "at thresholds we do not see, where

they sniff some 'present beyond,'" and in doing so live a "questioning" existence that is particularly instructive for the writer and the philosopher (in Steve Baker, *The Postmodern Animal* [London: Reaktion Books, 2000], 184).

24. Jacques Derrida, *Of Spirit: Heidegger and the Question,* trans. Geoffrey Bennington and Rachel Bowlby (Chicago: University of Chicago Press, 1989), 11. Subsequent references are given in the text. See Derrida's own partial list of his texts in which the animal has appeared, in "The Animal That Therefore I Am (More to Follow)," 403–6.

25. Derrida's essay has appeared in French in the volume of essays that grew out of the conference dedicated to his work, titled *L'Animal autobiographique: Autour de Jacques Derrida,* ed. Marie-Louise Mallet (Paris: Galilée, 1999). Here, I will be working from the text of David Wills's English translation published in *Critical Inquiry* 28:2 (winter 2002): 369–418.

26. Jacques Derrida, "*Geschlecht* II: Heidegger's Hand," trans. John P. Leavey Jr., in *Deconstruction and Philosophy,* ed. John Sallis (Chicago: University of Chicago Press, 1986), 173; emphasis in the original. Subsequent references are given in the text.

27. We should remember that Heidegger's larger political interest—an altogether understandable one, as Derrida notes—in thinking the meaning of *Geschlecht* (the *genre humaine* or species being, "the humanity of man" [163]) is to "distinguish between the national and nationalism, that is, between the national and a biologicist and racist ideology" (165). See also *Of Spirit,* where Derrida writes: "I do not mean to criticize this humanist teleology. It is no doubt more urgent to recall that, in spite of all the denegations or all the avoidances one could wish, it has remained *up till now* (in Heidegger's time and situation, but this has not radically changed today) the price to be paid in the ethico-political denunciation of biologism, racism, naturalism, etc. . . . . Can one transform this program? I do not know" (56). The recent work from Cerisy suggests, however, that Derrida will continue trying to theorize just such a transformation and that, in truth, he has all along been engaged in just such a project—hence this statement is perhaps too modest.

28. On the point of technology, see especially the discussion of Heidegger's opposition of handwriting and the typewriter in Derrida's "*Geschlecht* II," 178–81, which condenses many of these themes. As he puts it, for Heidegger, "Typographic mechanization destroys this unity of the world, this integral identity, this proper integrity of the spoken word that writing manuscripts, at once because it appears closer to the voice or body proper and because it ties together the letters, conserves and gathers together" (178). It is thus "a-signifying" because "it loses the hand," hence, as Heidegger puts it, "In typewriting, all men resemble one another" (179). "The protest against the typewriter," Derrida notes, "also belongs—

this is a matter of course—to an interpretation of technology *[technique]*, to an interpretation of politics starting from technology," but also, and more importantly, to a "devaluation of writing in general" as "the increasing destruction of the word or of speech" in which "The typewriter is only a modern aggravation of the evil" (180).

29. Jacques Derrida, "'Eating Well' or the Calculation of the Subject," in *Who Comes after the Subject?*, ed. Eduardo Cadava, Peter Connor, and Jean-Luc Nancy (New York: Routledge, 1991).

30. For Derrida, this "vulnerability" and "passivity" connects very directly to the question of shame and the motif of nakedness before the gaze of the other that structures the entire essay. In what sense can one be naked—and perhaps naked as before no *other* other—before the gaze of animal? "I often ask myself," he writes, "just to see, *who I am* (following) at the moment when, caught naked, in silence, by the gaze of an animal, for example the eyes of a cat, I have trouble, yes, a bad time, overcoming my embarrassment" (372). In a sense, this means nothing more than the fact that Derrida sees *himself* as a philosopher, for, as he notes, Descartes, Kant, Heidegger, Lacan, and Levinas produce discourses that are "sound and profound, but everything goes on as if they themselves had never been looked at, and especially not naked, by an animal that addressed them. At least everything goes on as though this troubling experience had not been theoretically registered, supposing they had experienced it at all, at the precise moment"—and here we recall Heidegger's use of the form of the *thesis*—"when they made of the animal a *theorem*" (20). Derrida, on the other hand, wants to insist on the "unsubstitutable singularity" of the animal (in this case "a real cat") and suggests that our readiness to turn it into a "theorem" is at base a panicked horror at our own vulnerability, our own passivity—in the end, our own mortality. "As with every bottomless gaze," he writes, "as with the eyes of the other, the gaze called animal offers to my sight the abyssal limit of the human: the inhuman or the ahuman, the ends of man. . . . And in these moments of nakedness, under the gaze of the animal, everything can happen to me, I am like a child ready for the apocalypse" (381).

31. Richard Beardsworth, *Derrida and the Political* (London: Routledge, 1996), 129. Subsequent references are given in the text.

32. See my "Old Orders for New" and "Faux Post-Humanism" for a critical overview of Singer's utilitarianism.

33. It should be noted here that, for Singer's own part, there appears to be no love lost either. When asked recently about the relevance of theory associated with "postmodernism" to bioethics, he replied, "Life's too short for that sort of thing." See Jeff Sharlet, "Why Are We Afraid of Peter Singer?" *Chronicle of Higher Education* 46:27 (March 10, 2000): A22.

34. And here we should remember the second half of the interview's title: "The Calculation of the Subject."

35. See, for example, "*Geschlecht* II" and "*Geschlecht*: Sexual Difference, Onto-logical Difference," trans. Ruben Berezdivin, in *A Derrida Reader: Between the Blinds,* ed. Peggy Kamuf (New York: Columbia University Press, 1991), 380–402. For Levinas, see Jacques Derrida, "At this very moment in this work here I am," in Llewelyn, *Rereading Levinas,* 11–48, and the selection from "Choreographies," trans. Christie V. McDonald, in *A Derrida Reader,* 440–56. Subsequent references are given in the text.

36. Quoted in Vicki Kirby, *Telling Flesh: The Substance of the Corporeal* (New York: Routledge, 1997), 90. Subsequent references to Kirby's book are given in the text.

37. J. T. Fraser, *Of Time, Passion, and Knowledge: Reflections on the Strategy of Existence* (New York: George Braziller, 1975). I am drawing on the popularization given in Jeremy Rifkin's *Algeny* (New York: Penguin, 1984), 186–91.

38. Eva M. Knodt, "Foreword" to Niklas Luhmann, *Social Systems,* trans. John Bednarz Jr. with Dirk Baecker (Stanford, Calif.: Stanford University Press, 1995), xxxi.

39. Derrida's theorization of language in terms of the inhuman trace pushes in a fundamental sense in exactly the opposite direction of Lyotard's strongly vertical sense of language, and would seem in many ways closer to more sophisti-cated contemporary notions of *communication* as an essentially ahuman dynam-ic. Here, one would eventually want to distinguish between second-wave systems theory of the sort found in Niklas Luhmann or Humberto Maturana and Francisco Varela—for whom difference is "not 'noise' that occludes the brighter pattern to be captured in its true essence," nor "a step toward something else," but is rather "how we arrive and where we stay"—and earlier theories with which Derrida, we can be sure, would have little patience, as he makes clear, among other places, in *Limited, Inc.* In any event, it is worth pausing over the point for a moment, because Lyotard would seem to prevent himself from radicalizing his concept of language in this direction precisely because of his suspicion (in *The Postmodern Condition*) of the sciences and, especially, of systems theory—the very domain of contemporary science in which the models of communication and meaning closest to those of poststructuralism have been developed. See Francisco J. Varela, "The Reenchantment of the Concrete," in *Incorporations,* ed. Jonathan Crary and Sanford Kwinter (New York: Zone Books, 1992), 320.

40. But for useful overviews of this material, see, for example *The Great Ape Project: Equality Beyond Humanity,* ed. Paola Cavalieri and Peter Singer (New York: St. Martin's Press, 1993) and *Anthropomorphism, Anecdotes, and Animals,*

ed. Robert W. Mitchell, Nicholas S. Thompson, and H. Lyn Miles (Albany: State University of New York Press, 1997).

41. Humberto Maturana and Francisco Varela, *The Tree of Knowledge: The Biological Roots of Human Understanding,* rev. ed., trans. Robert Paolucci, foreword J. Z. Young (Boston: Shambhala Press, 1992), 165. Subsequent references are given in the text.

42. This is true even in animals with the most minimal cephalization, such as the social insects, whose third-order couplings are, however, markedly rigid and inflexible because of the limits placed upon the possible concentration of nervous tissue by their hard exteriors of chitin (ibid., 188). Hence, their plasticity is limited and their individual ontogenies are of little importance in our explanation of their behavior, even though we cannot understand their behavior without understanding their broadly shared co-ontogenies.

43. This is why, according to Maturana and Varela, the so-called language of bees is not a language; it is a largely fixed system of interactions "whose stability depends on the genetic stability of the species and not on the cultural stability of the social system in which they take place" (ibid., 208).

44. The example Maturana and Varela give is of the chimp Lucy who, on the verge of a tantrum upon seeing her human "parents" about to leave, turned to her keepers and signed in Ameslan "Lucy cry"—a "linguistic distinction of an action performed" (ibid., 215).

45. For example, drawing on language experiments with chimps, they argue that animals equipped with a signifying repertoire, like humans, develop their ability to participate in linguistic domains in proportion to their interpersonal interactions with other languaging beings (ibid., 217). When they are permitted to live in an environment rich in opportunities for "linguistic coupling," they can communicate and express their subjectivities in ways more and more identifiably like our own—which suggests, of course, that such subjectivities are not given as ontological differences in kind, but rather emerge as overlapping possibilities and shared repertoires in the dynamic and recursive processes of their production. (The reverse is true as well; when animals and humans are deprived of opportunities for third-order couplings in social interactions and communications, their behaviors become more mechanical and "instinctive," as their ontogenies are severely limited and invariable.) Here, one might readily think of the example of animals used in factory farming, but also—on the other, human hand—of the example of the "wolf children" cited by Maturana and Varela, of two Hindu girls who were raised by a pack of wolves, without human contact, whose behaviors (modes of ambulation, dietary preferences, signifying repertoires, and so on) were in all significant respects canid and not human (128–30).

46. Gregory Bateson, "A Theory of Play and Fantasy," in *Steps to an Ecology*

of Mind (New York: Ballantine, 1972), 179. Subsequent references are given in the text.

47. This is why, according to Bateson, we "have many taboos on observing one another's kinesics, because too much information can be got that way" (ibid., 378). And, one might add by way of an example many of us have experienced, it is also the very absence of which that makes e-mail such an unnerving and explosive form of communicative exchange—there is no damping or comparative modulation of the digital message by any accompanying analogical signals.

48. For example, Maturana and Varela discuss a well-known experiment in which a gorilla is shown his reflection in a mirror, is then anesthetized, has a red dot painted between his eyes, and is then awakened and shown his reflection again, at which point the ape immediately, upon seeing the dot, points to his own forehead—not that of the mirror image. "[T]his experiment," they argue, "suggests that the gorilla can generate a domain of self through social distinctions. . . . How this happened we do not know. But we presume it has to do with conditions similar to those leading to the evolution of human linguistic domains" (*Tree*, 224–25).

49. It is significant in this regard—though not at all surprising—that Maturana and Varela are therefore willing to grant the existence of "cultural behaviors" in nonhuman social groups (ibid., 194–201).

50. Danial C. Dennett, *Consciousness Explained* (Boston: Little, Brown, 1991), 447. Subsequent references are given in the text.

51. See Wolfe, *Critical Environments,* 57ff. on Bateson, and, on representationalism, xi–xxiv, 12–22, and 41–71. On Dennett, see Richard Rorty's critique of Dennett's view in *Consciousness Explained* that it is possible to construct an "objective" "heterophenomenological text," in the same way that it is possible to provide a "correct" interpretation of a literary text. As Rorty puts it, "no up-to-date practitioner of hermeneutics—the sort who agrees with Derrida that there is no transcendental signified and with Gadamer that all readings are prejudiced— would be caught dead talking about the 'right interpretation'" (Richard Rorty, "Comments on Dennett," *Synthese* 53 [1982]: 184).

52. Dietrich Schwanitz, "Systems Theory according to Niklas Luhmann—Its Environment and Conceptual Strategies," *Cultural Critique* 30 (spring 1995): 156.

53. And it is also this very circularity, of course, that prevents the relationship between physical substratum (cephalization) and phenomenological domain (languaging) in Maturana and Varela from devolving into a type of positivism.

54. Humberto R. Maturana, "Science and Daily Life: The Ontology of Scientific Explanations," in *Research and Reflexivity,* ed. Frederick Steier (London: Sage Publications, 1991), 34. Subsequent references are given in the text.

55. Rodolphe Gasché, *Inventions of Difference: On Jacques Derrida* (Cambridge: Harvard University Press, 1994), 4.

56. As Schwanitz puts it, "Both theories make difference their basic category, both temporalize difference and reconstruct meaning as . . . an independent process that constitutes the subject rather than lets itself be constituted by it" ("Systems Theory according to Niklas Luhmann," 153).

57. There is a difference of accent here, in other words, and the seriousness of that difference is of some moment, and rests in no small part on whether one shares, or not, this characterization of Derrida's view. As Schwanitz points out, in comparison to systems theory, "Derrida reverses the relation between disorder and order. According to him, the level of order consists of the text of Western metaphysics that is brought about by a fundamental attribution of meaning to the simultaneity of the idea and the use of signs. In terms of systems theory, constative language is a kind of self-simplification of writing for the benefit of logos. On the other hand, writing as the basic differentiation within the use of signs that is also inherent in the spoken word, undertakes a permanent renewal of complexity and contingency through dissemination and dispersion, which in turn is again reduced by logocentric self-simplification. According to Luhmann, however, the paradox of self-referentiality comes first and the asymmetry produced by temporalization comes second. The opposite is true for Derrida. The 'illegitimate' asymmetry as a form of domination comes first and is then dissolved in the paradox of time" (ibid., 155).

58. Carolyn Merchant, *Radical Ecology* (New York: Routledge, 1993), 107.

59. Niklas Luhmann, "Deconstruction as Second-Order Observing," *New Literary History* 24 (1993): 770.

60. Niklas Luhmann, *Observations on Modernity,* trans. William Whobrey (Stanford, Calif.: Stanford University Press, 1998), 108. Subsequent references are given in the text.

61. Humberto R. Maturana and Francisco J. Varela, *Autopoiesis and Cognition: The Realization of the Living* (Dordrecht: Reidel Publishing Co., 1980), 39.

From Extinction to Electronics: Dead Frogs, Live Dinosaurs, and Electric Sheep

Ursula K. Heise

Since the mid-1980s, the figure of the cyborg in literature and popular culture has received a great deal of critical attention as an important symbol through which hopes and anxieties related to recent technologies have been articulated. Most of these analyses have focused on the reconceptualization of the human body and human identity that the cyborg stands for, with its wide-ranging implications for the relationship between humans and "nature"—whether it be in a medical, military, or scientific context—and for considerations of gender and race.[1] Yet, in her seminal "Cyborg Manifesto" (1984), Donna Haraway had already pointed out that the fusion of human and machine also has important repercussions for other conceptual distinctions such as that between human and animal (151–52). In spite of this early suggestion, robotic or electronic animals have been discussed very little in studies of cyborgs, even though they, too, appear with some frequency in recent literature and culture, sometimes in combination with genetically altered animals. Brett Leonard's film *The Lawnmower Man* comes to mind, which features a chimpanzee being trained in virtual-reality gear, as do the cyborg dolphin Jones in William Gibson's short story "Johnny Mnemonic" and "Ratthing," the semielectronic, semiorganic watchdog in Neal Stephenson's novel *Snow Crash*.[2] Simulations of animals have also begun to appear in computer games: *SimLife,* one in a series of games that allow the player to manipulate the evolution of complex environments, lets the user design and alter ecosystems that include multiple evolving plant and animal species; *SimAnt,* focusing on an ant colony, functions in a similar fashion; and in 1996–97, a wave of enthusiasm for "virtual pets" swept Japan, the United States, and Western Europe with the introduction of Bandai Corporation's Tamagotchi, a birdlike creature in an egg-shaped mini-computer that the player has to feed, clean, and entertain through a life cycle that can last more than three weeks.[3] Not infrequently, electronically and genetically engineered animals in literature and film appear along-side humans whose bodies and minds have been altered by similar techniques, and thereby raise complex questions about the relationship between humans, animals, and machines and their respective status in worlds where little that is purely "natural" is left.

Such representations of artificial animals touch upon a broad range of issues, from practical ones such as the domestication of animals, their use in scientific and military experiments, and their commodification in circuits of economic exchange, to more theoretical ones such as animal perception and cognition or the functioning of "natural" evolutionary mechanisms in the context of technological innovation.[4] It would be im-possible to explore the full spectrum of these questions in one essay; rather, this analysis will focus on one issue that informs many of these re-cent representations of human-made animals, though it may be less ob-vious at first sight: namely, their relationship to the rapid loss of natural-ly occurring species in the second half of the twentieth century. Although in all of these investigations of artificial animal forms, important ele-ments of pure play and freewheeling scientific imagination are certainly at work, I will argue that sometimes implicitly, and often quite explicitly, the extinction of real animal species crucially shapes the way in which the artificial animal forms are approached and evaluated. What underlies the imaginative exploration of artificial animals, then, is the question of how much nature we can do without, to what extent simulations of nature can replace the "natural," and what role animals, both natural and artifi-cial, play in our self-definition as humans. Three very different artifacts will illustrate the narrative strategies and metaphors by means of which these questions have been addressed in American culture in the last few decades: Steven Spielberg's film *Jurassic Park,* Thomas Ray's computer-based Artificial Life project *Tierra,* and Philip K. Dick's by now classic science-fiction novel, *Do Androids Dream of Electric Sheep?*[5] All three ex-plicitly relate the emergence of artificially created animals to the extinc-tion of natural species; but each one takes a different perspective on this relationship and, implicitly, on the significance of the natural in an increasingly technologized environment.[6]

Jurassic Park: Prehistoric Cyborgs

Steven Spielberg's *Jurassic Park,* based on a novel by Michael Crichton, and its sequel *The Lost World* address the issue of contemporary losses in biodiversity obliquely through their focus on the best-known historical extinction of an entire group of species, that of the dinosaurs. At first sight, both films seem to fit comfortably into the well-worn plot stereotype of the artificially created monsters that turn against their creators, as well as that of the overweening scientist who believes he can control nature only to find that such perfect mastery slips from his hands: from Mary Shelley's *Frankenstein* and H. G. Wells's *Island of Dr. Moreau* to the monster animals that populate 1950s Hollywood films, this formula is too well known to need any rehearsing.[7] But W. J. T. Mitchell, in the *Last Dinosaur Book,* places Spielberg's films into a somewhat different context when he notes that "the greatest epidemic of dinosaur images occurs in the late twentieth century, just at the moment when widespread public awareness of ecological catastrophe is dawning, and the possibility of irreversible extinction is becoming widely evident."[8] Mitchell does not discuss this aspect in any further detail, but his observation—derived from his survey of a long history of dinosaur representations—opens the way for an analysis of how the resurrection of a long-extinct group of species in *Jurassic Park* can be read not only as the horror and suspense device that it undoubtedly is, but also as an imaginative scenario that deflects possible anxieties over contemporary losses in species diversity.

Explicitly, this topic surfaces briefly early on in the film, when the visionary entrepreneur John Hammond presents his project, a natural history theme park with real dinosaurs re-created from prehistoric DNA as its main attraction, to a group of consultants consisting of three scientists and a lawyer. Contrary to Hammond's expectation, only the lawyer expresses enthusiasm about the planned park, predictably because of the profits it might earn. The three scientists all voice serious reservations vis-à-vis the attempt to put genetically engineered dinosaur species into an environment that only partially corresponds to the ecosystems in which they originally existed, and that they have to share with a species—humans—they had never previously encountered in their long history on the planet. Hammond, who is fundamentally more interested in the imaginative potential of his project than its financial possibilities, expresses deep disappointment that only the "bloodsucking lawyer" approves of his project; if he were breeding condors instead, he notes in a dejected voice, the scientists would all no doubt back him with enthusiasm. What is the difference, he implies, between genetically reconstructing species that have recently gone extinct or are currently endangered, and re-creating a group of species that disappeared 65 million years ago? Why would the former be desirable and the latter objectionable?

This juxtaposition of prehistoric with present-day species, along with the scientists' warnings about the appropriateness of the ecosystems Hammond has devised, raises the question of how Spielberg's film conceptualizes the relationship of a species to its environment. In discussions of contemporary species extinction, this relationship is often envisioned as a threatening gap or lack: biologists often warn that the disappearance of even a small number of species invariably has consequences for the food chains and ecosystems of which they formed part—consequences that are hard to predict accurately and can sometimes be catastrophic. Unlike condors, whales, or panda bears, however, dinosaurs in a late-twentieth-century setting are figures of excess rather than lack; they are not missing from any existing ecosystem but exceed their environment and break all its bounds when they emerge from extinction. This excessiveness is emphasized again and again in both *Jurassic Park* and *The Lost World* through the dinosaurs' monstrous size, the insatiable appetite of the carnivorous varieties for human flesh, and their relentless persistence in hunting down their prey. Dinosaurs in these films seem out of proportion to their environment and barely containable by any natural or technological system. Hammond's suggestion that these creatures are comparable to present-day animals such as the condor, therefore, establishes a first association between contemporary endangered species and this visual rhetoric of excess.

A further link is created by the movie within the movie toward the beginning of *Jurassic Park,* which explains the mechanism of the genetic reconstruction. According to this documentary, the reconstruction was enabled by dinosaur blood found in the sting of a prehistoric mosquito embedded in amber (a detail that establishes a humorous parallel to the "bloodsucking lawyer," another parasite who wishes to make a living off dinosaurs). From this blood, DNA sequences were extracted, and the gaps in them supplemented with frog DNA (the documentary does not explain how a single discovery of dinosaur blood could have led to the reconstruction of as many different prehistoric species as are presented in the theme park later on). The dinosaurs in the theme park, therefore, are not genetically pure, but partially frogs. Not only does this genetic mix turn them into creatures that are partially prehistoric and partially contemporary, it also associates them with another family of animals that is threatened by species loss. As it turns out, the composite DNA is crucially important because it is what allows the dinosaurs to procreate: Hammond had populated the park exclusively with females so as to prevent uncontrolled offspring, but when one of the scientists later discovers eggs from which young dinosaurs have hatched, he concludes that some of the adult dinosaurs must have changed their gender, an ability that, according to him, would have derived from their frog genes. This rather far-fetched turn of the plot becomes quite significant when we understand it as another strategy by means of which one group of species, many of which are currently endangered, turns out to be associated with the excess and havoc wrought by a quite different group of species in Hammond's theme park.

Perhaps even more important, the fantastic extrapolation of currently available genetic engineering techniques documented by the movie within the movie establishes a scenario in which species extinction is reversible and therefore no cause for concern: if minute amounts of DNA suffice to re-create a whole range of species, then no loss of biodiversity need be permanent, because extinct species can be brought back at will. The possibilities inherent in such a technology are so far-reaching that one might wonder why the visionary John Hammond, instead of fantasizing about a theme park, does not market his patent to any of the many institutions that would unquestionably be eager to use it, from pharmaceutical companies to agribusiness corporations and all the way to environmental associations. Such usage of his innovative technique of genetic engineering would seem to be a much more lucrative source of income than a theme park on an island more than a hundred miles off the coast of Costa Rica; but then, Hammond is portrayed as an entrepreneur driven by imagination rather than lust for profit, and the recuperation of a past that humans have never seen with their own eyes is clearly more attractive to him than merely practical applications of the technology. Yet it is precisely the ability genetically to return to the past that makes species extinction, in the world of *Jurassic Park,* a reversible and negligible affair.

Or so it looks at the beginning. Much of the film and its sequel, of course, are designed to show that resurrecting the genetic past is not as uncomplicated a project as Hammond imagines. Species restitution quickly reveals itself to be a dangerous and horrific enterprise as it turns into a persistent threat to human life: by the end, the two films seem to be suggesting that even if future advances in genetic engineering were to make the re-creation of lost species possible, this would certainly prove to be thoroughly undesirable. This impression is centrally conveyed through the sense of excess mentioned earlier, which accompanies almost every appearance of dinosaurs in the two films. The sense of wonder that their gigantic stature at first evokes in both scientists and children vanishes quickly. Instead, the animals turn out to be persistently associated with uncontrollable fluids and repulsive body secretions: in both films, their appearance is accompanied by tropical storms that turn the islands into unnavigable swamps of mud. In *Jurassic Park* in particular, humans are again and again confronted with dinosaurs' bodily secretions, from the oversized piles of stegosaurus dung that the team's paleobotanist delves into, to the sticky black fluid that a small dinosaur squirts into a computer programmer's face before devouring him; and even an otherwise friendly brontosaurus ends up sneezing full force into Hammond's granddaughter's face just when she had begun to feel a bit of reluctant sympathy for the creature. Beyond this emphasis on the dinosaurs' physically repulsive aspects, both films foreground the carnivorous species and present them as perpetually hungry, aggressive, and violent predators who pursue humans into the most unlikely hiding places—from the park's computer control room to the restaurant kitchen and the basement where the central electric panels are located. As the plot unfolds, the viewer is less and less able to sympathize with the dinosaurs, except when they efficiently dispose of characters that the spectator has come to despise. But by the end of each of the two films, it is difficult not to conclude that species extinction may not be such a bad thing if the life of animals so persistently interferes with the well-being of humans. Extinct species, in other words, end up seeming expendable and undesirable, an excessive presence that humans are better off without.

Understood as an oblique reflection on contemporary species loss, then, *Jurassic Park* wards off potential anxieties over the decrease in biodiversity both by suggesting that advances in gene technology might make species extinction reversible and by presenting the return of extinct species as a dangerous excess rather than the filling in of a lack. Yet it would be too simple to reduce the film and its sequel to this perspective, dominant as it may appear. Clearly, there is also an obverse side to its depiction of dinosaurs as relentlessly aggressive and violent destroyers, which emerges in the leitmotif that is repeated through both movies, "Life will find a way." As a summary comment on the plot of *Jurassic Park* and *The Lost World,* this motto seems preposterous, both because life processes are constantly being manipulated by humans and because the organisms that result are extremely destructive to other life-forms. But it does reveal a wishful thinking that underlies the two movies: the recurring images of gigantic creatures able to inflict significant damage on humans and their technological tools of mastery over nature may well express nostalgia for the return of a natural world that would be a match for human technology and not just a helpless victim. This fantasy may be the reason why Spielberg, in both films, shows extended sequences of dinosaurs battling not humans per se, but their technology, primarily automobiles: "If the dinosaur is the monstrous double of the skyscraper and the railroad, it also finds its counterpart in the world's largest consumer of fossil fuels, the automobile. *T. rex* can recognize a worthy antagonist when he sees one, so he attacks the park vehicle . . . and pushes it over a cliff" in a scene that, as Mitchell notes, is repeated and extended in *The Lost World* (222). This uprising of the animal world against technology comes to a climax when the velociraptors wreak havoc on the computer station that controls the functioning of the entire park. If the two films persistently foreground scenes in which extinct species come back to smash products of high technology, it is to show a natural world with the ability to fight back against the encroachments of a human civilization that leaves little that is "natural" in place. This struggle is, needless to say, temporary and doomed to failure, as is the fantasy that subtends it: the deadly rampage of a Tyrannosaurus rex through San Diego in *The Lost World* makes it clear that the cost—in human life as well as expensive equipment and urban structures—of seeing such a fantasy translated into reality is simply too high. Only when the excess of nature that the resurrection of extinct species represents is removed (by containing the dinosaurs on isolated islands far from human populations) can human society continue to function.

More broadly, such scenes can be understood as symptomatic of a certain mainstream interest in endangered wildlife that is sustained only so long as it does not interfere with human well-being (or what Western societies in the late twentieth century conceive of as such); extinction of other species becomes acceptable when they encroach upon human society. Yet it is worth remembering that the dinosaurs in these films, considered at another level, are of course *not* representations of the wildlife that humans usually encounter—not only because they are specimens of the fauna of a historical period in which humans did not exist, but also because they are products of computer technology; every step of the cloning process through which they are created is controlled and adjusted by computers in a process that Mitchell calls "biocybernetic reproduction" (215–19). Hence,

> Spielberg's dinosaurs are pure creations of information science, at both the level of the representation (the digitally animated image) and the level of the represented (the fictional cloned creatures produced by biogenetic engineering). . . . The architectural and mechanical models of the organism give way to (and are absorbed by) informational models: the species becomes a message, an algorithm: the boundary between organism and machine, natural and artificial intelligence, begins to waver. (213)

Advanced digital technologies, in other words, become a means of, on the one hand, generating an artificial version of the natural and, on the other, re-creating a prehistoric version of the natural to which humans normally have no direct access. In this sense, Spielberg's prehistoric cyborgs are creatures that not only bridge the gap between widely separated time periods and disparate animal species, but also between the natural and the digital—between extinction and electronics. It is through this bridging that digitally orchestrated resurrection can become a response to natural extinction.

Tierra: Electronic Evolution

This attempt to revert to earlier stages of animal life on Earth is not pure cinematic fantasy; certain projects that are currently being undertaken in the field of computer science that has become known as "Artificial Life" or AL also aim at reproducing, in the digital medium, some of the organic processes that shaped natural life-forms on planet Earth. One of these projects, Thomas Ray's *Tierra* (Spanish for "earth"), hints by its very name at its objective of creating a computer-based equivalent of species evolution and biodiversity; moreover, Ray explicitly links it to biological preservation projects in Costa Rica—the country that already figured in the background of Spielberg's imaginary species resurrection. *Tierra*, however, forges a different type of link between contemporary species loss and the creation of artificial animal life.

   In general, Artificial Life encompasses a wide variety of projects that attempt to simulate digitally the development and/or behavior of an organism, the evolution of a group of organisms, or the functioning of complex ecosystems. Some AL researchers view their work principally as an attempt to develop models for biological and ecological processes such as the flight patterns of birds in a flock or the cooperation among ants or bees. Others, however—Thomas Ray among them—make a much stronger claim for the discipline in that they understand it as a synthetic biology, a biology that studies possible evolutions of life, in contrast to analytic biology, which examines actually existing organic forms. What this implies is that the self-replicating and evolving strings of computer code they design not only model forms and processes of "natural" biological life, but indeed constitute a life-form of their own, silicon- rather than carbon-based.[9] Clearly, this entails a very different understanding of the digital medium as not only a tool for representing and understanding nondigital phenomena, but as an environment that can function as an "alternative nature" with its own "ecosystems," "organisms," and "physical laws":

> in simulation, the data in the computer is treated as a representation of something else, such as a population of mosquitoes or trees. In instantiation, the data in the computer does not represent anything else. The data patterns in an instantiation are considered to be living forms in their own right and are not models of any natural life form. . . . The object of an AL instantiation is to introduce the natural form and process of life into an artificial medium. This results in an AL form in some medium other than carbon chemistry and is not a model of organic life forms. (Ray, "An Evolutionary Approach," 180)

Anthropologist Stefan Helmreich and literary critic Katherine Hayles have analyzed in some detail the philosophical assumptions that such claims rely on; centrally, they argue, this kind of hypothesis replicates the conventional Western assumption that form is more essential than matter in determining identity: the A-lifers' claim is precisely that their digital populations replicate the *patterns* of life rather than its specific material incarnations. Both Helmreich and Hayles strenuously object to what they see as the devaluation of the body and embodied life in such scenarios.[10] Whereas this may be true of the philosophy that underlies AL in general, Ray's *Tierra* establishes a complex connection between the natural and the digital that is not exhaustively described by this critique.

Among the wide variety of AL projects that have been undertaken since the early 1990s, with very different goals and terminologies, *Tierra* is particularly illuminating because it links digital concerns quite explicitly to species preservation. In this project, a string of code called the "ancestor" with a program for self-replication is allotted a certain amount of memory space and allowed to reproduce; in order to imitate the workings of natural evolution in the digital medium, certain instructions effect random changes in the code of the evolving "creatures" as an equivalent to genetic mutations, and others mimic mortality by queuing the creatures up for erasure according to criteria such as age and success at performing their tasks. The functioning of sexual reproduction is simulated through the exchange of code segments between two creatures, who then transfer it to the next generation in their own replication process. When allowed to reproduce in this fashion over a period of time, an entire "population" of strings of varying lengths and composition develops that can be considered different species; these engage in complex relations such as "parasitism," one string using another's replication instructions to "procreate." In other words, in Ray's view, a veritable ecosystem with varied relations between different types of species evolves. Even though the biological terminology suggests animal-like organisms, there is no graphic representation attached to these entities that would make *Tierra* resemble computer games such as *SimLife;* the "creatures" are simply strings of computer code.[11]

Two aspects of this project are particularly noteworthy for the purposes of this analysis. First, Ray's plan is not to contain this experiment on a single computer or mainframe, but to create what he calls a "digital reserve" on the World Wide Web for these organisms. Second, he explicitly establishes a parallel between this digital exploration and a rain-forest conservation plan in northern Costa Rica that he himself is involved in (and where he owns land that is to be part of the reserve). He joins these two projects together in a paper titled "A Proposal to Create Two Biodiversity Reserves: One Digital and One Organic," which characterizes them as follows:

> The digital reserve will be distributed across the global net, and will create a space for the evolution of new virtual life forms. The organic reserve will be located in the rain forests of northern Costa Rica, and will secure the future of existing organic life forms.
>
> The proposed project will create a very large, complex and interconnected region of cyberspace that will be inoculated with digital organisms which will be allowed to evolve freely through natural selection. The objective is to set off a digital analog to the Cambrian explosion of diversity, in which multi-cellular digital organisms (parallel MIMD processes) will spontaneously increase in diversity and complexity. If successful, this evolutionary process will allow us to find the natural form of parallel processes, and will generate extremely complex digital information processes that fully utilize the capacities inherent in our parallel and networked hardware.[12]

This project of creating a reserve for digital organisms on the global computer network shares with the Jurassic Park of Michael Crichton's and Steven Spielberg's imagination the endeavor to recapture a part of nature's past that is usually inaccessible to humans. Both *Jurassic Park* and *Tierra* therefore have a historical dimension that is implicit in their biological project. Specifically, it is an ancient diversity of species that both projects are designed to re-create: unlike other AL researchers, Ray emphasizes, he aims at simulating not the moment of the emergence of life as such, but the "origin of biological diversity" in the "Cambrian explosion 600 million years ago" which "involved a riotous diversification of life-forms" ("An Approach to the Synthesis of Life," 112–13). But, of course, Ray does not conceive of his project as mere simulation: as Katherine Hayles has pointed out, he never hesitates to use the adjective *natural* in referring to digital processes, implying that the populations he designs would develop according to an evolutionary logic that is fully equivalent to that of the natural world.[13]

"A Proposal to Create Two Biodiversity Reserves," however, which establishes this equivalence clearly through the juxtaposition of the digital and biological projects, remains at the same time curiously elusive about what exactly the relationship between the computer experiment and a particular rain-forest conservation project really is assumed to consist of. Obviously, their appearance side by side is meant to make the proposal for a digital reserve appear as serious and important as attempts to safeguard the natural environment. But beyond that, both the natural and the digital projects seem to form part of one overarching purpose, to preserve and perpetuate life in both the forms that we currently know and the ones that might yet emerge. If a "Cambrian explosion" of digital life is in some respects a repetition of processes that have historically taken place in nature, it might in another sense also be understood as a continuation, an extension of the evolutionary narrative to as yet unheard-of life-forms. If this is so, then Ray's project participates at least implicitly in a relatively long history of envisioning computer networks as the next step in evolution, although this has usually been understood to refer to human evolution; from French theologian and paleontologist Pierre Teilhard de Chardin and media theorist Marshall McLuhan to some of the fringes of the contemporary computer culture, the emergence of digital networks has repeatedly been interpreted as the prelude to the birth of a new form of collective human consciousness that would be equivalent to the next major step in human evolution.[14] Ray's project operates less anthropocentrically by focusing on life in general rather than on human life specifically, but it belongs to the same complex of ideas.[15]

Yet there remains a curious tension between the prospect of an explosive multiplication of life-forms in the digital sphere and the threats to habitats and species diversity in the natural world that make the creation of biological conservation areas necessary in the first place. Seen from this perspective, the motives for creating each of the two reserves come to seem radically different; whereas the Costa Rican reserve would be intended to protect the *reduced biodiversity* that can still be saved from the spread of human populations and their environmental impact, the digital one is designed to give rise to a *rapid increase of diversity* among cyberspecies. Biological conservation, in other words, is a last attempt to ward off further loss, whereas digital conservation is, on the contrary, meant to trigger huge gains in species diversity. This fundamental difference between the two projects, which in Ray's article appear to be seamlessly connected, raises the question to what extent setting off a "Cambrian explosion" of life-forms in cyberspace is a strategy of compensating at least imaginatively for the current rapid loss of biodiversity in the natural world. To ask this question is not in any way to cast doubt on Ray's environmental commitment and the seriousness of his ecological project, but rather to explore one of the reasons—*especially* for a computer programmer who is also a biologist and deeply concerned about environmental issues—that might lie behind the insistence that digital organisms be considered genuine life-forms of their own rather than simulations of natural ones.

Much has been written about the way in which electronic culture might come to reshape current social structures and the experience of space that goes along with them. Frequently, in such analyses, the World Wide Web is envisioned as an analogue to the metropolis and urban space.[16] The question that projects such as Ray's *Tierra* and Spielberg's cyberbiology raise is to what extent computer technologies will also remold our perception and experience of the natural world and other living species. Ray himself clearly sees his concerns with ecology and digitality as not only compatible, but indeed complementary, aspects of the same overriding exploration of life in different forms. The danger that this view brings with it from an environmentalist perspective is that it might reinforce the neglect of problems that beset natural wildlife in the late twentieth century in favor of the more appealing prospects of digital populations of "creatures"; if the latter really are equivalent to the former, they can offer a convenient means of escape from the unpleasant realities of ecological deterioration and species extinction into a digital world that is not subject to the same sets of problems. The lack created by diminishing nature and disappearing species, in other words, may come to be filled in the cultural imagination of computer-literate societies by alternative life-forms on the global Web. This is no doubt far from the vision that Ray intends; but if studying populations of digital organisms and their evolution can become an incentive for rethinking similar phenomena in nature, it can also, and by the same logic, become a substitute for concerning oneself with the natural world itself and the dangers that it faces.

Dreams about Electric Toads

This possibility is realized in what is probably the best-known vision of a world in which the natural world and wild animal species have disappeared and been replaced by human-made animals: Philip K. Dick's classic science-fiction novel *Do Androids Dream of Electric Sheep?* (1968). Dick's novel does not yet envision the kind of species extinction owing to pollution and habitat destruction that biologists and environmentalists are currently most concerned about; rather, the world it describes has been devastated by "World War Terminus," a nuclear war that has laid the natural world to waste and covered it with a layer of radioactive dust. Most humans have left Earth for extraterrestrial colonies, and those that remain are threatened by infertility and degradation of their mental capacities. There are no wild animals left: the few live animals that still exist are carefully bred and sold as coveted private possessions. Unlike scores of other postnuclear sci-fi scenarios that seem by now hopelessly dated, Dick's novel has preserved an eerie relevance because it does not focus on nuclear warfare as such but on the daily lives of fairly ordinary people in a world in which few vestiges of the "natural" remain. Humans' changed relationship to animals in such a world emerges as one of the central topics of the novel.[17]

In this context, one scene toward the end of the text takes on particular significance. Rick Deckard, a bounty hunter and the novel's protagonist, flies from San Francisco to the radioactive northern Californian desert. After experiencing an almost mystical identification with the religious idol Wilbur Mercer in the middle of this bleak landscape, he gets back into his hovercar and is just about ready to fly back to the city when a slight movement among the rocks catches his eye. "An animal, he said to himself. And his heart lugged under the excessive load, the shock of recognition. I know what it is, he realized; I've never seen one before but I know it from the old nature films they show on Government TV. They're extinct! he said to himself" (236). The animal moving among the rocks is a frog—a toad, to be exact, and Deckard, who has spent the last 48 hours killing six androids of the most advanced and intelligent type, cautiously lifts it up, puts it in a cardboard box, and flies home both shocked and elated. On top of his achievement with the androids, he expects, he will now be honored as the rediscoverer of an animal species believed extinct. Because such rediscoveries happen so rarely, he cannot quite remember what the reward for it is: "Something about a star of honor from the U.N. and a stipend. A reward running into the millions of dollars" (237). Because Deckard had used up his bounty money for the androids just a few hours earlier as a down payment for a live goat that it will take him years to pay off, this reward would relieve a considerable financial burden for him. But what most deeply thrills him about his discovery is not the potential financial benefit, but the encounter with a living, organic animal that is, in addition, one of the two that are sacred to Wilbur Mercer. This scene repeats, at a smaller scale, the imaginative gesture that also shapes *Jurassic Park* and the *Tierra* project—the recuperation by humans of lost animal species.

As in Spielberg's film and Ray's AL project, however, this recuperation is mediated and in the end contained by advanced human technology. When Deckard arrives home, he finds out not only that another android has avenged her friend's death by killing his newly purchased goat, but also that the frog is electric. Like the sheep Deckard has long owned, it is just another one of the countless artificial animals that populate Dick's futuristic San Francisco, robot specimens so sophisticated and lifelike in their appearance and behavior that only the discovery of their well-hidden electric control panels will give them away. When Deckard finds this out, he is disappointed, but not devastated; his wife orders a supply of electric flies to feed the toad, and Deckard admits that "it doesn't matter. The electric things have their lives, too. Paltry as those lives are" (241).

This discovery is so crucial to the novel that Dick originally intended to call it *The Electric Toad: How Androids Dream.*[18] But Deckard's statement may come as a surprise at the end of a novel that has persistently emphasized the difference between the real and the fake, and privileged the authentic over the false. Even though electric animals are common in Dick's world because many people cannot afford live animals, their artificiality is carefully concealed from the neighbors. Androids are mass-produced and used as a menial labor force in the extraterrestrial colonies, but mercilessly hunted down and exterminated when they escape from their owners or travel to Earth. And yet Deckard's admission that electric life is also a kind of life may be understandable in the context of his society, where most humans can only experience other species through the intermediary of electric artifacts. Indeed, in his world, concern over and empathy with animals has become the principal defining characteristic of what it means to be human. After World War Terminus, the novel indicates, all citizens were obligated by law to take care of at least one animal; this law no longer exists but has mutated into social custom—a custom so strong that those who are unable to afford real animals acquire electric ones to remain socially reputable.

Even more important, concern for animal welfare is the central recurring topic in the question-and-answer test that bounty hunter Deckard routinely administers to ascertain whether an individual he has apprehended is human or android. The test equipment measures the emotional reaction of the subject to scenarios that include deer antlers mounted on walls, collections of butterflies, meals of oysters, bullfight posters, or a naked woman sprawling on a bearskin rug (the point of the scenario being the bearskin rug, not feminine nudity). Humans, theoretically at least, will display instinctive reactions of repulsion at such scenarios of animal death and exploitation, whereas androids typically will not. This criterion of distinction is interesting because the general claim in Deckard's society is that androids do not have empathy with other beings; presumably, to the extent that such an emotional capability is testable at all, it could be assessed through scenarios involving humans as well as animals. But of all the questions in Deckard's repertoire, only one involves humans; all the other ones hinge on references to humans' exploitation of animals.

The fact that most of these scenarios would appear entirely commonplace and hardly a reason for particular disgust to most late-twentieth-century Westerners has sometimes been interpreted to mean that Dick intends to ridicule the way in which the boundary between humans and androids is drawn in this culture, and to suggest that it is all mere ideology—an ideology that the protagonist in the end recognizes as such and transcends.[19] I do not believe that the novel actually sustains this post-Haraway perspective;[20] that the test scenarios seem commonplace to Dick's average reader could just as well be his indictment of Western culture's fundamental insensitivity to and relentless exploitation of animals. And although it is true that much of the first half of the text seems designed to make the reader side with the android characters and to blur the boundaries between them and their human antagonists, later plot developments radically shift reader sympathies. In one of the novel's most excruciating scenes, a human who has befriended several androids, John Isidore, watches with horror as his android friends willfully and thoughtlessly cut the legs off a spider one by one to see how many it needs still to be able to walk. In this scene, the difference between humans and androids could not be more marked: not only do the androids think gradually mutilating the spider is excellent fun, they also fail completely, at first, to understand Isidore's reaction, interpreting his horror as a response to unsavory revelations on the TV program running in the background rather than to their own actions. Combined with the other android's revenge killing of Deckard's goat, this scene confirms precisely the perception of androids as incapable of understanding and feeling with other living beings that much of the preceding text had seemed to portray as mere prejudice.

What follows from this shifting representation of the androids is that the distinction between humans and androids is not exactly symmetrical in the novel to the one between real and electric animals, as one might at first assume. Deckard's final assertion that electric things have their own lives does not automatically extend to androids—among other things because androids are not really electric: unlike the artificial animals, they have no electronic circuits and no hidden switch plates, but are organically indistinguishable from humans (hence the necessity for psychological testing). They are not, like Deckard's electric sheep and toad, mechanical but organic artifacts. Dick seems willing to blur the line between real and electric animals because both types of animals help to define what is uniquely human; if he is in the end unwilling also to accept androids as humans' equals, it may be precisely because being an android, in the novel, is not so much equivalent to being a technological object as equivalent to having a certain attitude toward the natural world. The inability to empathize with other living beings that characterizes one dominant perspective on nature in the Western world is precisely the one Dick rejects as inhuman by contrasting the human-looking androids with advanced humans who are no longer capable of such insensitivity. Viewed on these terms, Dick's novel remains a complex critique of some of the social and cultural forces that have brought about ecological deterioration and species extinction, at the same time that it accepts technology to a certain extent as a replacement for irrecuperably lost nature.

Toward Cyborg Environmentalism

All three of the cultural products I have discussed can be understood as attempts to envision and redefine the role of nature in general and the animal in particular in a world that is almost entirely shaped by human culture and technology. In all three, technology comes to serve as a means of recuperating a lost species diversity; but whereas *Jurassic Park* ultimately rejects this attempt as excessive and dangerous to human well-being, Ray's *Tierra* project views the diversification of electronic life-forms as not only a repetition of animal evolution, but an extension of it. And Dick's *Do Androids Dream of Electric Sheep?*, while it posits the animal other as crucial to the definition of what is human, accepts that the technological simulation of animal life may be able to fulfill the same function. From an environmentalist perspective, one might want to reject all three approaches: Spielberg's because it implies a trivialization of the dangers of species extinction, Ray's and Dick's because their acceptance of electronic or electric life-forms as equivalent to organic ones could well entail diminished concern over the fate of actual animal populations.[21] Although I am not unsympathetic to such criticism, it seems to me worthwhile to suspend it at least temporarily so as to explore the implications of the three works more fully.

The merit of Spielberg's, Ray's, and Dick's imaginative scenarios, even and particularly from an environmentalist viewpoint, lies in the fact that they capture something that is indeed essential about the human relationship to nature in the late twentieth century: the fact that for the majority of the population of industrialized nations (and of an increasing number of developing ones), the experience of nature is heavily mediated by technology. One need not even point to such events as the cloning of Dolly the sheep, the recently begun production by Mitsubishi of battery-run replicas of extinct marine species, or the release by Sony Corporation, in May 1999, of the first robotic pet dog, AIBO (retailing at $2,500), to illustrate the "realism" of Spielberg's and Dick's visions;[22] it is sufficient to note that especially for urban populations, biological diversity has already become a virtual reality of sorts, one that is conveyed centrally by a wide array of TV documentaries and entire channels devoted to nature and exotic wildlife, whereas everyday urban life exposes humans to an extremely limited number of animal species. Dick anticipates this situation most explicitly through his protagonist Rick Deckard, who reflects at one point that "[n]ever in his life had he personally seen a raccoon. He knew the animal only from 3–D films shown on television" (40), just as he only recognizes the toad for what it is by remembering televised images. In Western societies, even the disappearance of nature—including species extinction—has become a televised spectacle. Given that—ecotourism notwithstanding—the role of such mediations in shaping experiences of nature is likely to increase rather than diminish in the future, and that it would be difficult or impossible for most of the population of industrialized countries to return to a more direct exposure to the natural world, the three works I have discussed raise the important question of how best to envision the relationship between the natural world and simulations of it in their role for late-twentieth-century human culture, science, and society.[23]

To say this, however, is to point not only to the merit of these works but also to their weakness, for it implies that all three envision the issue of species extinction and the relationship between real and artificial nature from a relentlessly speciesist perspective. Animals are envisioned and assessed in terms of the benefits or drawbacks they bring to human knowledge, experience, and comfort, not as beings with an independent right to existence. The dinosaurs of *Jurassic Park* are created for the entertainment of humans, Ray's electronic creatures for the sake of scientific study, and Dick's animals to enhance the experience of being human (as well as, not unimportantly, indicators of social status). Dick's novel in particular explicitly emphasizes the protagonist's "need for a real animal" (42) and his sense that he "couldn't go on with the electric sheep any longer; it sapped [his] morale" (170). Animals in particular and the natural world in general seem to have no intrinsic value in these works apart from their functionality for humans and their needs and desires. As a consequence, if simulations can be shown to fulfill the same functions adequately, the imperative to preserve or protect what is left of the natural world is considerably diminished in importance. If Ray's and Dick's works in particular are understood to make claims in favor of electronic and electric life-forms that at least implicitly reduce the significance of organic life—which one could sum up in Rick Deckard's discovery, at the end of Dick's novel, that "electric things have their lives, too"—these claims would have to be rejected from an environmentalist or animal rights perspective.

But Ray's and Dick's approach to "cyborg" animals cannot be summed up quite so neatly; upon closer inspection, a somewhat different conclusion imposes itself. Especially when one considers that Dick's protagonist is a hunter of androids, his insight actually amounts to an acknowledgment that the lives and needs of his species, organic humans, are not the only ones that count. In an oblique fashion, Deckard renounces the speciesist viewpoint that had guided him earlier when he accepts the electric toad as its own kind of living being. Such an acknowledgment is even more pronounced in Ray's *Tierra* project. In several essays on *Tierra*, Ray emphasizes that biology currently has to base all its conclusions about life on one type only, the carbon-based life that dominates the planet Earth. Short of traveling to other planets with alternative life-forms, an option that is not currently available, humans must study artificial life processes on their own planet so as to gain a sense of alternative types of species evolution ("An Approach to the Synthesis of Life," 111; "An Evolutionary Approach," 179). Of course, this argument is not directed against a speciesist perspective that would insist on the primacy of humans so much as one that would much more broadly emphasize the primacy of organic life. Still, the thrust of Ray's essays is similar to that of Dick's novel insofar as its aim is, in the end, to broaden claims on behalf of one species or set of species to include a wider variety of life-forms. Clearly, one of Ray's objectives in bringing together plans for a digital and a biological reserve is precisely to give a sense of this greater diversity. What I am arguing, therefore, is that the endorsement of technologically generated life-forms in both Ray and Dick need not be understood as a threat to the claims an environmentalist might want to make on behalf of natural life-forms; rather, the advocacy of the cyborg animal can be viewed as at least in part a call to abandon speciesist prejudice and to accept alternative life-forms as beings with an existence and rights of their own.

It is my contention that if we accept this reading—or at least accept that it coexists with a more antienvironmentalist interpretation—it could become a point of departure for rereading the figure of the cyborg from an ecological perspective. In a sense, this rereading would be complementary to Donna Haraway's well-known interpretation of the cyborg in her "Cyborg Manifesto." Haraway's objective in this seminal essay was to break the persistent associations of the feminine with the natural, and to turn the potential of technology (typically linked to masculinity) and fusions of the organic and the technological into imaginative tools for redefining femininity. More than a decade later, the crucial conceptual task for environmentalists in their encounter with a profusion of images and narratives that privilege recent technologies is, in some respects, the opposite one: how to reconnect this explosion of the technological imagination with a concern for the rapidly diminishing natural world. In this context, the figure of the cyborg, and in particular that of the animal rather than the human cyborg, takes on a somewhat different significance. Not merely the symbol of a nature finally vanquished by technology that it sometimes can be, the animal cyborg also points to the possibility of a different relationship between species: one that no longer privileges the rights of humans—feminine or masculine—over those of all other forms of life, but that recognizes the value and rights of nonhuman species along with those of humans. Viewed in this way, the animal cyborg can take us, through the discovery of otherness in our own technological creations, to the recognition of and respect for the nonhuman others we did not make. If the recuperation of extinct animal species by technological means in the works discussed earlier points to this possibility, they open the way for reconsidering the imaginative functions of technology from an environmentalist perspective.

Notes

1. Some of the most important studies of the cyborg include the following: Donna Haraway's groundbreaking "A Cyborg Manifesto: Science, Technology, and Socialist-Feminism in the Late Twentieth Century," in her *Simians, Cyborgs, and Women: The Reinvention of Nature* (New York: Routledge, 1991), 149–81, and her later interview with Constance Penley and Andrew Ross, "The Actors Are Cyborg, Nature Is Coyote, and the Geography Is Elsewhere: Postscript to 'Cyborgs at Large,'" in *Technoculture,* ed. Constance Penley and Andrew Ross (Minneapolis: University of Minnesota Press, 1991), 21–26; Patricia Warrick, *The Cybernetic Imagination in Science Fiction* (Cambridge: MIT Press, 1980); Chris Hables Gray's comprehensive anthology of essays, *The Cyborg Handbook* (New York: Routledge, 1995); Mark Seltzer, *Bodies and Machines* (New York: Routledge, 1992); and Katherine Hayles, *How We Became Posthuman: Virtual Bodies in Cybernetics, Literature, and Informatics* (Chicago: University of Chicago Press, 1999). Subsequent references to Haraway and Hayles are given in the text.

2. William Gibson's "Johnny Mnemonic" appears in his collection *Burning Chrome* (New York: Ace, 1987), 1–22; Neal Stephenson, *Snow Crash* (New York: Bantam, 1993); *The Lawnmower Man,* dir. Brett Leonard, perf. Jeff Fahey, Pierce Brosnan, Jenny Wright, and Geoffrey Lewis, Allied Vision Lane Pringle/Fuji Eight Co., 1992. Subsequent references to these works are given in the text.

3. In somewhat different form, the Tamagotchi craze was echoed in 1999–2000 by the widespread enthusiasm of children in the United States and Western Europe for *Pokémon* creatures that formed the core of computer games, an animated television series, a movie, and an abundance of toy products. Their creator, Tajiri Satoshi, was an avid insect watcher and collector in his childhood and sees Pokémon as, among other things, an opportunity for a new generation of children to participate in this hobby. See Howard Chua-Eoan and Tim Larimer, "PokéMania," *Time* 154 (November 22, 1999): 84.

4. Some works also include remote echoes of Descartes's categorization of animals as clockwork-like mechanisms.

5. For Ray, see the following: Thomas S. Ray, "An Evolutionary Approach to

Synthetic Biology: Zen and the Art of Creating Life," in *Artificial Life: An Overview*, ed. Christopher G. Langton (Cambridge: MIT Press, 1995), 179–209; "An Approach to the Synthesis of Life," in *The Philosophy of Artificial Life*, ed. Margaret A. Boden (Oxford: Oxford University Press, 1996), 111–45; and "A Proposal to Create Two Biodiversity Reserves: One Digital and One Organic," http://www.hip.atr.co. jp/~ray/pubs/reserves/reserves.html. See also Philip K. Dick, *Do Androids Dream of Electric Sheep?* (New York: Ballantine, 1996); *Jurassic Park,* dir. Steven Spielberg, perf. Sam Neill, Laura Dern, Jeff Goldblum, and Richard Attenborough, Amblin Entertainment/Universal, 1993; *The Lost World: Jurassic Park*, dir. Steven Spielberg, perf. Jeff Goldblum, Richard Attenborough, Julianne Moore, Pete Postlethwaite, Arliss Howard, Vince Vaughn, and Vanessa Lee Chester, Universal, 1997. Subsequent references to Ray and to Dick are given in the text.

6. For a survey of issues related to contemporary species loss, see E. O. Wilson and Frances M. Peter's collection of essays *Biodiversity* (Washington, D.C.: National Academy Press, 1988); Les Kaufman and Kenneth Mallory, *The Last Extinction,* 2d ed. (Cambridge: MIT Press, 1993); and Paul Ehrlich, *Extinction: The Causes and Consequences of the Disappearance of Species* (New York: Random House, 1981). A controversial debate on the subject is recorded in Norman Myers and Julian Simon, *Scarcity or Abundance? A Debate on the Environment* (New York: Norton, 1994).

7. Mary Shelley, *Frankenstein* (Oxford: Oxford University Press, 1994); H. G. Wells, *The Island of Dr. Moreau* (New York: Dover, 1996).

8. W. J. T. Mitchell, *The Last Dinosaur Book* (Chicago: University of Chicago Press, 1998), 19. Subsequent references are given in the text.

9. For an introduction to Artificial Life as a discipline, see Claus Emmeche, *The Garden in the Machine: The Emerging Science of Artificial Life,* trans. Steven Sampson (Princeton, N.J.: Princeton University Press, 1994); Julio Fernández Ostolaza and Álvaro Moreno Bergareche, *Vida artificial* (Madrid: EUDEMA, 1992); and Stefan Helmreich, *Silicon Second Nature: Culturing Artificial Life in a Digital World* (Berkeley: University of California Press, 1998).

10. Helmreich, *Silicon Second Nature,* chapter 3; Hayles, *How We Became Posthuman,* chapter 9, and Katharine Hayles, "Simulated Nature and Natural Simulations: Rethinking the Relation between the Beholder and the World," in *Uncommon Ground: Toward Reinventing Nature,* ed. William Cronon (New York: Norton, 1995), 418–25.

11. The best source of information on *Tierra* is Thomas Ray's home page on the World Wide Web at http://www.hip.atr.co.jp/~ray/, which provides links to the program and many of Ray's publications about it; for descriptions of his project, see also his articles "An Approach to the Synthesis of Life" and "An Evolutionary Approach to Synthetic Biology."

12. See Ray's link, http://www.hip.atr.co.jp/~ray/pubs/reserves/reserves.html.

13. "In Ray's rhetoric, the computer codes composing these 'creatures' become natural forms of life; only the medium is artificial" (Hayles, *How We Became Posthuman*, 224).

14. See Pierre Teilhard de Chardin, "Une interprétation plausible de l'Histoire Humaine: La formation de la 'Noosphère,'" *Revue des questions scientifiques* 118 (1947): 7–37; Marshall McLuhan, "Interview," *Playboy* (March 1969): 53–74+; and Douglas Rushkoff's more recent restatement of this idea in *Cyberia: Life in the Trenches of Hyperspace* (San Francisco: HarperCollins, 1994). Mark Dery briefly comments on this evolutionary narrative in *Escape Velocity: Cyberculture at the End of the Century* (New York: Grove, 1996), 45–46.

15. See also Hayles's discussion of the fundamental role that evolutionary narrative plays in Ray's presentations of the *Tierra* project both in his writings and in a videotape released by the Santa Fe Institute (*How We Became Posthuman,* 225–31).

16. William J. Mitchell's *City of Bits: Space, Place and the Infobahn* (Cambridge: MIT Press, 1995) is a book-length exploration of this analogy.

17. Ridley Scott's film *Blade Runner,* which is loosely based on this novel and a classic in its own right, significantly reduces the importance of animals to the plot; whereas a "replicant" owl and an artificial snake do appear in the movie, their role is entirely marginal, as opposed to the central significance of electric animals in the novel. *Blade Runner,* dir. Ridley Scott, perf. Harrison Ford, Rutger Hauer, Sean Young, Daryl Hannah, and William Sanderson, Blade Runner Partnership/Ladd Co./Sir Run Run Shaw/Warner, 1982.

18. See Lawrence Sutin, *Divine Invasions: A Life of Philip K. Dick* (New York: Harmony, 1989), 306–7.

19. See Jill Galvan, "Entering the Posthuman Collective in Philip K. Dick's *Do Androids Dream of Electric Sheep?*," *Science-Fiction Studies* 24 (1997): 414, 427–28.

20. This is confirmed, among other things, by Dick's own reflections on humans and androids in his essays "Man, Android, and Machine," "The Android and the Human," and "Notes on *Do Androids Dream of Electric Sheep?*" For Dick, the blurring of boundaries between machine and human is tragic and not, as in Haraway, a phenomenon to be celebrated for its emancipatory potential. See Dick's "Man, Android, and Machine," "Notes on *Do Androids Dream of Electric Sheep?*," and "The Android and the Human," in *The Shifting Realities of Philip K. Dick: Selected Literary and Philosophical Writings,* ed. Lawrence Sutin (New York: Pantheon, 1995), 211–32, 155–61, 183–210, respectively.

21. As mentioned earlier, Ray's and Dick's approaches could also be criticized in terms of their underlying understanding of the concept of "life." Because such

a critique has already been elaborated in detail by Helmreich and Hayles, I will not pursue this aspect further here.

22. For Mitsubishi's robot sea bream and Sony's AIBO, see "The Call of Nature," *Economist* 351 (June 5, 1999): 78–79. Information and images of AIBO can also be accessed at Sony's Web site: http://world.sony.com/robot.

23. Akira Mizuta Lippit's *Electric Animal: Toward a Rhetoric of Wildlife* (Minneapolis: University of Minnesota Press, 2000), which appeared after the initial draft of this essay was completed, asks a related question about the disappearance of wildlife and the function of technology in the late nineteenth and early twentieth centuries. Lippit's central claim—which he discusses specifically with regard to photography and film, though he also seems to extend it to other fields ranging from electricity to quantum mechanics (see chapter 5, nn. 72–75)—is that "modern technology can be seen as a massive mourning apparatus, summoned to incorporate a disappearing animal presence that could not be properly mourned because, following the paradox to its logical conclusion, animals could not die. It was necessary to find a place in which animal being could be transferred, maintained in its distance from the world" (188–89). In its broad generality, Lippit's claim is not supported by the evidence and argument he presents. Although certain instances of animal representation in early photography and film he discusses are fascinating, this does not warrant the conclusion that these technologies in and of themselves are a response to the loss of animal life—a claim that Lippit supports by recurring to late-twentieth-century theories of these media whose applicability to the late nineteenth century remains unproblematized. It is, at any rate, not clear exactly what Lippit means by the "disappearing animal presence"; although he sometimes seems to refer primarily to the diminishing importance of animals in modern urban life (187), he seems to be thinking of actual species loss at other times (1–3, 184). But if species extinction is the reality he has in mind, then the assumption that animals are unable to die loses much of its meaning; as Lippit himself argues, the sense that animals cannot die is predicated both on their inability to speak (and therefore to "experience death as death" [170]) and on the perception that "animal being cannot be reduced to individual identities. It is dispersed thoughout the pack or horde, which preserves the individual organism's death within the framework of a group body or identity" (172–73). Consequently, it would seem, if the pack or entire species goes extinct, animals do acquire the ability to die, which would undercut the logic of the mourning process Lippit attributes to the technological apparatus. The generality of Lippit's claims and his lack of specificity in discussing both the status of animals and the conditions under which particular technologies emerge in the nineteenth century undermine the persuasiveness of an analysis that might otherwise have revealed potentially interesting parallels with the one I am proposing here.

Language, Power, and the Training of Horses

Paul Patton

People love horses for all kinds of reasons. For some, it is a matter of the simple aesthetic appreciation embodied in the idea that "horses make a landscape look more beautiful."[1] For others, it is the horse's power, speed, intelligence, and infinite capacity to respond to human desires. In my own case, the love of some memorable horses came about through the experience of learning to train them. A few years ago, the contingencies of career and personal life allowed me to spend time on a farm rediscovering a childhood passion for playing with horses. Some of these were Quarter Horses, but for the most part they were Australian Stock Horses, a breed of working horses prized for their skill with cattle. Their origins lie in horses brought to the colony in order to breed cavalry mounts, but over time they became the kinds of horses epitomized in Banjo Patterson's epic poem *The Man from Snowy River*: tough and wiry animals "with a touch of timor pony, three parts thoroughbred at least, and such as are by mountain horsemen prized." They are now used for all kinds of equestrian sport, from working-horse events such as cutting or campdrafting to more refined pursuits such as polo, eventing, and dressage.

It was only after I undertook to "break in" some of the progeny of our homegrown breeding program that the simple pleasures of trail riding and mustering sheep and cattle gave way to a more reflective interest in our relations with animals. Perhaps because I was teaching a course on

83

Foucault and the ways in which power helps to create forms of subjectivity, horse-training manuals became a source of intellectual fascination as well as practical instruction. At this point, my love of horses connected with my love of philosophy in a way that I thought nobody shared before I discovered Vicki Hearne's wonderful book *Adam's Task: Calling Animals by Name*.[2] Like Hearne, I had read with interest Peter Singer's *Animal Liberation* but come away dissatisfied with its lack of attention to the ways we interact with domestic animals such as dogs and horses.[3] His utilitarian approach to human–animal relations did not provide a sufficiently fine-grained basis for discrimination between the many ways in which we use animals for our own purposes. The qualitative differences between hunting animals for sport, raising them for consumption, or training them for jumping or dressage are not readily captured by the calculus of pleasures and pains. In the course of endorsing the trainer's saying that you don't know what it is to love a dog until you've trained one, Hearne describes the special kind of respect, awe, and delight that result from prolonged engagement with the character and capacities of a particular animal (93–94). Like her, I was interested in the complexity of training, the peculiar richness it brought to the relationship with the animal, and the ways in which training and riding could benefit from awareness of and respect for the being of the animal. Her book was an inspiration to pursue this idiosyncratic interest in the philosophy of training horses as well as a model for the kind of double writing that could come of an engagement with both the practice of training and the practice of philosophy.

It was only later, when I had read more widely on the subject, that I realized how fortunate I had been that my initial clumsy efforts at training had led to no serious damage to horse or rider. I put this down to the calm and generous response from Eulabah, my first trainee, and to the relatively gentle methods I had employed. These were drawn from a book that advocated a "nonviolent" technique of handling young horses, in opposition to the rough tactics that were still common in the bush.[4] The "Jeffery method" described in this book argued against the cruder forms of restraint formerly used to convert wild horses to saddle mounts. These included the use of leg ropes, fixed side reins, and other cruel practices designed to wear down the animal's capacity to resist. Tying up the horse and hitting it all over the body with a sack was known as "bagging" or "sacking out." The purpose of this activity, which was terrifying to young, unhandled horses, was to dull their sensitivity to touch and sudden movement. In his best-selling book *The Man Who Listens to Horses*, Monty

Roberts describes these techniques as the basis of his father's cowboy method for breaking the willpower of horses.[5] Roberts's own strategy for "starting" rather than "breaking" young horses was devised in explicit opposition to the cruelty of the conventional method. He refused the use of ropes, whips, or any of the traditional apparatus of domination in favor of a nonviolent approach relying on body language and occasional use of the voice. From the outset, he wanted an approach that recognized that horses can either accept or refuse to cooperate in the training process, and that sought to engage their trust rather than their fear. More recently, Roberts insists even more strongly that violence and confrontation are not the best way to obtain cooperation (90–91).[6]

The Man Who Listens to Horses had not been published when I first began training young horses. But he was by no means the first to advocate a nonviolent approach to horse training. I discovered a similar ethos in the work of the English cavalry-trained Henry Wynmalen, written in the 1930s. Wynmalen describes a method of schooling young horses that relied on repetition, infinite patience, and unlimited time and resources. Although the lungeing whip remains an important training aid, it is never employed to strike the horse. Wynmalen describes its use with exemplary understatement as a "gentle art" that "the inexperienced will do well to practise . . . in a quiet corner, well away from any horse."[7] Although Wynmalen allows that there will be occasions when the whip should be used, his was definitely an improvement on the Jeffery method, which relied on a control technique unselfconsciously called a "choke rope," consisting of a slipknot around the horse's windpipe that could be tightened at any moment it became necessary to remind the animal who was in charge. Even Hearne stresses the importance of corrections in training when the horse fails to give the proper response to a given command: a sharp jerk on the horse's sensitive mouth to ensure that the next time it will give the proper response. Clearly, there are degrees of nonviolence in the training of horses. Roberts insists that he will never hit, kick, jerk, pull, tie, or restrain the horse, but still includes the caveat that "if we are forced to use some restraint, we want it to be of the mildest nature and without the feeling 'You Must' communicated to the horse" (*The Man Who Listens*, 350).

Could there ever be a purely nonviolent method of training horses, or is the very idea of training inseparable from a kind of violence to the horse's intrinsic untrained nature? Wynmalen appeared to suggest the possibility of a completely nonviolent relationship when he described riding as an art whose supreme principle was "to endeavour always to detect what is the lightest possible aid to which our horse will respond, and, on the discovery of this lightest possible aid, to continue trying to obtain response to a lighter one still" (193). A mode of relating to the horse free of any trace of violence figures here as a Kantian idea of reason, always on the horizon of our techniques of riding and training, if never fully attained in practice. Appealing as I found this ideal, I could not help but think that it was also a lure or an illusion that served only to mask the reality of a relationship that was fundamentally coercive.

From Wynmalen I also learned something of the arcane rules of dressage and the complex system of commands or aids employed to produce particular movements in the horse. In stark contrast with the unsubtle bush methods of riding and training, these aids provide a sophisticated language that enables riders to communicate with the horse by ever more subtle movement and gesture. They rely on the horse's extremely fine sense of touch, and the ability to use them well requires a no less extraordinary degree of sensitivity both to one's own body and that of the horse. At higher levels of skill such as those found in Grand Prix dressage, this corporeal communication between rider and horse is largely invisible even to the trained observer. Hearne describes watching a film of the Spanish Riding School instructor Colonel Podhajsky working with a highly educated horse in which, even in slow-motion close-up, there was no detectable movement of the legs and hands that executed the aids (112). She argues that this kind of riding presupposes in the rider a degree of responsiveness to the horse that in turn enables communication in both directions, such that there is an ongoing conversation between horse and rider. A true rider, she suggests, is someone who has earned the right to continuously "question the horse and the horse's performance," while in turn it is the horse's performance that "answers the rider's questioning" (162).

Having developed an interest in training techniques more sensitive to the situation and capacities of the horses, it seemed to me a natural progression to want to expand the vocabulary and syntax of my own means of communication with them. As a result, when I later went to teach at the Australian National University in Canberra, I took the biggest and best of my young Stockhorses along and boarded him at an equestrian center a few miles out of town. My plan was to complete Flash's basic schooling and for both of us to learn some dressage. We did this and successfully completed some elementary tests before becoming completely absorbed in show jumping. We competed for several years in low-level competitions with mixed success. I divided my time between the classroom and the riding arena, enjoying the enormous cultural differences between them, but also the points at which my interests in the two worlds leached into one another.

As much as I tried to inhabit the moral universe of the classically trained horseman, I often found it difficult to do so with the required seriousness of purpose. Flash's first reactions were those of a horse raised in the bush among his own kind, far from the formal routines of the school and the arena. He was prone to outbursts of herd behavior that were inappropriate in this context, and any new jump was met with great wariness. I could not help being amused as he would round the corner on course only to stiffen with surprise at the obstacle ahead and prick his ears forward and back as if to say "Surely you don't expect us to go over that monstrosity." I was astounded at the agility with which, entirely of his own volition, he could perform a flying change at the canter and vary his line of approach in order to slide around the obstacle he was supposed to jump. In part, it was my personal involvement with the history and personality of this particular horse that got in the way of providing the necessary corrections to improper reactions on his part.

However, I also like to think that this problem arose because of my awareness of the historically and culturally contingent nature of the training techniques and standards of horsemanship. While there was much overlap in the skills and attitudes required of the good rider in the different worlds, working-horse culture favored a somewhat different set of characteristics, abilities, and movements on the part of the horse from those prized in dressage and show jumping. It was difficult to see these capacities as any less grounded in the nature of these extraordinary animals. Rather, each of the different cultures of horsemanship seemed to have its own "final vocabulary" in the sense that Richard Rorty uses this term, whereas I found myself in the position of ironist in relation to all of these: aware of their historical contingency, their susceptibility to change, and their lack of foundation in any natural order of human–horse relations.[8] As an intellectual observer of the influential final vocabularies of horse culture, I was free to adopt this attitude in private. However, just as Rorty suggests we cannot envisage an ironist public culture, I found it difficult to reconcile the ironist stance of the postmodern intellectual with the commitment required of a dressage rider. In Hearne's terms, I lacked a good story to tell myself about my horse's and my own participation in this activity. This essay records some of my efforts to work out such a story. Although I sympathized with her aim, stated at the outset of *Adam's Task*, "to find an accurate way of talking about our relationships with domestic animals," I remained skeptical of some of her more poetic conclusions (3).

Trainers and riders tell themselves all kinds of stories about why their animals cooperate in the ways that they do, but the more enlightened among them place great importance on communication between humans and horses. They reject the idea that training proceeds by domination or coercion in favor of seeing it as a form of dialogue or negotiation. Roberts, for example, insists that training should proceed by offer and counteroffer rather than anything that resembles "you must." He describes his "Join-Up" method as a means of communicating and connecting with the horse: "Join-Up is a consistent set of principles that I developed as a trainer of horses over many years, using the horse's own language, designed to let the horse know that he has freedom of choice" (*Join-Up*, 2). His technique for starting young horses relies on his appropriation of elements of the system of nonverbal communication that horses use among themselves. He employs his eyes, body language, and gesture to challenge the horse and put it into flight mode. He then waits for the horse's own signs of willingness to submit before proceeding to the next stage of familiarizing the horse with some of the trainer's own signs and equipment.

Hearne offers a compelling story about the capacity of horses and dogs for language where this means something like their capacity for submission to the formal demands of certain kinds of structured activity. She argues that training establishes a linguistic form of life within which humans and animals are able to communicate with one another. Her anecdotes of linguistic creativity on the part of animals involved in training, including jokes and evasions, are familiar to anyone who has worked with dogs or horses. They are also examples of the capacity of these animals to respond rather than merely react to the speech acts of their trainers.[9] But the "language" employed in the early stages of training the horse is not the same as the structured system of commands employed in dressage or other forms of advanced riding. It is not obvious where language resides in the training relation between humans and horses. Perhaps there is no univocal answer to the question "What is linguistic in this relation?"

It is true that there is nothing self-evident about any of the means by which riders communicate with their horses. The most remarkable feature of this kind of interspecies communication between such different kinds of being is that it takes place at all. To begin with, communication between horse and rider is a case of "radical communication" in the sense that Quine speaks of radical translation.[10] However much one knows about horses' means of communication with other horses, however much one has prepared the untrained horse by familiarizing it with bits, saddles, and additional weight on the back, there is still a void between the horse and the rider seated on its back for the first time; neither can be sure what the other expects or fears, neither can be sure how the other will react to their movements or what this reaction means. The apparatuses of bridles, bits, and spurs are entirely conventional devices that only the naive rider thinks of as means of forcing a horse to do what it does not want to do. For the most part, horses are stronger than their riders and if they obey the rider's commands it is because they are trained to do so. Even the most elementary aids are signs. The horse has to learn that pressure through the legs behind the girth means "go forward" or "go faster" and not "do everything in your power to rid yourself of this unpleasant parasite." These signs form a linguistic system to the extent that they are both arbitrary and relational. They are recognizable across physical differences of seat, leg position, and strength on the part of riders.

These are signs employed for the command of horses by humans, but this "language" of command only works because it is integrated within a larger, somatic framework of interspecies communication. The aids employed in riding work because they are embedded within a larger sensory field of touch, pressure, body contact, and attitude, including eye contact, which enables humans and horses to communicate with one another. This system of eye and body language is like an operating system within which the software of particular riding styles (dressage, western, Australian working horse, etc.) can be implemented. It also forms the common basis of riding and training aids and the intraspecies system of communication that Roberts first observed among mustangs in the wild. Watching the body language employed by the dominant mare in a herd to discipline an unruly young horse gave him clues to decipher this "silent language":

> As I watched the mare's training procedures with this and other adolescents, I began to cotton on to the language she used, and it was exciting to be able to recognise the exact sequence of signals that would pass between her and the adolescents. It really was a language—predictable, discernible and effective. First and foremost it was a silent language. . . . Body language is not confined to humans, nor to horses; it constitutes the most often used form of communication between animate objects on dry land. (*The Man Who Listens*, 101)

Even the most basic interaction with horses demands a certain level of knowledge about their behavior; flattened ears, swishing tails, a threatened kick are signs that every rider soon learns to read. Roberts's "Join-Up" technique involves an extended version of this kind of knowledge and its integration into the training process.

Although this nonverbal "language" undoubtedly allows for communication in both directions between horse and human, the rhetoric of dialogue and partnership remains misleading so far as training is concerned. After all, the signs employed by Roberts are modeled on those of a dominant mare controlling a young horse. Like the precise system of signs employed in dressage, where each sign corresponds to a discrete action on the part of the horse, they enable commands. Although good trainers allow considerable latitude in acceptable responses to a given command in the early stages, ultimately what they aim to achieve is absolute obedience from the trained animal. Hearne argues that "absolute obedience" here means not only immediate compliance with a given command, but also commitment to performing what is required as though it were a sacred duty. She praises the trainer William Koehler for his rigorous commitment to the view that the goal of training ought to be to obtain "absolute obedience" from a dog (43). Similarly, Henry Wynmalen asserts at the outset of his *Equitation* that the primary object of schooling the horse is to make him "perfectly obedient to his rider," where perfect obedience implies "that the rider, without effort, strength or fuss, be able to obtain from his horse any movement, any pace, any speed, at any time" (34). Horse trainers often speak as though it were a matter of horse and rider becoming one body, in which the human is the head that commands while the horse is the body that executes the movements. Hearne suggests that the relation is even closer, not simply the control of one part by another but "the collapse of command and obedience into a single supple relation." It is not merely, as Podhajsky and others have suggested, "as though the rider thinks and the horse executes the thought," but also the other way around, "as though the horse thinks and the rider creates, or becomes, a space and direction for the execution of the horse's thoughts" (Hearne, *Adam's Task*, 163). Yet although training both involves and enables a form of linguistic communication, there remains a fundamental asymmetry at the heart of the relation between horse and rider. The conversation between horse and rider in the arena takes place entirely in respect of tasks that are set by the rider. The primary purpose of the communication between them is the transmission of orders.

Absolute obedience is undoubtedly a goal or limit that is only attained, if at all, in rare moments of sublime performance. But the importance of this goal as the transcendental object of the trainer's art shows that the training relationship is fundamentally a relation of command that is superimposed on the difference between species. Locating the language of aids employed in riding and training within the larger context of forms of nonverbal communication between humans and horses allows us to disentangle, in theory, the elements of communication and command that are inextricably intertwined in the training relationship. Both training and riding involve the exercise of power over the animal and, contrary to the view of many philosophers and trainers, relations of communication are not external but immanent to relations of power.

Hearne objects strongly to the language of power on the grounds that it is inaccurate, inefficient, and, as we will see, ugly. She prefers the anthropomorphic and morally loaded language of the animal trainers. This is a language that allows trainers to speak of the character, understanding, responsibility, honesty, and courage of their animals. It supposes that dogs and horses are capable not only of intelligent, conscious thought, but also of "a complex and delicate (though not infallible) moral understanding that is so inextricably a function of their relationships with human beings that it may well be said to constitute those relationships" (8). Hearne does not deny the importance of command and obedience to the forms of life within which animals and trainers interact, but she renders this relationship as a kind of sacred duty that is binding on trainer and trainee alike. By way of illustration, she tells the story of Drummer Girl, a thoroughbred mare who was brought to her as a crazy horse for retraining. On her account, Drummer Girl's problem was not unwillingness or inability to respond to commands but, on the contrary, an "enormous capacity for precision and elegance" that made her intolerant of less demanding or less coherent commands. Her method of dealing with this problem was not to coerce, but rather to appeal to the horse's own intelligence and desire by setting up situations in which the horse's own preference for balance and precision made her do the right thing. Although Hearne admits that "it would not be hard to make this out to be a tale of coercion," such a story would be ineffective because "it would be impossible to get the response I have described [from Drummer Girl] by using such a philosophy" (129–34).[11]

At this point, however, the requirements of an effective story and those of an accurate one seem to pull in different directions. In explicit rejection of a remark attributed to Foucault that defines dressage as an "uninterrupted, constant coercion" of the body and its forces, Hearne argues for a distinction "between education as coercion and dressage or any other genuine discipline" (123).[12] Yet, if by coercion we understand causing the animal to perform a certain action against its will or by force, then it is difficult not to see techniques such as administering "corrections" or "getting on the ear" of the inept dog as coercion pure and simple. Hearne's technique for curing Drummer Girl of a tendency to rush at jumps by asking for a halt immediately after each jump is a less direct way of acting upon the horse's actions. But if we understand coercion to mean causing the animal to act in ways that it would not otherwise have acted, then even such indirect techniques are coercive in the broader sense. The difference here is between more and less sophisticated techniques of exercising power over other beings.

Hearne describes her technique of asking Drummer Girl for a halt soon after the jump as setting up "a situation in which she had available to her certain clear decisions" (132). Roberts also talks of relying on the horse's own capacity to choose whether or not to cooperate, even though the circumstances of its choice are constrained by his technique of putting pressure on the horse, using the body language of the dominant mare, before backing off and allowing it to choose. In both cases, the trainer engages in precisely the kind of action upon the actions of others that Foucault calls "government."[13] Coercion may well be ineffective, uneconomic, and unpleasant for trainer and trainee, but it is nonetheless a mode of government. So too are the more effective as well as more humane methods that rely on the animal's own capacity to integrate and coordinate its movements. The difference between the conventional cowboy methods that employ leg ropes and "sacking out" and the methods of Hearne, Roberts, and others is not a difference between the exercise of power over animals and communication with them. It is a difference between less and more sophisticated techniques of exercising power over others.

Does this mean that there is no significant difference between the various techniques we employ in the exercise of power over horses? Not really. Good training both relies on and enhances the means of communication between humans and animals. Even though it remains a difference within forms of exercise of power over the animal, the difference relates to the degree to which good training is grounded in understanding of and respect for the being of the animal. This is a difference of degree that gives rise to a qualitative difference in the nature of these activities. The commitment to understanding and respect for the nature of horses is what lies behind the language of freedom and choice that both Hearne and Roberts use to recount their training techniques. In less anthropomorphic terms, we might describe the difference between their training and conventional methods as that between an exercise of power that blindly seeks to capture some of the powers of the animal for human purposes, and an exercise of power that seeks to capture the powers of the animal in ways that enhance both those powers and the animal's enjoyment of them.

Hearne's stories about tracking dogs and jumping horses are not only intended to point us toward the right language to use in describing our relationships with animals we train; they are also supposed to provide a defense of these relationships and of the activities in which they are embedded. Ultimately, this is an aesthetico-moral defense that relies on the idea that training "results in ennoblement, in the development of the animal's character and in the development of both the animal's *and the handler's* sense of responsibility and honesty." She admits that this attempt to ground the value of training in the development of the animal's beauty and character "is either hopelessly corrupt, in a sense that *The Genealogy of Morals* might unfold, or else it can tell us something about not only what goes on in training but also what it might mean to respond fully as human beings to 'character,' 'responsibility' and 'honesty'" (43).

I think, in fact, that it is both corrupt and informative in the manner suggested, and the remainder of this essay will be concerned to spell out why. The sense in which *The Genealogy of Morals* shows slave morality to be corrupt is by showing how it inverts the values of the masters and projects a self-serving conception of human character onto those others in order to be able to condemn them in the name of supposedly shared values. The aesthetico-moral defense of the activities for which animals are trained is corrupt in the same manner to the extent that it misrepresents what, anthropomorphically, we might call the "values" of the animals involved and it projects onto them as natural certain aptitudes and airs that are valued by their all too human trainers. Nonetheless, as we shall see, there are lessons to be learned from a proper understanding of the training relationship and the differences between good and bad training.

Classical accounts of the art of training and riding horses by Podhajsky, Wynmalen, and others often refer to the achievement of grace and beauty in the horse's bearing. Following this long tradition, which may be traced back to Xenophon, Hearne also asserts a connection between training and the resultant beauty of the horse and its movement. For the trainer, "Beauty is a sign, even a criterion of truth," and the good technique is the one that leads to the development or enhancement of the horse's beauty

(124). Moreover, the argument goes, the beauty that is the aim of good riding is a beauty that belongs to the nature of the horse. A mimetic principle comes into play at this point, for it is argued that in properly training horses and dogs we do nothing that is incompatible with their nature: "The jump, like the complicated movements of dressage, is an imitation of nature" (160).[14] Similarly, the positions and movements of dressage, along with the collection and lightness of step associated with them, are displayed by horses themselves under certain conditions, especially in the course of sexual display. Xenophon provides the classic expression of this idea when he argues that

> if you teach your horse to go with a light hand on the bit, and yet to hold his head well up and to arch his neck, you will be making him do just what the animal himself glories and delights in. A proof that he really delights in it is that when a horse is turned loose and runs off to join other horses and especially towards mares, then he holds his head up as high as he can, arches his neck in the most spirited style, lifts his legs with free action, and raises his tail. So when he is induced by a man to assume all the airs and graces which he puts on himself when he is showing off voluntarily, the result is a horse that likes to be ridden, that presents a magnificent sight, that looks alert.[15]

But this is ultimately a slender thread on which to hang the defense of the kinds of training that produce the formal routines of modern-day jumping and dressage. In the end, it seems no more than a rationalization of certain human, all too human, tastes and preferences. After all, it is particular gaits and body shapes, such as the bowed head with the neck bent at the poll, that are valued as the standard of beauty. Nor should we forget that the classic texts of modern dressage date from the seventeenth and eighteenth centuries, the same period in which the techniques of discipline to which Foucault drew our attention were being applied to the bearing and movement of human bodies. This was also a period in which art was supposed to improve upon nature and landscape gardening was counted among the fine arts. That is why Kant could assert an equivalence between artistic genius and the performance of a well-trained horse.[16] We should also remember that although horses in their natural state can jump fences and other obstacles, they rarely do so if left to their own devices. When they do jump, it is in order to flee, to get to water or to other horses, and not in order to overcome a complicated series of obstacles in a certain order and time. Similarly, the movements undertaken in high school dressage may well be the re-creation of movements, postures, and gestures that horses undertake of their own accord. Horses do lift their knees and arch their necks in moments of erotic display, in ways that accord with human criteria of grace and beauty. But they do not perform the complicated sequences of movements and gaits expected in dressage competitions. When horses compete in jumping and dressage, it is because they have been trained to do so in order to satisfy the culturally acquired desires of their trainers and riders.

Does this mean that training horses to perform classical disciplines such as dressage is irredeemably corrupt? Is training of any kind an indefensible form of co-optation of the animal's powers? To see why the answers to these questions should be in the negative, we need to hold apart the elements of the training relationship: the disciplinary relations of command and obedience, the relation to animals, and the languages that enable us to interact with them. Disciplinary relations of command and obedience are precisely a means to create and maintain stable and civil relations between different kinds of beings, not only among individuals of the same species, but also between representatives of different species. Trainers such as Hearne and Roberts argue that in training dogs and horses we create forms of society that establish domestic animals not only as our interlocutors in certain contexts, but as moral beings capable of being endowed with certain rights and duties.

The philosophical interest of this claim emerges when we consider that philosophers such as Nietzsche and Foucault are widely condemned for their insistence that all human social relations are power relations, in part on the grounds that if this were true it would amount to a denial of the possibility of ethical relations. The assumption here is that justice, fair treatment, and respect for others are possible only outside of or apart from relations of power. Power relations are relations of inequality, whereas the presumption of contemporary political theory is the moral equality of all the parties concerned. This leaves it open to suppose that moral equality does not extend to animals and that, as a result, we have no obligations toward them. By contrast, what we learn from the disciplines of animal training is that hierarchical forms of society between unequals are by no means incompatible with ethical relations and obligations toward other beings.

Some of these are intrinsic to the nature of disciplines as coherent and rule-governed activities and only incidentally connected to the interspecies relation—for example, the strict obligations that absolute obedience places on those who would command. In a chapter titled "How to Say 'Fetch,'" Hearne argues that would-be trainers have to learn how to utter commands to their dogs. In this sense, just as the dog has the right to the consequences of its actions, so the trainer must have a heightened awareness of the consequences of his or her actions. A consequence of trainers appreciating this is that they become more careful about the frequency and the conditions under which they utter commands. In effect, trainers must become like those whom Nietzsche says have acquired the right to make promises. These are beings "who promise like sovereigns, reluctantly, rarely, slowly." Trainers, too, must become like sovereign individuals, aware of "the extraordinary privilege of responsibility" and conscious of the "power over oneself and fate" that this implies.[17] The overlap between the moral cosmos of the trainer and the one we encounter in Nietzsche's writings is also evident in Hearne's remark that, for the trainee dog, "Freedom is being on an 'Okay' command" (54). In other words, freedom only makes sense within a system of constraints; it presupposes both capacities of the subject and their location within relations of power.

Some of the ethical relations that are inseparable from training derive from the fact that this is a communicative relationship, where it is also incidental that the communication takes place between animals of different species. Just as communication among humans presupposes a degree of trust, so it is apparent that to establish means of communication between humans and animals is also to establish a basis for trust. Hearne points out that the better a dog (or a horse) is trained, "which is to say, the greater his 'vocabulary'—the more mutual trust there is, the more dog [or horse] and human can rely on each other to behave responsibly" (21). Roberts also insists that the point of his method is to create a relationship based on mutual trust and confidence (*Join-Up*, 8, 93ff.).

Relationships involving communication and command-obedience are, of course, common within human social life. That is why, in *Join-Up: Horse Sense for People*, Roberts can argue for the extension of the principles of his horse-training techniques to the whole gamut of human relations involving differences of power and capacity. He suggests that relations between parents and children, women and men, managers and employees will all be better served by an approach that employs nonverbal as well as verbal means to establish trust and invite cooperation. Hearne also points out that much of human social life presupposes relationships of command and obedience. We expect obedience to some at least of our own basic needs and desires on the part of other people and we teach obedience to our children. The import of this line of thought in both Hearne and Roberts is to suggest that we do well to attend to the requirements of the hierarchical and communicative relations in which we live, and that certain kinds of emphasis on equality in all contexts are not only misleading but dangerous. Be that as it may, the trainer's relation to animals provides an important qualification to the presumption that ethical relations only obtain between beings of the same natural kind.

Finally, there is an ethical dimension to the training relationship that relates to the fact that it is an interspecies relationship. One of the most appealing features of Hearne's defense of training is her insistence that this involves relations between beings that are unequally endowed with capacities for language, for hearing and scent discrimination, or for movement and kinesthetic sensation. As a consequence, human–animal relations cannot be regarded as incomplete versions of human–human relations but must be regarded as complete versions of relations between different kinds of animals. Hearne points to the similarities between the moral cosmos of training and that of the older forms of human society in which "obedience was a part of human *virtu*," thereby drawing attention to the fact that the idea of society that is expressed in the practice of training is at odds with our modern egalitarian ethos (43). But whereas the differences between the sexes, races, and social classes in those older forms of society were only purportedly based in nature, the differences between trainers and their subjects are natural differences between animal kinds endowed with different powers and capacities. The good trainer is the one who appreciates these differences, who both understands and respects the specific nature of the animal. Thus Roberts's "Join-Up" technique makes use of the fact that horses are herd animals whose first instinct is to run, but whose second instinct is to negotiate. Hearne argues that good training recognizes and engages with those things that are important to horse being: not only sensitivity to body language and touch, but also the desire for balance, for rhythm and precision of movement. In a reworking of the story of our expulsion from paradise, she suggests that our fallen relation to animals is one in which a gap has opened up between "the ability to command and the full acknowledgment of the personhood of the being so commanded" (47). Good training establishes a form of language that closes that gap, which is another way of saying that it enables a form of interaction that enhances the power and the feeling of power of both horse and rider.

Notes

Moira Gatens read several earlier drafts of this essay. I am very grateful for her helpful comments and for the many conversations we have had about horses and riding.

1. This is the title of a collection of poems by Alice Walker, *Horses Make a Landscape Look More Beautiful* (New York: Harcourt Brace Jovanovich, 1984). Walker attributes this phrase to Lame Deer, who recounts that his people had no word for the strange animal acquired from the white man that they called "holy dog."

2. Vicki Hearne, *Adam's Task: Calling Animals by Name* (New York: Alfred A. Knopf, 1986). Subsequent references are given in the text.

3. Peter Singer, *Animal Liberation* (London: Jonathan Cape, 1976).

4. Maurice Wright, *The Jeffery Method of Horse Handling: An Introduction to a New Approach to the Handling of Horses* (Prospect, South Africa: R. M. Williams, 1973).

5. Monty Roberts, *The Man Who Listens to Horses* (New York: Random House, 1997), 21–23. The novel and film character of the "horse whisperer" are based on Roberts, who writes at one point: "A good trainer can hear a horse speak to him. A great trainer can hear him whisper" (31). Subsequent references are given in the text.

6. Monty Roberts, *Join-Up: Horse Sense for People* (London: HarperCollins, 2000). Subsequent references are given in the text.

7. Henry Wynmalen, *Equitation* (London: J. A. Allen & Co., 1938; 2nd rev. ed. 1971), 48. Subsequent references are given in the text.

8. Richard Rorty, *Contingency, Irony, Solidarity* (Cambridge: Cambridge University Press, 1989), 73–95.

9. As Derrida points out, one of the ways in which philosophers since Aristotle have sought to argue that animals are without language is by suggesting that they are unable to respond "with a response that could be precisely and rigorously distinguished from a reaction." See Jacques Derrida, "The Animal That Therefore I Am (More to Follow)," trans. David Wills, *Critical Inquiry* 28:2 (winter 2002): 369–418.

10. W. V. O. Quine, *Word and Object* (Cambridge: MIT Press, 1960), 26ff.

11. Hearne makes a similar point in her comments on the story of Hans Winkler's heroic ride on a difficult mare named Halla at the Stockhom Grand Prix in 1956, suggesting that part of the explanation for Winkler's success with Halla is that "he had a better story to tell himself and her about the nature of horsemanship and horses than riders who failed with her did" (122).

12. No citation is given for this remark and it does not strictly correspond to anything that occurs in Foucault's *Discipline and Punish*. Moreover, the only context in this book in which Foucault uses the term *dressage* makes it clear that he was concerned with the dressage of men rather than horses. See Michel Foucault, *Discipline and Punish* (London: Allen Lane, Penguin, 1977), 136ff., where he refers to La Mettrie's *L'Homme-Machine* as both a materialist reduc-

tion of the soul and a general theory of *dressage,* at the center of which reigns the notion of "docility."

13. See Michel Foucault, "The Subject and Power," Afterword to Hubert L. Dreyfus and Paul Rabinow, *Michel Foucault: Beyond Structuralism and Hermeneutics* (Chicago: University of Chicago Press, 1983), 208–16. Foucault specifies that "Basically power is less a confrontation between two adversaries or the linking of one to the other than a question of government. . . . To govern, in this sense, is to structure the possible field of action of others" (221).

14. Earlier Hearne suggests that "dog training is one of the arts concerned with the imitation of nature" (55).

15. Xenophon, *Art of Horsemanship,* trans. M. H. Morgan (London: J. Allen and Company, 1962), 56.

16. "Shallow minds fancy that the best evidence they can give of their being full-blown geniuses is by emancipating themselves from all academic constraint of rules, in the belief that one cuts a finer figure on the back of an ill-tempered than of a trained horse" (Immanuel Kant, *Critique of Judgement,* trans. J. C. Meredith [Oxford: Oxford University Press, 1952], Part I, book 2, no. 47).

17. Friedrich Nietzsche, *On the Genealogy of Morals,* second essay, section 2, available in many translations, including Walter Kaufman and R. J. Hollingdale, *On the Genealogy of Morals and Ecce Homo, with 75 Aphorisms* (New York: Random House, 1967).

From Protista to DNA (and Back Again): Freud's Psychoanalysis of the Single-Celled Organism

Judith Roof

> The external pressure which provokes a constantly increasing extent of develop-
> ment has not imposed itself upon *every* organism. Many have succeeded in re-
> maining up to the present time at their lowly level. Many, though not all, such
> creatures, which must resemble the earliest stages of the higher animals and
> plants, are, indeed, living to-day.
>
> **Sigmund Freud, *Beyond the Pleasure Principle***

For Sigmund Freud, the protist is an instrumental interspecies example
of the wider truth of his psychodynamic formulations. Standing (or
swimming) at the base of the complex ontogenetic/phylogenetic architecture of Freud's thought, the protist and its twin the "germ-plasm" are
primal, deathless reference points for Freud's thinking about life processes. The protist is both tabula rasa and antediluvian archetype that proves
the elemental antiquity and universality of the drives (death and pleasure) and instincts (sexuality) governing vital impulses. Freud's two versions of this seminal single cell—the independently surviving protoplas-
mic organism and the germ-plasm (or reproductive cells) that form a
central but separable part of all other species—are obligingly stable, simple,
persistent, and flexible. Occupying a large share of Freud's sparse references to animals, the single-celled organism both is and is not "human";
its difference from humanity both is and is not a positive feature. This

ambivalent status makes the example of the protista valuable as a link be-tween the human and the animal, as well as between the animate and the inanimate, the simple and the complex, the mortal and the immortal, its dual position guaranteeing the commonality of fundamental processes throughout a range of species. At the same time, the protist is the anthro-pomorphized subject of a psychoanalysis as Freud interprets its impuls-es, demonstrating how even the microbiological is ultimately a mirror for the human. Freud's intercalation of human and protozoa rendered sometimes as evolution, sometimes as phylogenesis, sustains simultane-ously two somewhat contradictory ideas about the interrelation of species: a theory of species hierarchy and a perception of species' independent equality. Together these positions produce an economy of conflict and exception that underwrites Freud's formulations of life forces.

Freud selects the example of the protist or single-celled organism not so much because its physiochemical processes are simpler, closer to the hy-pothesized chemical bases of behavior, and more easily distinguishable than those of more complex creatures, but because the single-celled or-ganism (which he equates with gametes or "germ-cells") has the happy feature of reproducing "asexually" through simple cell division or fission. In a pre-DNA universe, this fission would appear to preserve a portion of the original cell ad infinitum. But these versatile protista also reproduce through conjugation or a mingling of their cellular matter (later under-stood to be the recombination of DNA). Single-celled organisms are thus so multifaceted that they provide a model for almost any sexual practice, while also appearing to be devoid of other complicated structures and behaviors.

   Cell biology is meaningful as example for Freud solely within a Darwinian perspective. Only if we understand human beings to be the most complexly developed organisms in a chain of beings who presum-ably derive, through an evolutionary process, from one another can less complex species plausibly provide basic and reliable analogies for human physiology. The leap from physiology to psychology—from body (or soma) to mind—depends on the presumed unity of life, the common rule of dynamic principles, the relation among species, and species' pre-sumed intrarelation. The idea that less complex (and presumably earlier) forms of life survive as parts of later and more complex forms derives primarily from the phylogeny (and a hidden ontogeny) that Freud com-bines with his Darwinism.

   Initially interested in biology, Freud was greatly influenced by Darwin, whose ideas had found a receptive German audience. Devising his own mixture of evolution, phylogeny, and ontogeny, Freud adopted Darwin's claim that "psychology will be based on a new foundation, that of the necessary acquirement of each mental power and capacity by gradation."[1] Freud "weds evolution to Ernst Haeckel's 'biogenetic law' which holds that 'ontogeny recapitulates phylogeny,' or the development of the individual member of a particular species (ontogeny) recapitulates the history of the development of the entire species (phylogeny)."[2] Forging a series of parallels among evolution, human development, psychic development, and cultural change, Freud outlined not only opportunities for interspecies comparison, but also a unified theory of life processes that makes each species an example for all others. Just as animals develop into increasingly complex species, so each individual species becomes increasingly complex, so each individual develops from simple fetus to complex adult, so the psyche matures from simple to complicated, so culture evolves from primitive to sophisticated.

For Freud, however, phylogeny's recapitulation is not complete; organisms are littered with primitive holdovers coexisting with more developed forms. Like the archaeology Freud was so fond of using as an analogy for analysis, physiology becomes an unlayering of multiple developmental histories: that of the species and the individual.[3] And Freud goes even further; not only are these lines of development parallel, they are interconnected so that primitive types are contained within more complex species, producing a layering that provides a chronological, developmental basis for Freud's topological models of the psyche. At the same time, the coexistence of these developmental layers—these vestigial tokens—supplies a locus for the instinctive tendencies Freud elaborates in *Beyond the Pleasure Principle*.

Freud's appropriation of Darwinian evolution is not entirely an effect of his education and the scientific thinking of the time. The Goethean notions of the unity of life, subscribed to by his teachers Claus and Brücke, place basic principles of physics and chemistry as the foundation for all processes, even if they cannot yet be specified. In his early "Project for a Scientific Psychology" (1895), Freud tried to account for psychological processes through neurophysiology, drawing from his early experiments with the nervous systems of crayfish. Although he found neurophysiology to be too limited at the time to account adequately for the phenomena he was trying to explain, he persisted in his belief that when science had advanced sufficiently, such explanations would be possible. Twenty-five years later in *Beyond the Pleasure Principle* (1920), he suggests again that "the deficiencies in our description would probably vanish if we were already in a position to replace the psychological terms by the physiological or chemical ones."[4] Because physiology and chemistry are inadequate to the task, Freud substitutes for them the biology of more "primitive" organisms.[5]

Although these single-celled organisms are usefully primitive, Freud's phylogenous evolutionary logic is ultimately circular. Just as psychological processes might be glossed through the example of protista biology, so biological processes might be seen as manifestations of a psychology that operates even at the simplest level. The basic framework of Freud's metapsychological considerations in works such as *Beyond the Pleasure Principle* depends on the idea that "high" reflects "low" because high is comprised of low and low reflects high because the dynamics exemplified by the high are general principles of organic existence. This produces what seems to be a contradiction: if more complex species derive from lower forms and yet develop or elaborate those forms, how can the same dynamics already be at work in lower forms? Freud himself points to this dilemma: "The question arises here . . . whether we do right in ascribing to protista those characteristics alone which they actually exhibit, and whether it is correct to assume that forces and processes which become visible only in the higher organisms originated in those organisms for the first time" (51).

Freud does so assume, in regard not only to protista, but to animals in general, and his phylogeny does not limit itself to biochemistry and physiology, but extends to the psychic life. Noting that Karl Abraham and Carl Jung were "aware that the principle 'ontogeny is a repetition of phylogeny' must be applicable to mental life," Freud believed that traces of an animal past not only remain in the individual psyche, but remain and are indignantly denied in human culture.[6] The psychic phylogeny of human beings is evident, Freud believed, in the "early efflorescence [of sexual life] which comes to an end about the fifth year and is followed by what is known as the period of latency (till puberty)."[7] Freud concludes that this infantile sexuality "leads us to suppose that the human race is descended from a species of animal which reached sexual maturity in five years."[8] The descent from animals is denied through the "arrogance" of modern man, although the erasure of "the bond of community between him and the animal kingdom . . . is still foreign to children, just as it is to primitive and primaeval man. It is the result of a later, more pretentious stage of development."[9] Because Freud saw animals and humans existing phylogenetically through an evolutionary logic, it is entirely plausible that protista, regarded as evolution's simplest organisms, not only exhibit elements of psychodynamics, but also represent a link between humans and the biochemical elements that might ultimately provide a molecular explanation for life processes.

But although they exist at the intersection of old and new, biochemistry and life, and animal and human, protista are both the common denominators of and the exception to evolution's rule. Protista are the remainder, those organisms that "have succeeded in remaining up to the present time at their lowly level" (34), which already, always, and seemingly eternally represent the very dynamic that higher organisms only arrive at later. In fact, these surviving lower organisms incarnate the rules of survival, functioning both literally and figuratively as the germ-plasm into which they will evolve (in Freud's narrative), bearing in their economy the seeds of an entire dynamic—a fight between life and death. These protista are exceptional—they did not evolve, they are potentially immortal—and, for Freud, the exception always proves the rule, even if the exception seems to fly in the face of rules and external pressures. Relying on what seems to be the exception, Freud forges the rule that makes the protista the exception, the important leftover that provides hope in the face of determinism and strength in the simplest processes.

Freud deploys the example of the protista strategically in *Beyond the Pleasure Principle* as an illumination of the hidden "other" pressure that prevents individuals from rapidly settling for the pleasure principle's desired quiescence. Why do things continue to live, Freud queries, when death is so much more like the originary state of quiescence to which individuals, driven by the pleasure principle, would wish to return? The answer to Freud's question turns in part on his understanding of "instincts," the "forces originating in the interior of the body"—in other words, on an impetus not instigated by an outside stimulus but coming from something already inherent to the body of the organism (28). Positing that the "manifestations of a compulsion to repeat . . . exhibit to a high degree an instinctual character," but that they also seem to conflict with the pleasure principle, Freud demonstrates how repetition's "fort/da" provision of mastery actually produces pleasure and thus does not diverge from the pleasure principle at all (29). But when the repetition is of something unpleasant such as a trauma, the repetition compulsion seems to "disregard the pleasure principle in every way" (30). At the point of this apparent contradiction, Freud reexamines his original assertion about the instinctual nature of repetition, asking "how is the predicate of being 'instinctual' related to the compulsion to repeat?" (ibid.).

Like the tautology of phylogeny where low and high anticipate one another, the instinctual is already what it will become in Freud's argument: a primary axiom whose rule of conservatism is linked to animals and whose position as a fundamental precept parallels the phylogenetic position of the animal in the evolution of individual (psychic and physical) human development. This is the case even as Freud's formulation of the instincts seems (to him) to fly in the face of evolutionary sense. Reaffirming that the compulsion to repeat is instinctual (without ever really defining how), Freud declares:

> At this point we can not escape a suspicion that we may have come upon the track of a universal attribute of instincts and perhaps of organic life in general which has not hitherto been clearly recognized or at least not explicitly stressed. *It seems, then, that an instinct is an urge inherent in organic life to restore to an earlier state of things* which the living entity has been obliged to abandon under the pressure of external disturbing forces; that is, it is a kind of organic elasticity, or, to put it another way, the expression of the inertia inherent in organic life. (Ibid.)

Freud goes on to suggest that "this view of instincts strikes us as strange because we have become used to seeing in them a factor impelling towards change and development" (ibid).

To substantiate his theory that instincts are "an expression of the *conservative* nature of living substance," Freud calls up animal examples, not of instinct and repetition, but of how in animals the instinct to repeat is itself an ontogenetic expression of phylogenesis (ibid.). Instinct is a repetition of both individual and species history, as fish returning to spawn and birds migrating serve to illustrate. But Freud's "most impressive proof" is his version of Ernst Haeckel's "biogenetic law" that "ontogeny recapitulates phylogeny" (Hoffer, "Freud's 'Phylogenetic Fantasy,'" 18). In the "phenomena of heredity and the facts of embryology," Freud declares, "we see how the germ of a living animal is obliged in the course of its development to recapitulate (even if only in a transient and abbreviated fashion) the structures of all of the forms from which it is sprung" (31). Instinct thus derives phylogenetically not only from the animal forms recapitulated in human development, but also from the "germ" as the primal form of all organic existence. This "germ," which is obliged to live out its species history, already contains the instinct to repeat or it would not comply with biogenetic law and we would be a culture of animalcules.

The germ of an idea, the germ of an instinct, the germ of a living animal—the germ is a fertile, if microscopic, and thus almost fantasmatic, field of projection. Not only can it propel the past forward, it also becomes the site for projections about the primal urges that account for the apparently contradictory impulses of the drives. In Freud's evolutionary logic, the germ is "the earlier state of things," the conservative state organic instincts strive to repeat, an earlier condition Freud finally links to death. "Those instincts," Freud concludes, "are therefore bound to give a deceptive appearance of being forces tending towards change and progress, whilst in fact they are merely seeking to reach an ancient goal by paths alike old and new" (32). This ancient goal is not development, but death, a return to the inanimate, because *"inanimate things existed before living ones"* (ibid.). Organisms, therefore, live out their history through a dynamic of clashing but cooperative instincts: those that pressure repetition, or a return to an inanimate state, and those that constitute a history of detours—"self-preservation," "self-assertion," and "mastery"— "whose function it is to assure that the organism shall follow its own path to death" (33).

At this point in his argument about instincts Freud pauses. Instincts preserve life and yet are the "myrmidons of death" (ibid.). An organism struggles against the "short-circuits" of premature death in order "to die only in its own fashion" (ibid.). But Freud warns, "It cannot be so" (ibid.). There are "sexual instincts" (ibid.). They have "a special place" in the theory of neuroses. They present another possible exception to the rule that we all seek to return to a low-energy state. How do we understand the sexual in the grand scheme of instincts and drives? Here Freud's sexual objection becomes the germinal exception, evoking that hardy surviving throwback, the protista, which have "succeeded in remaining up to the present time at their lowly level. Many, though not all, such creatures, which must resemble the earliest stages of the higher animals and plants, are, indeed, living to-day" (33–34). The protista seem to be an exception to the evolutionary rule of increasing complexity; their twins, the germ-cells, which "probably retain the original structure of living matter," do not "trod" "the whole path of development to natural death" (34). Instead, the germ-cells are exceptional in another way, "separat[ing] themselves from the organism as a whole," "with their full complement of inherited and freshly acquired instinctual dispositions" (ibid.). In their analogy to the survivalist protista—to the most basic form of life—germ-cells "repeat the performance to which they owe their existence" (ibid.). In other words, germ-cells, like protista, simply split, enacting in this splitting what Freud regards as the primal moment of reproduction and the sexual instinct. "The instincts which watch over the destinies of these elementary organisms that survive the whole individual, which provide them with a safe shelter while they are defenseless against the stimuli of the external world, which bring about their meeting with other germ cells, and so on—these constitute the group of the sexual instincts" (ibid.). Sexual instinct exists to preserve the germ-cell; the "high" envelops the "low," which persists as the immortally existing site of immortality.

That germ cells are synecdoches of sexual instincts depends on their analogy to independently existing single-celled organisms. Their detachment from the rest of the organism with its moribund future parallels the exceptional antievolutionary survival of those protozoic organisms that represent the earliest stages of "higher animals and plants." The paradigm of fission that grounds germ-cell reproduction ("the performance to which they owe their existence") becomes the model for the counterimpulses of the sexual instincts, which include the importation of both immortality and other modes of temporality. Like the protista, the germ-cells divide into two parts; in both protista and germ-cell one part retains the original cellular material, the other a copy. If a single-celled organism continues to reproduce by simple fission and the animalcules exist in an optimal environment, the original cell could theoretically persist forever. Citing the findings of the biologists August Weismann and L. L. Woodruff (whose animalcules persisted through fission until the 3,029th generation where they quit counting), Freud grants the potential immortality of the protista, employing it as a model for the potential immortality of the germ-cell.

But not all of the germ-cells. Unlike the protista, who simply stay themselves for infinite generations, the split germ-cell develops two different ways; one part matures into a complex organism and the other remains a germ-cell. The developed or somatic portion dies eventually, whereas the germ-cell lives on, like the protista, preserving a reproductive immortality Freud regards as sexual. The protista/germ-cells that constantly reiterate the earliest state of living substance provide a conservative model "in that they preserve life itself for a comparatively long period" (ibid.). They thus represent the "true life instincts" that "operate against the purpose of the other instincts," the death instincts, producing an opposition that renders existence a matter of constant conflict between sex and death (ibid.). Freud's evocation of conflict harks back to Darwin, whose "survival of the fittest" made prominent the model of conflict that pervades Freud's understandings of development, neuroses, and psychic topography.[10] And even if the example of single-celled organisms is not sexual in the sense that their fission does not reflect any notion of sexual difference or conjugation, Freud grants that "the possibility remains that the instincts which were later to be described as sexual may have been in operation from the very first, and it may not be true that it was only at a later time that they started upon their work of opposing the activities of the 'ego-instincts'" (35).

These "ego-instincts" derive, the footnote tells us, from the "earliest psycho-analytical terminology" (ibid.). Freud calls them "provisional," and they are as provisional as the asexual animalcule will have been as its exceptional immortality gives way to what Freud sees as the more advantageous mingling of genetic matter. The "ego-instincts," Freud tells us, "exercise pressure towards death"; the sexual instincts pressure toward "a prolongation of life" (38). "But what," Freud asks, "is the important event in the development of living substance which is being repeated in sexual reproduction, or in its fore-runner, the conjugation of two protista?" (ibid.). Admitting that he cannot answer this question, Freud considers how it can be that the sexual instinct, present in single-celled organisms, can precede the introduction of a death instinct. In other words, if death is a primal drive, how can it be that single-celled organisms do not seem to have it—that it is not a "primal characteristic of living matter?" (41). It must be, of course, that single-celled organisms do manifest a death drive; the model of fission he had employed must therefore be in error. Discerning, thus, that Weismann and Woodruff find immortality in unlikely circumstances, Freud rejects their example for the researches of E. Maupas and Gary N. Calkins, who found that repeated fission wore organisms out, weakening them unless they were infused with new matter. The nature of life's prolongation shifts from the simple immortal survival of a single-celled organism through asexual fission to the urge to coalesce with another cell that will "prolong the cell's life and lend it the appearance of immortality" (38). This leads Freud to conclude (with some relief) that protista indeed do die after a period of senescence "exactly like the higher animal" (42) and that they are saved from senescence by conjugation—"the fore-runner of the sexual reproduction of higher creatures" (ibid.).

Rejecting the model of fission and the theoretical immortality of the protist, Freud can thus locate a death instinct in the single-celled organism's primal living matter. As he quibbles with the conditions of the various biological researchers to arrive at the conclusion he wants, single-celled organisms fortunately are flexible enough—or researches about them are indeterminate enough—that Freud can make them stand for any proposition he wishes them to stand for. Beginning with fission, a model that does not suit his needs with its potential immortality and seeming denial of the death instinct, he moves on to conjugation and with it to additional evidence that if protozoa die of their own accord, they exemplify the primacy of the sexual instinct and the death drive. The protozoan model thus shifts to suit Freud's needs. Although he himself raises the question of the usefulness of the protozoan example—"At this point the question may well arise in our minds whether any object whatever is served by trying to solve the problem of natural death from a study of the protozoa"—he persists with the example precisely because he can make it solve "the problem of natural death" and protista serve admirably as a flexible field for theoretical projections. At the same time, the validity of any theory of warring instincts and drives appears to lie in their palpable operation in the simplest forms of life. The function of the single-celled organism is to be an example of a scientific "truth" that will then come back as if from the protista as an objective forerunner. The evidentiary logic here is circular, but what is more important is the way the protista exception has become the incarnation of a rule.

Freud often disputed any notion of a clear boundary between animals and humans as he disputed the idea of boundaries between any of the opposing structural forces in the psyche he outlined. His reliance on the protista example is an instance of the dissolution of boundaries; life can illustrate the principles of life because all life is connected. His rhetorical deployment of the single-celled organism, however, also suggests a disregard for its independent status as Freud shops among various and probably incommensurable modes of cellular life from the perspective of the human as the model. If he did not already have sexual instincts in mind as a possible hitch in the neat workings of the pleasure principle, he would not necessarily have found them in the observation of the protozoa. Understanding fission as a form of reproduction linked to his concepts of Eros (the desire to come together with a primevally lost other half) comes from looking for such a concept in the protista life cycle. In a sense, this is the same as seeing, as early researchers did, tiny little human beings fully formed in the heads of sperm. Instead of seeing humans as the development of primitive instincts, the primal must reflect what exists in the human, making Freud's use of other species not surprisingly a very anthropocentric (and anthropomorphic) endeavor. Through the example of the protista, the human is finally primal and the lonely fission of the single cell's solitary self prefigures materially the split subject—the relation between the conscious and the unconscious—as well as the tensions between this split and the conflicting impetuses of the drives.

This is nowhere more evident than in Freud's psychoanalysis of the single-celled organism, to which he turns after rejecting the probability that biology would prove the nonuniversality of death instincts. Because the protist tells us nothing definitive, Freud tells it something about itself in what he calls "a bold step forward" into Eros, or the libido that compels cells to seek out other cells and mingle their matter. Freud's libido theory is suggested by research that indicates that protozoa prolong their existence if they share matter with other protozoa during conjugation. In addition, the development of cell communities permits cells to help one another and survive as a species, if not individually. "Accordingly," Freud says, "we might attempt to apply the libido theory which has been arrived at in psycho-analysis to the mutual relationship of cells" (44). Through the libido theory (or a theory of drives), the single cell impels itself into groups where fission is supplanted by conjugation, the singular subordinated to the plural, the immortal substantiality of the splitting cell giving way to the compulsion of drives that make profitable use of others.

With these anthropomorphized protista Freud constructs a fantasmatic account of a cellular romance scenario that arrives at narcissism. "We might suppose," he explains, "that the life instincts or sexual instincts which are active in each cell take the other cells as their object, that they partly neutralize the death instincts (that is, the processes set up by them) in those cells and thus preserve their life; while other cells do the same for *them,* and still others sacrifice themselves in the performance of this libidinal function" (ibid.). In this happy cellular community, the germ-cells, like cancer cells, are exceptions, behaving in a "completely 'narcissistic' fashion" as they "require their libido, the activity of their life instincts, for themselves, as a reserve against their later momentous constructive activity" (ibid.).

Under the aegis of the drives, cells constitute a community of cooperative and self-sacrificing individuals resembling civilized culture. In the midst of this community are the narcissists, the self-serving malignancies, and the reproducers who take for themselves even if the germ-cells ultimately expend themselves for the perpetuation of the tribe. The libidinal glue of cell attraction in this infinitesimal culture brings sexuality together with more poetic forces: "the libido of our sexual instincts would coincide with the Eros of the poets and philosophers which holds all living things together" (ibid.). Human civilization is already inscribed in the history of the microscopic. But more important, the relation between the germ-cell, libido, and self-preservation provides an instructive instance of the relation between the libido and the ego in humans. The cell becomes the matrix upon which Freud can map out the complex and contradictory forces that merge the ego with Eros and make sexual instincts a mode of self-preservation. The unicellular character of the protista example suggests that the forces that govern their behavior must be intrinsic to cell matter itself, and if intrinsic to the cell, which comprises life, then intrinsic to all life as well.

Discerning the nature of living matter with its ineffable libidos and its clashing community values provides Freud with the opportunity to look back "over the slow development of our libido theory" in humans. In his careful analysis of the transference neuroses, Freud concludes as a first step that there is an opposition between "sexual instincts" that take as an object something outside of themselves and ego-instincts dedicated to self-preservation. In trying to discern the other aims of the libido, "psychoanalysis" noted the incidence of introversion, where the libido is directed inward. "Studying the libidinal development of children in its earliest phases" (an ontogenetic procedure), Freud concludes that the "ego is the true and original reservoir of libido" (45), which makes the ego itself a kind of a sexual object. If the libido fixes on the ego, then such an attachment is narcissistic, but it also serves the ends of self-preservation. Thus, Freud concludes, the libido and the ego are not necessarily in opposition to one another after all. But with the ambivalence that has characterized his entire cellular discussion, he also asserts that, given this understanding of the cooperation between the libido and the ego-instincts, their conflict need not be rejected as a basis for psychoneuroses.

How, then, can we have both conflict and cooperation, identity and difference at the same time? The ambivalent status of the protista has been displaced onto psychic mechanisms themselves (and vice versa), and the germ-plasm has become a fetish that negotiates potential clashes and differences. Freud's notion of fetishism, E. L. McCallum points out, includes both the idea of a fetish object and the ways subjects deploy fetishes. "The most important thing about fetishism," McCallum urges, "is not its complex arbitration of sexual differences, but more generally how it enables us to accommodate both desire and knowledge, even when the two conflict."[11] In this sense, the protozoan indeed is an arbitrator, an object that enables Freud to bring together (to conjugate?) basic forces—ego and libido—that otherwise clash and to negotiate the gaps between his knowledge of these principles and his desire that they form a coherent, consistent whole. Freud's deployment of the protista as fetish that mediates the tricky collision of sex and death as well as problems in theory is not so much owing to an overdetermined quality of the species (the protista embody on many levels the conflicts he wishes to untangle) as it is that the tiny and malleable spot that constitutes the protozoa (the inevitable glint on the nose) enables a denial of interspecies differences. The protista's position at the bottom of the phylogenetic scale allows Freud to employ it as evidence that all species—and principles—are connected.

Freud reconciles the microlevel clashes of ego and libido by re-characterizing the quality of the instinct (sexual, self-preservative) as a matter of topography. Its spatial metaphor permits both ego and libido to share in the same impulses, though they may aim in different directions. Employing a topographical field has the effect of unifying instincts by rendering them all as part of the same spatial matrix just as it unifies scientific disciplines by making biology, chemistry, and psychoanalysis different expressions of the same phenomenon. If the sexual instincts come from the same egoistic pool as the self-preservative instincts and if both are manifestations of Eros, "the preserver of all things" (46), then, as Freud queries, "there are perhaps no other instincts whatever but the libidinal ones?" (ibid.). Acknowledging that there are "none other visible"—an ironic admission given the relative invisibility of his specimens—Freud seems almost ready to grant the insight of critics who accuse psychoanalysis of making everything sexual or the "hasty judgment" of Jung, who uses the word "libido to mean instinctual force in general" (ibid.). But the invisible protista salvages Freud's theory of conflicting impulses again. Objecting that he had begun his discussion with a clear idea of the opposition between the death drive, ego-instincts, and the life-affirming sexual instincts, Freud returns again to the protista's conjugation, which this time exemplifies the idea that while the internal life processes of individual cells tend to the "abolition of chemical tensions," "the influx of fresh amounts of stimulus" coming from "the coalescence of two only slightly different cells" increases the chemical tensions "which must then be lived off" (49). This mechanical economy imagined on the level of the single-celled organism thus grounds Freud's dualistic theory of the drives.

But he has one last detail to account for: how it is that the sexual instincts are aligned with the compulsion to repeat with which he began the discussion? In his phylogenetic universe, this means that Freud must discern the origins of sexuality. Again he returns to the protista, whose conjugation (rather than simple fission), he notes, might provide a slight advantage in a Darwinian scheme. But if, in the evolutionary theater, cell conjugation were merely a happy accident, then sexuality is not a very ancient (i.e., originary) process at all. Freud again raises the objection he had raised earlier: "whether we do right in ascribing to protista those characteristics alone which they actually exhibit, and whether it is correct to assume that forces and processes which become visible only in the higher organisms originated in those organisms for the first time" (51). But the point of origination of both sexual and death instincts—the protista—becomes dark for Freud. He can no longer see the origin of sexuality, which has become "a darkness into which not so much as a ray of a hypothesis has penetrated" (ibid.).

But just as Freud has looked to the supposed phylogenetic forebears of humanity for answers, so he finally returns to mythology for an explanation that will illuminate "the origin of an instinct to *a need to restore an earlier state of things*," which, it turns out, is an originary splitting that serves as model and motive for all splitting (ibid.). Citing Aristophanes' myth in Plato's *Symposium*, Freud imagines the originary duplicity of all beings, who, split apart by Zeus, doom humanity to forever trying to re-find their lost halves—to return quite literally to an earlier state of things. This mythical state of *sparagmos* provides Freud with yet another way to understand the impetus behind evolution. Envisioning single-celled organisms as fragments of a larger living substance, Freud accounts for evolution as a drive to reassemble ever larger and more complex organisms, the germ-cells embodying a particularly concentrated form of the instinct for reuniting.

From Animalcule to Molecule

Freud's idea that behaviors were ultimately governed by chemical processes was not so far wrong, however, in light of the discovery of DNA. Heralded as "the fundamental genetic material," DNA promised a specific site for the unraveling of life's mysteries, including the physiochemical bases of both existence and behaviors. Combining Freud's ideas of cellular fission with the idea of conjugation, DNA relocates reproductive processes from the level of the cell to the level of the molecule. Posited as a "law-code and executive power" or "architect's plan and builder's craft" that works the same way but with slightly different combinations throughout the range of terran life, DNA supplants Freud's protista with what appears to be a primal molecular structure that better defines life through chemistry.[12] Like the protista, DNA suggests the fundamental interconnection of living things; the repetition of portions of DNA structures from species to species suggests the same kind of evolutionary phylogeny suggested by Freud's notion of the holdover germ cells.

The study of this chemical interconnection has been primarily conducted on another minute animalcule, the drosophila fly, whose genetic strands and their study provided the template for knowledge about where genes are located and how they function. Seymour Benzer's experiments with fruit flies not only developed the art of mapping of genes on the chromosomes begun by Alfred Sturtevant, but also suggested that genes governed both physical and behavioral patterns.[13] Using a mutated virus, RII, Benzer devised a way to map and cut specific genes. The ability to link specific traits with specific genes spurred Benzer and his associates into looking into the possibility that behavior too might be inherited, a Lamarckian idea also promulgated by Darwin's cousin Francis Galton.[14] Although it was well established that genes determined features such as eye color, wing shape, and other morphologies, Benzer and his associates showed that they also governed certain basic behaviors such as waking/sleeping rhythms, courtship practices, and the ability to remember.

For example, using a countercurrent machine (a series of interconnected test tubes), Benzer demonstrated that some, but not all, flies are attracted by light. Working with a mutagen, Benzer encouraged variation, then sorted out and bred flies that did not go toward light or that moved slowly or that flew in irregular patterns, establishing that behaviors are linked to genes and may be inherited. His associate Ronald Konopka looked for and discovered genes governing circadian rhythms by looking for time mutants—flies whose daily processes deviated largely from the norm. Another associate, Jeff Hall, mapped courtship and copulation mutants. If, for Freud, the exception proved the rule, for molecular biologists, the mutation provides the useful example. Looking for variations seems to suggest that rather than negotiating differences as Freud's fetishized protista do, mutants enable science to capitalize on difference. Mutant difference, however, ultimately demonstrates the common substratum of DNA that may itself function as something like Freud's protista fetish. In all, mapping genes for behaviors does seem to establish that at least some of the instincts Freud was trying to fathom do exist as chemical processes in DNA.

The research of Benzer and others focuses more certainly on DNA as a site of truth than Freud did with his example of the protista. The visibility of DNA, sought by James Watson and Francis Crick and others as the key to its operation, situates it as a code that will unravel all of the mysteries of life, because with DNA we seem to have gotten to the most minute level possible. Genetic research thus seems to advance knowledge about human behavior from Freud's notion of instinct to a well-delineated chain of amino acids. What had seemed to Freud to be a complex psychological mystery of competing and conflicting aims and drives is to molecular biologists the intricate operation of multiple genetic sites, protein and amino acid synthesis, and the extended chemistries of life processes.

The shift from a dynamic theory to a chemical one also seems to represent a shift from superficial deductive empiricism to disciplined inductive experimentation. As Jonathan Weiner observes, "Freud worked by introspection, which is looking from the outside inward," whereas molecular biologists worked "from the bottom up and from the inside out" (66). As Freud predicted, the psychological is indeed reduced to the chemical, but how that chemistry works is still mysterious, despite the obsessive thoroughness of the human genome project, which intends to map every gene in the twenty-three human chromosome pairs. As a chemistry to be laboriously discovered and mapped, genes, however, are seen less and less as the complicated cooperative site that might illuminate complex behavioral dynamics and become more the chopped-up proprietary interests of biotechnology companies who patent specific genes and even knowledge about them. That information about genes becomes property signals a transition from the dynamic science of Freud to an object-centered, commodity-driven science that treats DNA like a computer chip.

Reducible always to its component elements, DNA is figured as working like language (or even phonemes) where meaning is built from a grammar of phoneme-like constituent parts, but where the exact nature of the necessary connection between signifier (gene) and signified (trait) is not quite known. The transition to DNA as an object rather than a dynamic process seems to signal that DNA, too, has become a fetish that arbitrates the conflicts between desire and knowledge. DNA seems to provide a fetish in that it operates as a visible site for negotiating (and explaining and eliminating) differences in appearance, behavior, and among species by reducing everything to four basic compounds. As the study of behaviors shifts to the molecular level, difference represented by mutation becomes more a matter of variation than of conflict or opposition. The image of the molecule smooths out the much more violent differences that emerge in the being for which DNA is presumably a recipe. But, as what appears to be the basic, most minute site of knowledge about life processes—as Francis Crick saw it, "the borderline between the living and the nonliving"—DNA seems less a fetish than an authentic key, the terms of an explanation that will reduce inexplicable differences (the death drive, the sexual instinct, animate, inanimate) to manifestations of the same chemical operations.[15] Its very precise chemical information seems to render DNA objective and nonambiguous, truth rather than phantasm, source of information rather than site of projection. And given contemporary understandings of digital mechanics, the idea of bits operating to produce patterns (software) or data is more than plausible and seems to provide the finite end to decades of questions.

But what kinds of answers does DNA provide? We know, for example, where certain genes are located on chromosomes. We begin to discern the chemical processes of combining amino acids and proteins defined by DNA's amino acid template. We suspect that certain aspects of human behavior are inherited rather than learned, though it is difficult to find a single gene for them. We can clone sheep and make crop seeds proprietary. What DNA does not tell us, finally, are the answers to some of the questions Freud asked about the dynamics of human existence, about desire and drives. Or, as R. C. Lewontin, noted critic of DNA as the ultimate answer, points out, it also does not explain violence, hunger, politics, cruelty, or any of the other behaviors that plague society.[16]

This is not to say that deductions about the locations and functions of specific genes may not inform us of ways in which chemical information is transferred, nor that such processes might not constitute a general rule about the relations between life and heredity. It is to suggest that, unlike Freud's protistic deductions about life dynamics, those who see DNA as a master code with all the answers may miss some of the point. Freud used the protista as an example of a set of common dynamics that characterize existence; while it is a far cry from a protozoan to a human, both belonged to the category of living things. Molecular biologists try to find the chemical coding point for particular behaviors they already observe, behaviors parsed and separated according to current notions of what elemental behavior is. Research proceeds from the behavior to the gene (despite the observation that molecular biologists work from the inside out), so that DNA, rather than being a key, may finally be more of a shadow lure whose chemical code is divided according to functions and morphologies we have already identified. This is most certainly true in popularizations of DNA as a kind of recipe through which we arrive at the result we already know is there—that is, the human or the fly.

In this sense, DNA functions more as a lure than a fetish; it appears in the place of knowledge as an answering border, the link between inanimate and animate, mystery and science (a position attributed both by Crick and Erwin Schrödinger), but in itself does not provide insight into extended processes or dynamics. The "answers" are somewhere else, located in the processes by which code becomes flesh, the less definable, loadable, messier, more multifarious interchanges by which the information becomes life. DNA's graphically coiled snake of information mesmerizes in its promise of exactitude and detail, but its ordered molecular code, though it looks like what we understand to be a code and may function as a code of sorts, is not a legend to the complexities that have vexed human existence. In attending to the details of this DNA lure and in thinking that somehow, someday if we completely map this code, it will answer all questions about human nature, we may be ignoring other possible causes and solutions to very complex problems of human behavior and interaction.

This is certainly Lewontin's argument. For Lewontin, focusing on DNA as the site of knowledge means that we do not focus on really resolving the problems that plague contemporary culture. But Lewontin's critique of biotech's ideologies includes his reservation about the possible relation between animal and human DNA. One procedural problem for Lewontin is the use of analogy by which animal traits become human traits. "Analogy," he says, "is in the eye of the observer":

> How do we decide that the coyness we see in people is the same as the behavior in animals called coyness? What happens is that human categories are laid on animals by analogy, partly as a matter of convenience of language, and then these traits are "discovered" in animals and laid back on humans as if they had a common origin. There is in fact not a shred of evidence that the anatomical, physiological, and genetic basis of what is called aggression in rats had anything in common with the German invasion of Poland in 1939. (96)

The hyperbole of Lewontin's analogy makes it clear how he misses the point; what behavioral genetics in animals suggests is that there may be a similar genetic basis for some human behaviors, not that human behaviors have exactly the same genetic basis as the behaviors of animals. What Lewontin's complaint reveals, however, are certain intellectual alliances. On the one hand, both Freud and molecular biologists believe in the common genetic legacy of life; on the other, humanist critics such as Lewontin (whose analysis of biotechnology's various ideological presumptions is often useful) deny the commonality of species and question DNA's status as answer.

It would seem, in fact, that believing in the fundamental status of DNA requires a belief in the commonality of life. The emergence of protista or DNA as fetishes or lures may be a necessary by-product of the belief in the continuity of life processes throughout the species, negotiating not differences between species, but ideologies about the superior status—the ultimate difference—between humanity and everything else. Molecular biologists believe in commonality—in fact seem to gaze on the miracle of life and the potential unities of the universe with Tao-like wonderment—but their faith in DNA also provides the illusion of a mastery of all life located, via knowledge of DNA, in science and in the human. That this surreptitious mastery requires a fetish suggests both the immense scope of this unity and the strength of pro-human prejudice, a prejudice that still permeates the work of both Freud and Benzer and his associates as they willingly deploy other species to find some truth about humans. But the connection between questioning DNA's status and asserting the primacy of humanity represented by Lewontin suggests more insidiously that not to be fooled by the lure of DNA's answers and to critique ideology means believing uncritically in the ideology of the privileged perspective of the human. Simply, Lewontin cannot believe in DNA because doing so would destroy the biological basis for human superiority. Ironically, perhaps Lewontin believes more fully in DNA's potential power than the molecular biologists he critiques, not because of what is produced in the realm of capitalist biotechnology, but in what DNA may suggest about the common basis of behaviors—that humans are not in conscious control. In the age of DNA the lesson of Freud and the single-celled organism remains a psychoanalytic lesson as the battle over the status and possibilities of DNA engages once again the conflicting forces—desire for mastery, trauma, forgetting—that defined life for Freud.

Notes

1. Charles Darwin, *Origin of the Species,* quoted in Lucille Ritvo, *Darwin's Influence on Freud* (New Haven: Yale University Press, 1990), 21.

2. Peter T. Hoffer, "Freud's 'Phylogenetic Fantasy': Poetry or Truth?" *Proteus: A Journal of Ideas* 6:2 (fall 1989): 18. Subsequent references are given in the text.

3. For example, in his "Fragment of an Analysis of a Case of Hysteria," Freud uses the metaphor of archaeology to describe the processes of analysis. See Sigmund Freud, *The Standard Edition of the Complete Psychological Works of Sigmund Freud,* trans. and ed. James Strachey (London: Hogarth Press, 1953–74), vol. 7, 3–122.

4. Sigmund Freud, *Beyond the Pleasure Principle,* trans. and ed. James Strachey (New York: Norton, 1961), 60. All subsequent references will be to this edition.

5. Freud's interest in microbes may well have been stirred by the series of late-nineteenth-century microbiological successes in discovering and treating diseases. See Paul de Kruif, *Microbe Hunters* (San Diego: Harcourt Brace, 1926).

6. Sigmund Freud, "The Claims of Psycho-analysis to Scientific Interest," in *Standard Edition*, vol. 13, 184; quoted in Ritvo, *Darwin's Influence on Freud*, 75.

7. Sigmund Freud, *An Outline of Psychoanalysis*, in *Standard Edition*, vol. 23, 74–75.

8. Ibid., 75. See also Ritvo, *Darwin's Influence on Freud*, 76–77.

9. Freud, *Standard Edition*, vol. 17, 140; quoted in Ritvo, *Darwin's Influence on Freud*, 76.

10. Ritvo's entire book traces Darwin's influence on Freud.

11. E. L. McCallum, *Object Lesson: How to Do Things with Fetishism* (Albany: State University of New York Press, 1999), 45.

12. Erwin Schrödinger, *What Is Life?* (Cambridge: Cambridge University Press, 1967), 22.

13. Benzer's activities are well described in Jonathan Weiner, *Time, Love, Memory: A Great Biologist and His Quest for the Origins of Behavior* (New York: Alfred A. Knopf, 1999). Subsequent references are given in the text. My characterizations of Benzer's work and its significance come primarily from this book.

14. See ibid., 90–95.

15. James Watson, *The Double Helix* (New York: Penguin, 1969), 61.

16. R. C. Lewontin, *Biology As Ideology: The Doctrine of DNA* (New York: HarperCollins, 1991). Subsequent references are given in the text.

And Say the Animal Responded?

Jacques Derrida

Translated by David Wills

Would an ethics be sufficient, as Levinas maintains, to remind the subject of its being-subject, its being-guest, host or hostage, that is to say its being-subjected-to-the-other, to the Wholly Other or to every single other?

I don't think so. It takes more than that to break with the Cartesian tradition of the animal-machine that exists without language and without the ability to respond.[1] It takes more than that, even within a logic or an ethics of the unconscious which, without renouncing the concept of the subject, somehow claims to "subvert" that subject.

By evoking this Lacanian title, "the subversion of the subject," we therefore move from one ethical disavowal to another. I have chosen, in this context, to trace that movement by following the paths that have just been opened, those of the other, of witnessing, and of the "signifiers without signifieds" that Levinas associates with the "simian." In Lacan's 1960 text, "The Subversion of the Subject and the Dialectic of Desire in the Freudian Unconscious," a certain passage names "the animal" or "an animal," in the singular and without any further details. It perhaps marks what is at one and the same time a step beyond and a step this side of Freud with respect to the relations among the human, the unconscious, and the *animot*.[2] This remarkable passage at first gives the impression, and raises hope, that things are going to change, notably concerning the concept of communication or information that is assigned to what one

121

calls the animal, the animal in general. It is thought that "the animal" is capable only of a coded message or of a meaning that is narrowly indicative, strictly constrained; one that is fixed in its programming. Lacan begins by taking to task the platitude of the "modern theory of communication." It is true that at that point he is talking about the human subject and not the animal, but he writes the following, which seems to announce, or allow one to hope for, a further note:

> The Other as previous site of the pure subject of the signifier holds the master position, even before coming into existence, to use Hegel's term against him, as absolute Master. For what is omitted in the platitude of modern information theory is the fact that one can speak of a code only if it is already the code of the Other, and that is something quite different from what is in question in the message, since it is from this code that the subject is constituted, which means that it is from the Other that the subject receives even the message that he emits.[3]

Following a digression, we will come back to this page of "The Subversion of the Subject and the Dialectic of Desire in the Freudian Unconscious." It *poses* (and I emphasize the word *poses* because it puts forward in the form of a thesis, or presupposes without providing any proof) the idea of an animal characterized by an incapacity to *pretend to pretend (feindre de feindre)* or to *erase its traces,* an incapacity that makes it unable to be a "subject," that is to say, "subject of the signifier."

The digression I shall now make will allow us to identify in earlier texts by Lacan places where, it seems to me, they announce *at the same time* a theoretical mutation and a stagnant confirmation of inherited thinking, its presuppositions and its dogma.

What still held out hope for a decisive displacement of the traditional problematic was, for example, the taking into account of a specular function in the sexualization of the animal that can be identified, from 1936 on, in "the mirror stage." Such an idea was quite rare at the time. And that was the case even if—this amounts to a massive limitation—the passage through the mirror according to Lacan forever immobilized the animal within the snare of the imaginary, depriving it of any access to the symbolic, that is to say to the law and to whatever is held to be proper to the human. The animal will never be, as man is, "prey to language." Later, in "The Direction of the Treatment," we read: "It must be posited that, produced as it is by any animal at the mercy of language *[en proie au langage],* man's desire is the desire of the Other" (*Écrits,* 264). (This figure of the prey symptomatically and recurrently characterizes the "animal" obsession in Lacan at the very moment when he insists so strongly on dissociating the anthropological from the zoological; man is an animal but a speaking one, and he is less a beast of prey than a beast that is prey to language.) There is no desire, and thus no unconscious, except for the human; it in no way exists for the animal, unless that be as an effect of the human unconscious, as if the domestic or tamed animal translated within itself the unconscious of man by some contagious transfer or mute interiorization (the terms of which would, moreover, still need to be taken into account). Being careful to distinguish the unconscious drive from what limits the animal, namely, instinct or what is "genetic," in "Position de l'inconscient" Lacan holds that the animal could not itself have an unconscious, an unconscious of its own, if such a thing could be said and if the logic of the expression did not sound ridiculous. But, to begin with, it perhaps seems ridiculous to Lacan himself, because he writes that "in the propaedeutic experience one can illustrate the effect of enunciation, or at least some effect of language, and of human language, by asking the child if he can imagine the unconscious in the animal."[4]

Each word of this sentence deserves critical examination. Its thesis is clear: the animal has neither unconscious nor language, nor the other, except as an effect of the human order, that is, by contagion, appropriation, domestication.

No doubt the acceptation of sexualizing specularity in the animal is a remarkable advance even if it captures the *animot* in the mirror, and even if it keeps the hen pigeon or migrating locust in captivity within the imaginary. Referring to the effects of a Gestalt proven by a "biological experimentation" that is utterly refuted by the language of "psychic causality," Lacan nevertheless credits that theory with recognizing that "the maturation of the gonad in the hen pigeon" relies on the "sight of a fellow creature," that is to say another pigeon of either sex. And that is true even to the extent that a simple mirror reflection will suffice. It is also sufficient for a migrating locust to perceive a similar visual image in order to evolve from a solitary to a gregarious state. Lacan states, in a way that is for me significant, that this is a move from the "solitary to the gregarious form," and not to the social form, as if the difference between *gregarious* and *social* were the difference between animal and human. This motif, and the words *gregarious* and even *gregariousness,* reappear forcefully in the context of animality some ten years later, in "Propos sur la causalité psychique" (1946).[5] Moreover, this is a text at the end of which Lacan declares Descartes to be unsurpassable. The analysis of the specular effect in the pigeon is developed further in that text but it still works in the same direction: according to research by Harrisson (1939) the ovulation of the hen pigeon is produced by the simple *sight* of a form evoking another member of the species, of a visual reflection in short, even in the absence of an actual male.[6] It is indeed a matter of a specular gaze, by means of an image and a visual image, rather than identification by means of odor or sound. Even if the mating game is physically preempted by a sheet of glass, and even if the couple consists of two females, ovulation still takes place. It happens after twelve days when the couple is heterosexual, if we can use the term, and after a period of up to two months for two females. A mirror is all it takes.[7]

One of the interesting things about this interpretation is that, after all, as with Descartes, and according to the tried and true biblical and Promethean tradition that I keep coming back to, it relates the fixity of animal determinism within the context of information and communication to a type of originary perfection of that animal. Conversely, if "human knowledge has greater autonomy than animal knowledge in relation to the field of force of desire"[8] and if "the human order is distinguished from nature,"[9] it is paradoxically because of an imperfection, because of an originary fault in man, who has, in short, received speech and technics only inasmuch as he lacks something. Here I am speaking of what Lacan situates at the center of his "mirror stage," namely, the "fact of a real *specific prematurity of birth* in man" (4; Lacan's italics). The lack tied to this prematurity would correspond to the "objective notion of anatomical incompleteness of the pyramidal system," to what embryologists call *"fetalization,"* and which, Lacan recalls, is linked to a certain "intra-organic mirror" (ibid.). An autotelic specularity of the inside is thus linked to a lack, to a prematurity, to an incompleteness of the little man.

I have just referred, rather quickly, here on the threshold of "The Subversion of the Subject," to a limited but incontestable advance recognized by Lacan. But that has to be registered with the greatest caution. For not only is the animal held within the imaginary and unable to accede to the symbolic, to the unconscious, and to language (and hence, still following our general thread, to autobiographical auto-deixis),[10] but the description of its semiotic power remains determined, in the *Discours de Rome* ("The Function and Field of Speech and Language in Psychoanalysis," 1953), in the most dogmatically traditional manner, fixed within Cartesian fixity, within the presupposition of a code that only permits *reactions* to stimuli and not *responses* to questions. I refer to the "semiotic" system and not to "language," for Lacan also refuses the animal language, recognizing in its case only a "code," the "fixity of coding," or a "system of signalling." These are other ways of naming what, within a cognitivist problematic of the animal that often repeats the most worn-out truisms of metaphysics even as it appears to resist them, is called the "prewired response *[réponse précâblée]*" or "prewired behavior."[11]

Lacan is so precise and firm in accrediting the old, yet modernized topos of the bee that he seems, if I might say, not to have a clear conscience. I detect an unavowed anxiety underneath the authority of this new, yet so old, so old discourse concerning the bee. Lacan claims to be relying on what he blithely calls the "animal kingdom" in order to critique the current notion of "language as a sign" as opposed to "human languages." When bees appear to "respond" to a "message," they do not respond but react; they merely obey a fixed program, whereas the human subject responds to the other, to the question posed by the other. This discourse is quite literally Cartesian. Later, as we shall see, Lacan expressly contrasts *reaction* with *response* in conformity with his opposition between human and animal kingdom, and in the same way that he opposes nature and convention:

> I shall show the inadequacy of the conception of "language as a sign" by the very manifestation that best illustrates it in the animal kingdom, a manifestation which, if it had not recently been the object of an authentic discovery, it seems it would have been necessary to invent for this purpose.
>
> It is now generally admitted that when the bee returns to the hive from its honey-gathering it indicates to its companions by two sorts of dance the existence of nectar and its relative distance, near or far, from the hive. The second type of dance is the most remarkable, for the plane in which the bee traces the figure-of-eight curve—which is why it has been called the "wagging dance"—and the frequency of the figures executed within a given time, designate, on the one hand, exactly the direction to be followed, determined in relation to the inclination of the sun (on which bees are able to orient themselves in all weathers, thanks to their sensitivity to polarized light), and, on the other hand, the distance, up to several miles, at which the nectar is to be found. And the other bees respond to this message by setting off immediately for the place thus designated.
>
> It took some ten years of patient observation for Karl von Frisch to decode this kind of message, for it is certainly a code, or system of signalling, whose generic character alone forbids us to qualify it as conventional.
>
> But is it necessarily a language? We can say that it is distinguished from language precisely by the *fixed* [my italics, J. D.] correlation of its signs to the reality that they signify. For in a language signs take on their value

from their relations to each other in the lexical distribution of seman-
temes as much as in the positional, or even flectional, use of morphemes,
in sharp contrast to the *fixity* [my italics again, J. D.] of the coding used by
bees. And the diversity of human languages *(langues)* takes on its full
value from this enlightening discovery.

Furthermore, while the message of the kind described here determines
the action of the *socius,* it is never retransmitted by it. This means that the
message remains *fixed* [my italics still, J. D.] in its function as a relay of the
action, from which no subject detaches it as a symbol of communication
itself. (84–85)

Even if one were to subscribe provisionally to this logic (to which I do
not in fact object in the slightest, although I would want to reinscribe it
differently, beyond any simple opposition between animal and human),
it is difficult to reserve, as Lacan does, the differentiality of signs for
human language only, as opposed to animal coding. What he attributes
to signs that, "in a language" understood as belonging to the human
order, "take on their value from their relations to each other" and so on,
and not just from the "fixed correlation" between signs and reality, can
and must be accorded to any code, animal or human.

As for the absence of a response in the animal-machine, as for the
trenchant distinction between *reaction* and *response,* there is nothing for-
tuitous in the fact that the most Cartesian passage of all is found following the discourse on the bee, on its system of information, which would
exclude it from the "field of speech and language." It is indeed a matter of
the constitution of the subject as human subject to the extent that the latter crosses the frontier of information to gain access to speech:

For the function of language is not to inform but to evoke.

What I seek in speech is the response of the other. What constitutes me
as subject is my question. In order to be recognized by the other, I utter
what was only in view of what will be. In order to find him, I call him by a
name that he must assume or refuse in order to reply to me. . . .

If I now place myself in front of the other to question him, there is no
cybernetic computer imaginable that can make a *reaction out of what the
response is.* The definition of response as the second term in the "stimulus
response" circuit is simply a metaphor sustained by the subjectivity im-
puted to the animal, a subjectivity that is then ignored in the physical
schema to which the metaphor reduces it. This is what I have called putting the rabbit into the hat so as to be able to pull it out again later. *But a
reaction is not a response.*

If I press an electric button and a light goes on, there is no response except for *my* desire. (86; translation modified, my italics [J. D.], except for
Lacan's "*my* desire")

Once again, we are not concerned with erasing every difference between what we are calling *reaction* and what we commonly call *response*.
It is not a matter of confusing what happens when one presses a computer
key and what happens when one asks a question of an interlocutor. We
are even less concerned with attributing to what Lacan calls "the animal"
what he also calls a "subjectivity" or an "unconscious" such as would, for
example, allow us to put the said animal in an analytic situation (even if
such analogous scenarios cannot be completely excluded for *certain* animals, in *certain* contexts—and if time permitted we could imagine some
hypotheses that would allow us to refine that analogy). My hesitation
concerns only the purity, the rigor, and the indivisibility of the frontier
that separates—already with respect to "us humans"—reaction from response; and as a consequence, especially, the purity, rigor, and indivisibility of the concept of responsibility that ensues. The general concern that I
am thus formulating is aggravated in at least three ways:

1. when one is required to take account of an unconscious that should
   prevent us having any immediate and conscious assurance of the freedom presupposed by any notion of responsibility;
2. especially when—and this is singularly the case for Lacan—the logic of
   the unconscious is founded on a logic of repetition which, in my opin-
   ion, will always inscribe a destiny of iterability, hence some automaticity of the reaction in every response, however originary, free, deciding
   [*décisoire*] and a-reactional it might seem;
3. when, and this is true of Lacan in particular, one gives credence to the
   materiality of speech and to the corporality of language.

Lacan reminds us of this on the following page: "Speech is in fact a gift of
language, and language is not immaterial. It is a subtle body, but body it
is" (87). Yet in the interval he will have founded all "responsibility," and to
begin with all psychoanalytic responsibility, thus all psychoanalytic
ethics, in the distinction, that I find problematic, between *reaction* and
response. He will even have founded there—and this is precisely what I
wish to demonstrate—his concept of the *subject*:

Henceforth the decisive function of my own response appears, and this
function is not, as has been said, simply to be received by the subject as acceptance or rejection of his discourse, but really to recognize him or to

abolish him as subject. Such is the nature of the analyst's *responsibility* whenever he intervenes by means of speech. (87; translation modified)

Why do the stakes here seem to be so much higher? In problematizing, as I have done, the purity and indivisibility of a line between reaction and response, and especially the possibility of tracing such a line, between the human *in general* and the animal *in general,* one risks—anxiety about such an idea and the subsequent objections to it cannot but be forthcoming—casting doubt on all responsibility, every ethics, every decision, and so on. To that I would respond—for it is indeed a matter of responding—with what follows, schematically, by means of principles, with three points.

1. *On the one hand,* casting doubt on responsibility, on decision, on one's own being-ethical, seems to me to be—and is perhaps what should forever remain—the unrescindable essence of ethics: decision and responsibility. Every firm knowledge, certainty, and assurance on this subject would suffice, precisely, to confirm the very thing one wishes to disavow, namely, the reactionality in the response. I indeed said "to disavow" *[dénier],* and it is for that reason that I situate disavowal at the heart of all these discourses on the animal.

2. *On the other hand,* far from erasing the difference—a nonoppositional and infinitely differentiated, qualitative, and intensive difference between reaction and response—it is a matter, on the contrary, of taking that difference into account within the whole differentiated field of experience and of a world of life-forms. And that means refraining from reducing this differentiated and multiple difference, in a similarly massive and homogenizing manner, to one between the human subject, on the one hand, and the nonsubject that is the animal in general, on the other, by means of which the latter comes to be, in another sense, the nonsubject that is subjected to the human subject.

3. *Finally,* it would be a matter of developing another "logic" of decision, of the response and of the event—such as I have also attempted to deploy elsewhere and which seems to me less incompatible than one might think with what Lacan himself, in "The Subversion of the Subject," maintains concerning the code as "code of the Other." He refers to that Other as the one from whom "the subject receives even the message that he emits" (305). This axiom should complicate the simple distinction between *responsibility* and *reaction,* and all that follows from it. It would, therefore, be a matter of reinscribing this *difference* between reaction and response, and hence this historicity of ethical, juridical, or political re-

sponsibility, within another thinking of life, of the living, within a different relation of the living to their selfness [ipséité], to their autos, to their
own autokinesis and reactional automaticity, to death, to technics or to
the mechanical [machinique].

Following this digression, if we are now to come to the later text titled
"The Subversion of the Subject and the Dialectic of Desire in the Freudian
Unconscious," we will indeed follow this same logic and these same oppositions, namely, that between the imaginary and the symbolic, between
the specular capture of which the animal is capable and the symbolic
order of the signifier to which it does not have access. At the juncture between imaginary and symbolic is played out the whole question of autobiography, of autobiography in general no doubt, but also that of the
theoretician or of the institution within whose history the theoretician
articulates and signs his discourse on juncture, that is to say Lacan's discourse as autobiographical analysis. (Although we cannot undertake this
within the limits constraining us here, it would be necessary to give back
a more accurate perspective, some years after the War, with all the accompanying ideological stakes, to the whole essentially anthropological
design of the period with respect to its claim to transcend every positive
anthropology and every metaphysical and humanist anthropocentrism.
And especially, in a most legitimate way, to transcend biologism, physi-
calism, behaviorism, geneticism, and so on. For Heidegger as for Lacan
and many others, it was above all a matter of relying on a new fundamental anthropology and of rigorously responding to the question and answering for the question "What is the human?")

In "The Subversion of the Subject" the refining of the analysis is brought
to bear on other conceptual distinctions. They seem to me as problematic
as those we have just analyzed, and, moreover, they remain indissociable
from them. I am concerned in particular with what appears as a parenthesis ("Observe, in parentheses . . ."), but a parenthesis that is to my mind
capital. It relates to the testimonial dimension in general, that is to say to
what subtends the problematic we are dealing with here. Who witnesses
[témoigne] to what and for whom? Who proves, who looks, who observes
whom and what? What is there of knowledge, of certainty, and of truth?

> Observe, in parentheses, that this Other, which is distinguished as the
> locus of Speech, imposes itself no less as witness to the Truth. Without the
> dimension that it constitutes, the deception practised by Speech would be
> indistinguishable from the very different pretence to be found in physical
> combat or sexual display [parade]. (305)

The figure of the animal comes to the surface therefore in this difference between pretense *[feinte]* and deception *[tromperie]*. There is, according to Lacan, a clear distinction between what the animal is capable of, namely, strategic pretense (suit, pursuit, or persecution, in war or in seduction), and what it is incapable of and incapable of witnessing to, namely, the deception of speech *[la tromperie de la parole]* within the order of the signifier and of Truth. The deception of speech, of course, means, as we shall see, lying (and the animal would not properly know how to lie according to common sense, according to Lacan and to many others, even if, as one knows, it understands how to pretend); but more precisely, deception involves lying to the extent that, in promising what is true, it includes the supplementary possibility of telling the truth in order to lead the other astray, in order to have him believe something other than what is true (we know the Jewish story recounted by Freud and so often quoted by Lacan: "Why do you tell me that you are going to X in order to have me believe you are going to Y whereas you are indeed going to X?"). According to Lacan, the animal would be incapable of this type of lie, of this deceit, of this pretense in the second degree, whereas the "subject of the signifier," within the human order, would possess such a power and, better still, would emerge as subject, instituting itself and coming to itself as subject *by virtue of this power,* a second-degree reflexive power, a power that is *conscious* of being able to deceive by pretending to pretend. One of the interests of this analysis derives, no doubt, from the fact that in this essay Lacan gives much importance—in any case, more than anyone else in philosophy and more than he himself does in earlier writings—to the capacity to pretend that he attributes to what he still calls "the animal," "an animal," to what he nicknames here its *"dancity"* *[dansité]* with an "a."[12] *Dansity* refers to the capacity to pretend by means of a dance, lure, or parade, by means of the choreography of the hunt or seduction, the parade that is indulged in before it makes love or the movement of self-protection at the moment it makes war, hence all the forms of the "I am (following)" or "I am followed" that we are tracking here.[13] But in spite of what Lacan thus accords or lends to the animal, he keeps it within the imaginary or presymbolic (as we noted in the "mirror stage" and following the examples of the hen pigeon or migrating locust). He keeps "the animal" prisoner within the specularity of the imaginary; he keeps it more than the animal keeps itself in such captivity, speaking in this regard of "imaginary capture." Above all, he keeps "the animal" within the first degree of pretense (pretense without pretense of pretense) or, which here amounts to the same thing, within the first degree of the trace: the capacity to trace, to leave a track, and to track, but not to distract the tracking or lead the tracker astray by *erasing* its trace or covering its tracks.[14]

An important "But" will, in effect, fold this paragraph in two ("But an animal does not pretend to pretend" [305]). A balance sheet separates the accounting of what has to be accorded the animal (pretense and the trace, inscription of the trace) and what has to be denied it (deception, lying, pretense of pretense, and erasing of traces). But—what the articulation of the "But" perhaps leaves undetected, discreetly in the shadows, among all the traits that are listed, is a reference to life, to the "vital." Everything accorded the animal is conceded on the grounds of "vital situations," even though one would be tempted to conclude that the animal, whether hunter or game, is held to be incapable of an authentic relation to death or of testifying to an essential mortality in the heart of Truth or Speech. The animal is a living creature that is only living, as it were an "immortal" living thing. As Heidegger states—Lacan is here closer to him than ever—and, as we shall see, this is especially the case in terms of what binds the *logos* to the possibility of "deceiving" or "being deceived," the animal does not die.[15] For the same reason, moreover, it would also be ignorant of mourning, the tomb and the cadaver, which for Lacan constitutes a "signifier":

> Observe, in parentheses, that this Other, which is distinguished as the locus of Speech, imposes itself no less as witness to the Truth. Without the dimension that it constitutes, the *deception* practised by Speech would be indistinguishable from the very different *pretense* to be found in physical combat or sexual display *[parade]*. Pretense of this kind is deployed in imaginary capture, and is integrated into the play of approach and rejection that constituted the original dance, in which these two *vital* situations find their rhythm, and in accordance with which the partners ordered their movements—what I will dare to call their "dancity" *(dansité)*. Indeed, animals, too, show that they are capable of such behaviour when they are being hunted; they manage to put their pursuers off the scent *[dépister]*[16] by making a false start. This can go so far as to suggest on the part of the game animal the nobility of honoring the element of display to be found in the hunt. [Of course, that is only a figurative and anthropomorphic suggestion, like a "rabbit in the hat," for it will immediately be made clear by the ensuing "But" that honor and nobility, tied to vouching for one's word or the gift of speech *(la Parole donnée)* and to the symbolic, is precisely what the animal is incapable of. An animal does not give its

word and one does not give one's word, or attribute speech to the animal, except by means of a projection or anthropomorphic transference. One can't lie to an animal either, especially by pretending to hide from it something that one shows it. Isn't that patently obvious? True enough, though it remains to be seen *(Voire.)*. In any case it is this whole organization of Lacan's discourse that we are calling into question here.] *But an animal does not pretend to pretend.* He does not make tracks whose deception lies in the fact that they will be taken as false, while being in fact true ones, ones, that is, that indicate his true trail. *Nor does an animal cover up its tracks, which would be tantamount to making itself the subject of the signifier.*[17]

What does it mean to be (the) subject of/to the signifier, that which the animal is here reputed to be incapable of? What does it signify? Let us first note in passing that this confirms the old (Adamic and Promethean) theme of the animal's profound innocence, its incapacity with respect to the "signifier," to lying and deceit, to pretended pretense, which gets linked here, in a way that is also very traditional, to the theme of a cruelty that does not recognize itself as such; the cruel innocence, therefore, of a living creature to whom evil is foreign, living anterior to the difference between good and evil.[18]

But to be subject of the signifier also means, still yet, two indissociable things that are coupled within the subjecticity of the subject. The subject of the signifier is subject(ed) to the signifier. Lacan never stops insisting on the "dominance . . . of the signifier over the subject" and over "the symbolic order that is constitutive for the subject."[19] The "subject" does not have mastery over it. Its entry into the human order of the law presupposes this passive finitude, this infirmity, this lack that the animal does not suffer from. The animal does not know evil, lying, deceit. What it lacks is precisely the lack by virtue of which the human becomes subject of the signifier, subject subjected to the signifier. But to be subject of the signifier is also to be a subjecting subject, a subject as *master,* an active and deciding subject of the signifier, having in any case sufficient mastery to be capable of pretending to pretend and hence of being able to put into effect one's power to destroy the trace. This mastery is the superiority of man over the *animot,* even if it gains its assurance from the privilege constituted by a defect *[défaut],* a lack *[manque],* or a fault *[faute],* a failing *[défaillance]* that derives both from the generic prematurity of birth and from the castration complex, which Lacan designates, in a text I shall shortly cite, as the Freudian and scientific (or at least nonmythological) version of original sin or the Adamic fall.

It is there that the passage from imaginary to symbolic is determined as a passage from animal to human order. It is there that subjecticity, as order of the signifier from the place of the Other, appears as something missed by or lacking in the traditional philosophy of the subject, as a matter of relations between human and animal. That is at least what Lacan alleges at the moment he subtly reintroduces an anthropocentrist logic and strongly reinforces the *fixism* of the Cartesian *cogito* as a thesis on the animal-machine in general:

> All this has been articulated only in a confused way even by professional philosophers. But it is clear that Speech begins only with the passage from "pretence" to the order of the signifier, and that the signifier requires another locus—the locus of the Other, the Other witness, the witness Other than any of the partners—for the speech that it supports to be capable of lying, that is to say, of presenting itself as Truth.
>
> Thus it is from somewhere other than the Reality that it concerns that Truth derives its guarantee: it is from Speech. Just as it is from Speech that Truth receives the mark that establishes it in a fictional structure. (305–6)

This allusion to a "structure of fiction" would refer us back to the debate concerning "The Purloined Letter."[20] Without reopening it to that extent, let us note here the reflective sharpness of the word *fiction*. The concept it leads us toward is no longer merely that of the *figure* or simple *feint* but the reflexive and abyssal concept of a *feigned feint* or *pretended pretense*. It is by means of the power to pretend a pretense that one accedes to Speech, to the order of Truth, to the symbolic order—in short, to the order of the human.

(Even before detailing once more the principle behind the reading being attempted here, I would at least like to advance a hypothesis. Although Lacan often repeats that there is no Other of the Other [e.g., 316]; although for Levinas, on the other hand, and from another point of view, the question of justice is born from this request of the third [party] and from an other of the other who would not be "simply one's fellow [creature],"[21] one wonders whether the common if disavowed implication of these two discourses on the other and the third did not in fact amount to locating at least an instance of the animal, of the animal-*other*, of the other *as animal*, of the living-mortal-*other*, of the non-fellow in any case, the non-brother [divine or animal, here inseparable], in short of the ahuman combining god and animal according to whatever theo-zoomorphic possibilities there are that properly constitute the myths, religions, idolatries, and even sacrificial practices within the monotheisms that claim to break with idolatry. Moreover, the word *ahuman* does not scare Lacan because, in a postscript to "The Subversion of the Subject," he notes that he was in no way insulted by the epithet *ahuman* that one of the participants in the conference attributed to his talk [324].)

What is Lacan doing when he holds that "the signifier requires another locus—the locus of the Other, the Other witness, the witness Other than any of the partners"? In order to break with the image and with the likeness of a fellow must not this beyond of partnership—thus beyond the specular or imaginary duel—be at least situated in a place of alterity that is radical enough to break with every identification of an image of self, with every fellow living creature, and so with every fraternity or human proximity, with all humanity?[22] Must not this place of the Other be ahuman? If this is indeed the case, then the ahuman, or at least the figure of some—in a word—*divinanimality*, even if it were to be felt through the human, would be the quasi-transcendental referent, the excluded, foreclosed, disavowed, tamed, and sacrificed foundation of what it founds, namely, the symbolic order, the human order, law, and justice. Is not this necessity performed secretly in Levinas and in Lacan, who, moreover, cross paths so often in spite of all the differences in the world? That is one of the reasons why it is so difficult to utter a discourse of mastery or of transcendence with regard to the animal and to simultaneously claim to do it in the name of God, in the name of the name of the Father or in the name of the Law. Must not one recognize Father, Law, Animal, and so on, as being, in the final analysis, the same thing—or, rather, indissociable figures of the same Thing? One could conjoin the Mother within that juncture and it would probably not change anything. Nietzsche and Kafka perhaps understood that better than the philosophers or theoreticians, at least those who belong to the tradition that we are trying to analyze here.

Once more, of course, my prime concern is not to mount a frontal attack on the logic of this discourse and what it implies vis-à-vis the Lacan of the period of the *Écrits* (1966). For the moment, I shall have to leave in suspense the question of whether, in later texts or in the seminars (published or unpublished, accessible or inaccessible), the armature of this logic came to be explicitly reexamined—especially since the oppositional distinction between imaginary and symbolic that forms the very axiomatics of the discourse on the animal seems to be progressively abandoned, if not repudiated, by Lacan. As always, I am trying to take account of the strongest systematic organization of a discourse in the form in which it comes together at a relatively determinable moment of that process. The texts distributed over a thirty-year period and collected within a single volume, solidly bound to its own integrity [relié à soi], namely, the Écrits, provide us in this regard with a reliable purchase on that process and allow us to follow its tracks. Among the published and accessible texts that follow the Écrits, I think that one would have, in particular, to try to follow the path that leads, in an interesting but continuous way, to the analyses of animal mimetism, for example, those that still work from the perspective of the gaze precisely, of the image and the "seeing oneself looking," being seen looking even by a can of sardines that does not see me. ("To begin with, if what Petit-Jean said to me, namely, that the can did not see me, had any meaning, it was because in a sense, it was looking at me, all the same. It was looking at me at the level of the point of light, the point at which everything that looks at me is situated—and I am not speaking metaphorically.")[23]

Instead of objecting to this argument, therefore, I would be tempted to emphasize that the logical, and thus rational, fragility of certain of its articulations should induce us to recast in a general way the whole conceptual framework.

It seems difficult in the first place to identify or determine a limit, that is to say an indivisible threshold between pretense and pretense of pretense. Moreover, even supposing that that limit were conceptually accessible, something I do not think is so, one would still have to know in the name of what knowledge or what testimony (knowledge is not the same as testimony) it would be possible to calmly declare that the *animal in general* is incapable of pretending pretense. Lacan does not invoke here any ethological knowledge (whose increasingly spectacular refinement is proportional to the refinement of the *animot*), nor any experience, observation, or personal attestation that would be worthy of credence. The status of the affirmation that refuses the pretense of pretense to the animal is that of a simple dogma. But there is no doubt a dissimulated motivation to this humanist or anthropocentric dogmatism, and that is the probably obscure but indisputable feeling that it is indeed difficult, even impossible, to discern between pretense and a pretense of pretense, between an aptitude for pretense and an aptitude for the pretense of pretense. How could one distinguish, for example, in the most elementary sexual parade or mating game, between a feint and a feint of a feint? If it is impossible to provide the criterion for such a distinction, one can conclude that every pretense of pretense remains a simple pretense (animal or imaginary, in Lacan's terms), or else, on the contrary, and just as likely, that every pretense, however simple it may be, gets repeated and reposited undecidably, in its possibility, as pretense of pretense (human or symbolic in Lacan's terms). As I shall make clear in a moment, a symptomatology (and, of course, a psychoanalysis) can and must conclude with the possibility, for every pretense, of being pretense of pretense, and for every pretense of pretense of being a simple pretense. As a result, the distinction between lie and pretense becomes precarious, likewise that between speech and truth (in Lacan's sense), and everything he claims to separate from it. Pretense presupposes taking the other into account; it therefore supposes, simultaneously, the pretense of pretense—a simple supplementary move by the other within the strategy of the game. That supplementarity is at work from the moment of the first pretense. Moreover, Lacan cannot deny that the animal takes the other into account. In his article "On a Question Preliminary to Any Possible Treatment of Psychosis" (1957–58), there is a remark that goes in that direction and which I would have liked to insert into this network in a careful and patient manner: putting it at the same time into tension, if not in contradiction, with Lacan's discourse on the imaginary capture of the animal (thereby deprived of the other, in short), and into harmony with the discourse on pathology, evil, lack, or fault that marks the relation to the other as such in the human, but which is already announced in the animal:

> To take up Charcot's formula, which so delighted Freud, "this does not prevent [the Other] from existing" in his place O.
>
> For if he is taken away, man can no longer even sustain himself in the position of Narcissus. As if by elastic, the *anima* springs back on to the *animus* and the *animus* on to the animal, which between S and *o* sustains with its *Umwelt* "external relations" noticeably closer than ours, without, moreover, one being able to say that its relation with the Other is negligible, but only that it does not appear otherwise than in the sporadic sketches of neurosis. (*Écrits,* 195; translation modified)

In other words, the animal resembles the human and enters into relation with the Other (in a more feeble manner, and by reason of a more "restricted" adaptation to the milieu) only to the extent of being ill, of a neurotic defect that brings it closer to man, to man as failure [*défaut*] of the premature and still insufficiently determined animal. If there were a continuity between animal and human orders, as between animal psychology and human psychology, it would follow this line of evil, of fault and defect. Lacan, moreover, has argued against insisting on a discontinuity between the two psychologies (animal and human), *at least* as *psychologies*: "May this digression at least obviate the misunderstanding that we could thus have provided the occasion for in the eyes of some, that of imputing to us the doctrine of a discontinuity between animal psychology and human psychology that is far from being what we think."[24] What does that mean? That the radical discontinuity between animal and human, the absolute and indivisible discontinuity that he, however, confirms and compounds, no longer derives from the psychological as such, from *anima* and *psychē*, but instead from the appearance of a different order.

On the other hand, an analogous (not to say identical) conceptual undecidability comes to trouble the opposition that is so decisive for Lacan between leaving tracks *[tracer]* and covering one's tracks *[effacer ses traces]*. The animal can trace, inscribe, or leave a track or trace, but, Lacan adds, it "does not cover up its tracks, which would be tantamount to making itself the subject of the signifier." But there again, supposing one can trust the distinction, Lacan does not justify by means of either testimony or some ethological knowledge this affirmation that "the animal," as he calls it, the animal in general does not cover its tracks. Apart from the fact that, as I have tried to show elsewhere (and this is why so long ago I substituted the concept of trace for that of signifier), the structure of the trace presupposes that *to trace* amounts to *erasing a trace* as much as to imprinting it, all sorts of sometimes ritual animal practices, for example, in burial and mourning, associate the experience of the trace with that of the erasure of the trace. A pretense, moreover, and even a simple pretense, consists in rendering illegible or imperceptible a sensible trace. How can it be denied that the simple substitution of one trace for another, the marking of their diacritical difference in the most elementary inscription—which capacity Lacan concedes to the animal—involves erasure as much as it involves the imprint? It is as difficult to assign a frontier between pretense and pretense of pretense, to have an indivisible line pass through the middle of a feigned feint, as it is to assign one between inscription and erasure of the trace.

But let us take this further and pose a type of question that I would have wished, had I the time, to pose generally. It is less a matter of asking whether one has the right to refuse the animal such and such a power (speech, reason, experience of death, mourning, culture, institution, technics, clothing, lie, pretense of pretense, covering of tracks, gift, laughter, tears, respect, and so on—the list is necessarily without limit, and the most powerful philosophical tradition within which we live has refused the "animal" all those things) than of asking whether what calls itself human has the right to rigorously attribute to man, which means therefore to attribute to himself, what he refuses the animal, and whether he can ever possess the *pure, rigorous, indivisible* concept, as such, of that attribution. Thus, were we even to suppose—something I am not ready to concede—that the "animal" were incapable of covering its tracks, by what right could one concede that power to the human, to the "subject of the signifier"? Especially from a psychoanalytic point of view? Granted, every human can, within the space of doxic phenomenality, have *consciousness* of covering its tracks. But who could ever judge the effectivity of such a gesture? Is it necessary to recall that every erased trace, in consciousness, can leave a trace of its erasure whose symptom (individual, or social, historical, political, and so on) will always be capable of ensuring its return? And is it necessary, above all, to remind a psychoanalyst of that? And to recall that every reference to the capacity to erase the trace still speaks the language of the conscious, even imaginary ego? (One can sense all the virtual consequences crowding in here from the side of the question posed by this colloquium, namely, autobiography.)

All this will not amount to saying (something I have developed at length elsewhere) that the trace cannot be erased. On the contrary. A trace is such that it is always being erased and always able to be erased *[Il appartient à une trace de toujours s'effacer et de toujours pouvoir s'effacer]*. But the fact that it can *be* erased *[qu'elle s'efface]*, that it can always be erased or erase itself, and that from the first instant of its inscription, through and beyond any repression, does not mean that someone, God, human, or animal, can be its master subject and possess the power to erase it. On the contrary. In this regard, the human no more has the *power* to cover its tracks than does the so-called animal. To *radically* erase his traces, that is to say by the same token to *radically* destroy, deny, put to death, even put himself to death.

But let us especially not conclude, therefore, that the traces of the one and of the others are ineffaceable, or that death and destruction are impossible. Traces erase (themselves), like everything else, but the structure of the trace is such that it cannot be in anyone's *power* to erase it, and especially not to "judge" its erasure, even less by means of a constitutive power assured of being able to erase, performatively, what erases itself. The distinction might appear subtle and fragile but its fragility renders fragile all the solid oppositions that we are in the process of tracking down *[dé-pister]*, beginning with that between symbolic and imaginary which underwrites finally this whole anthropocentric reinstitution of the superiority of the human order over the animal order, of the law over the living, and so on, wherever such a subtle form of phallogocentrism seems in its way to testify to the panic Freud spoke of: the wounded reaction not to humanity's *first* trauma, the Copernican (the Earth revolves around the sun), nor its *third* trauma, the Freudian (the decentering of consciousness under the gaze of the unconscious), but rather to its *second* trauma, the Darwinian.

Before we leave, provisionally, Lacan's text, I would like to define a task and proffer a reminder. The task is one that would involve us, from the vantage of everything that we have here inscribed under the sign of the Cartesian *cogito,* in closely analyzing Lacan's references to Descartes. As is the case with references to Hegel, with which it is often associated, the appeal to Descartes, to the Cartesian *I think,* was constant, determinant, complex, and differentiated. Within that rich network and that wide-reaching process, a first signpost is set by our problematic. It can be found in the pages immediately following the paragraph on the difference between the nonpretending pretense of the animal and the pretending pretense of the human capable of erasing its own traces. Lacan shares out both praise and criticism.

On the one hand, the "Cartesian *cogito* did not fail to recognize" what is essential, namely, that the consciousness of existence, the *sum,* is not immanent to it but transcendent, and thus beyond specular or imaginary capture. That amounts to confirming that an animal *cogito* would remain a captive of the identificatory image, a situation that could be formalized by saying that the animal accedes to the ego *[moi]* only by lacking the I *[Je],* but an I that itself accedes to the signifier only from the perspective of a lack: the (animal) self lacks the lack. For example, Lacan writes:

> From this point on, the ego is a function of mastery, a play of presence, of bearing *(prestance),* and of constituted rivalry [all traits that are not refused the animal]. In the capture to which it is subjected by its imaginary nature, the ego masks its duplicity, that is to say, the consciousness in which it assures itself of an incontestable existence (a naivety to be found in the meditation of Fénelon) is in no way immanent in it, but, on the contrary, is transcendent, since it is supported by the unbroken line of the ego ideal (which the Cartesian *cogito* did not fail to recognize). As a result, the transcendental ego itself is relativized, implicated as it is in the *méconnaissance* in which the ego's identifications take root. (*Écrits,* 307)

But, *on the other hand,* therefore, the *ego cogito* gets dislodged from its position as central subject. It loses its mastery, its central power, it becomes subject subjected to the signifier.

The imaginary process extends thus from the specular image all the way to "the constitution of the ego by way of subjectification by the signifier" (ibid.). That seems to confirm that the becoming-subject of the ego passes by way of the signifier, Speech, Truth, and so on, that is to say by losing its immediate transparency, consciousness as consciousness of the self identical to itself. Which ends only in an apparent paradox: the subject is confirmed in the eminence of its power by being subverted and brought back to its own lack, meaning that animality is on the side of the conscious *ego* whereas the humanity of the human subject is on the side of the unconscious, the law of the signifier, Speech, the pretended pretense, and so on:

> The promotion of consciousness as being essential to the subject in the historical after-effects of the Cartesian *cogito* is for me the deceptive accentuation of the transparency of the I in action at the expense of the opacity of the signifier that determines the I; and the sliding movement *(glissement)* by which the *Bewusstsein* serves to cover up the confusion of the *Selbst* eventually reveals, with all Hegel's own rigour, the reason for his error in *The Phenomenology of Mind.* (Ibid.)

The accent on transparency is thus said to be "deceptive" *[trompeuse]*. That not only means a case of "being deceived" by the error, but of "being deceived" by the deceit, or lie, the lying-to-oneself as belief, the "making believe" in the transparency of the ego or of self to itself. Such would be the risk of the traditional interpretation of the Cartesian *cogito*, perhaps that of the autointerpretation of Descartes himself, of his intellectual autobiography, one never knows. Whence the Lacanian promotion of the *cogito* and his diagnosis of the lie, of deceit, and of a deceptive transparency in the very heart of the *cogito*.

"Hegel's rigor," he says. One would have then to follow the interpretation proposed by Lacan of the struggle between Master and Slave, there where it comes to a "decomposition of the equilibrium of counterpart *[semblable]* to counterpart" (308). The same motif of the "alienating dialectic of Master and Slave" appears in "Variantes de la cure-type" (1955). Animal specularity, with its lures and aberrations, comes to "durably structure the human subject" by reason of the prematurity of birth, said to be a "fact in which one apprehends this dehiscence in the natural harmony, demanded by Hegel as the fecund illness, the happy fault of life, where man, by being distinguished in his essence, discovers his existence" (*Écrits* [French], 345). We could situate the reinscription of the question of the animal, in our reinterpretation of Lacan's reinterpretation of Hegel, at the point where Lacan reintroduces this reminder regarding the imaginary, regarding "specular capture" and the "generic prematuration of birth," the "danger . . . which Hegel was unaware of" (*Écrits*, 308). There again it is life that is at stake, as Lacan makes clear, and the passage to the human order of the subject, beyond the animal imaginary, is indeed a question of life and death:

> The struggle that establishes this initial enslavement is rightly called a struggle of pure prestige [which means, according to Lacan, that it is no longer animal], and the stake, life itself, is well suited to echo that danger of the generic prematuration of birth, which Hegel was unaware of, and in which I see the dynamic motivation of specular capture. (Ibid.; translation modified)

How should we understand this word *generic,* for it qualifies so forcefully the insistent and determinant concept of "prematuration," namely, the absolute event without which the whole discourse would lose its "motivation" *[ressort],* as Lacan himself says, beginning with the relevance of the distinction between imaginary and symbolic? Is the "generic" a trait of "humankind" *[du genre humain]* as a kind of animal, or a trait of the human inasmuch as it escapes classification *[genre],* precisely, escaping the generic or the genetic—by means of the defect, precisely, of a certain de-generation *[dé-génération]* rather than de-generacy *[dégénérescence],* by means of a de-generation whose very defect engenders symbolic "generation," the relation between generations, the law of the Name of the Father, Speech, Truth, Deceit, the pretended pretense, the power to erase one's traces, and so on?

On the basis of this question, which we shall leave in suspense, as a task, there where it proceeds nevertheless from this traditional logic of the originary defect, I come back to what I announced as a final reminder, namely, what brings together this whole perspectival configuration of the defect within the history of original fault, of an original sin that finds its mythical relay in the story of Oedipus, then its nonmythic relay in the "castration complex," such as it was formulated by Freud. In the passage that follows, I shall underline lack and defect, and we shall find there again all the stages of our journey, Genesis, the serpent, the question of the I and the "Who Am I (Following)?"—a quotation from Valéry's *Ébauche d'un serpent* ("the universe is a *defect* in the purity of Non-Being"), and so on:

> This is what the subject lacks in order to think himself exhausted by his *cogito,* namely, that which is unthinkable for him. But where does this being, who appears in some way *defective [en défaut]* in the sea of proper nouns, originate?
>
> We cannot ask this question of the subject as "I." He *lacks* everything needed to know the answer, since if this subject "I" was dead, he would

not, as I said earlier, know it. He does not know, therefore, that I am alive. How, therefore, will "I" prove to myself that I am?

For I can only just prove to the Other that he exists, not, of course, with the proofs for the existence of God, with which over the centuries he has been killed off, but by loving him, a solution introduced by the Christian *kerygma*. Indeed, it is too precarious a solution for me even to think of using it as a means of circumventing our problem, namely: "What am 'I'?"

"I" am in the place from which a voice is heard clamouring "the universe is a *defect* in the purity of Non-Being."

And not without reason, for by protecting itself this place makes Being itself languish. This place is called *Jouissance*, and it is the *absence* of this that makes the universe vain.

Am I responsible for it, then? Yes, probably. Is this *Jouissance*, the *lack* of which makes the Other insubstantial, mine, then? Experience proves that it is usually forbidden me, not only, as certain fools believe, because of a bad arrangement of society, but rather because of the *fault (faute)* of the Other if he existed: and since the Other does not exist, all that remains to me is to assume the *fault* upon "I," that is to say, to believe in that to which experience leads us all, Freud in the vanguard, namely, to *original sin*. For even if we did not have Freud's express, and sorrowful avowal, the fact would remain that the myth Freud gave us—the latest-born myth in history—is no more use than that of the forbidden apple, except for the fact, and this has nothing to do with its power as myth, that, though more succinct, it is distinctly less stultifying *(crétinisant)*.

But what is not a myth, and which Freud nevertheless formulated soon after the Oedipus complex, is the castration complex. (*Écrits*, 317–18, translation modified)

Notes

This essay is part of an extended lecture given by Jacques Derrida at a conference devoted to his work in 1997 at Cerisy-la-Salle, France, titled "L'Animal auto-biographique." That lecture, from work in progress destined to appear in book form, included analyses of Descartes, Kant, Heidegger, Levinas, and Lacan. The introductory outline of that discussion appears as "L'animal que donc je suis" in *L'Animal autobiographique*, ed. Marie-Louise Mallet (Paris: Galilée, 1999). It appears as "The Animal That Therefore I Am (More to Follow)," trans. David Wills, *Critical Inquiry* 28: 2 (2002). The essay published here follows a chapter on the animal according to Levinas.—*Ed.*

1. Earlier in the lecture, in rereading Descartes, I elaborated at length upon what I shall here call the *question of the reply* or *response,* and defined the hegemonic permanence of the "Cartesianism" that dominates the discourse and practice of human or humanist modernity with respect to the animal. A programmed machine such as the animal is said to be incapable not of emitting signs, but rather, according to the fifth part of the *Discourse on Method,* of "responding." Like animals, machines with "the organs and outward form [*figure, face*] of a monkey . . . could never use words, or put together other signs, as we do in order to declare our thoughts to others. For we can certainly conceive of a machine so constructed that it utters words, and even utters words which correspond to bodily actions causing a change in its organs (e.g. if you touch it in one spot it asks what you want of it, if you touch it in another it cries out that you are hurting it, and so on). But it is not conceivable that such a machine should produce different arrangements of words so as to give an appropriately meaningful answer *[pour répondre]* to whatever is said in its presence, as the dullest of men can do" (René Descartes, *The Philosophical Writings of Descartes,* vol. 1, trans. John Cottingham, Robert Stoothoff, and Dugald Murdoch [Cambridge: Cambridge University Press], 139, 140).

2. [See "The Animal That Therefore I Am" for extended discussion of this neologism that phonically singularizes the plural of animal *(animaux)*—noting thus the habit of speaking of all animal species as if they were one—and combines it with the word for "word" *(mot).—Trans.*]

3. Jacques Lacan, "The Subversion of the Subject and the Dialectic of Desire in the Freudian Unconscious," in *Écrits: A Selection,* trans. Alan Sheridan (New York: Norton, 1977), 305. [Subsequent references to the Sheridan translation of *Écrits* are given in the text. Other translations from Lacan are my own.—*Trans.*]

4. Jacques Lacan, "Position de l'inconscient," in *Écrits* (Paris: Seuil, 1966), 834. [The original French version of *Écrits* will be henceforth identified as "*Écrits* (French)."—*Trans.*]

5. See especially *Écrits* (French), 190–91.

6. [*Proceedings of the Royal Society,* Series B (Biological Sciences), no. 845, February 3, 1939, vol. 126.—*Trans.*]

7. See ibid., 189–91, and also 342, 345–46, 452.

8. "The mirror stage as formative of the function of the I as revealed in the psychoanalytic experience" (*Écrits,* 3).

9. Jacques Lacan, "Variantes de la cure-type," in *Écrits* (French), 354: "For it is fitting to reflect on the fact that it is not only through a symbolic assumption that speech constitutes the being of the subject, but that, through the law of the alliance, wherein the human order is distinguished from nature, speech determines

not only the status of the subject but the coming-into-the-world of its biological being."

10. [See opening note on the title of the Cerisy-la-Salle conference and of Derrida's complete lecture, "The Animal That Therefore I Am."—*Trans.*]

11. Cf. Joëlle Proust, *Comment l'esprit vient aux bêtes. Essai sur la représentation* (Paris: Gallimard, 1997), 150. The same author does all she can to ensure that, in the case of the animal, the very word *response* signifies nothing more than a programmed *reaction,* deprived of all responsibility or even of any responsivity that I would cautiously call "intentional," given that that word is used with a confidence and an imprudence, not to say a level of phenomenological vulgarity, that is almost laughable. Concerning the syrphid, an insect that is "programmed to seek out females by automatically applying a pursuit trajectory in accordance with a given algorithm in order to intercept the pursued object," Joëlle Proust cites Ruth Millikan and comments thus: "What is interesting in this type of response is the fact that it is *inflexibly* provoked by certain precise characteristics in the *stimulus* (in the event its size and speed). The insect cannot respond to other characteristics, neither can it exclude targets manifesting characteristics that are incompatible with the desired function. It cannot abandon its course by 'perceiving' that it is not following a female. This insect appears not to have any means of evaluating the correctness of its own perceptions. It would therefore seem *exaggeratedly generous* to attribute to it a *properly intentional* capability. It *responds to signs, but* these signs are not characteristic of an independent object; they are characteristic of proximate stimuli. As Millikan states, it follows a 'proximal rule.' However, the prewired response aims to bring about the fecundation of a female syrphid, that is to say an object existing in the world" (228–29). I have underlined those words that, more than others, would call for a vigilant reading. The critical or deconstructive reading I am calling for would seek less to restitute to the animal or to such an insect the powers that it is not certain to possess (even if that sometimes seems possible) than to wonder whether one could not claim as much relevance for this type of analysis in the case of the human, with respect, for example, to the "wiring" of its sexual and reproductive behavior. And so on.

12. [Pronounced the same as *densité* (density).—*Trans.*]

13. [See "The Animal That Therefore I Am."—*Trans.*]

14. [*dé-pister le dé-pistage et d'*effacer *sa trace. Une piste* is a track and *pister* is sometimes used for "to follow (an animal's) tracks." However, *dépister,* which looks to have a privative sense, is the more usual word for "to follow tracks." Here Derrida is giving *dé-pister* that privative sense, following Lacan's usage as explained in note 15 below.—Trans.]

15. Allow me to refer the reader to my *Aporias,* trans. Thomas Dutoit (Stanford, Calif.: Stanford University Press, 1993), especially 35–38 and 74–76.

16. In an important note in the "Seminar on 'The Purloined Letter,'" Lacan explains the original usage of the word *dépister* that he is having recourse to here: not to track, follow a scent or tracks, but, on the contrary, as it were, to confuse the issue *[brouiller les pistes]* by covering one's tracks, *dé-pister*. In the same note he invokes both Freud's famous text on the "antithetical sense of words," "primal or not," the "magisterial rectification" that Benveniste contributed to it, and information from Bloch and Von Wartburg dating the second sense of the word *dépister* from 1875. The question of the antinomic sense of certain words, Lacan makes clear, "cannot be dispensed with *[reste entière]* if one is to bring out the instance of the signifier in all its rigor" (*Yale French Studies* 48 [1975]: 51; translation modified).

And, indeed, I would be tempted to add in order to raise the stakes, especially if, as is the case here, we are to put to the test the axioms of a logic of the signifier in its double relation to the distinction between animal (capture by the imaginary) and human (access to the symbolic and to the signifier) orders, on the one hand, and to another interpretive implementation of undecidability, on the other. The supposedly assured difference between *pister* and *dé-pister,* or rather, between *dépister* (track, or follow a track) and *dé-pister* (cover one's tracks and purposely lead the hunter off the track), coalesces and underwrites the whole distinction between human and animal, according to Lacan. It would be enough for this distinction to waver for the whole axiomatic to fall apart, in its very principle. That is what we are going to have to make clear.

17. Lacan, *Écrits*, 305. Italics are, of course, mine. Elsewhere I will analyze another text that, obeying the same logic ("the sexual instinct . . . crystallized in a relation . . . that is imaginary"), concerning precisely the stickleback and its "dance of copulation with the female," introduces the question of death, of the *being already dead*, and not just the being-mortal of the individual as a "type" of the species; not horses but the horse. Cf. *Les écrits techniques de Freud* (Paris: Seuil, 1975), 140–41.

18. "If instinct in effect signifies the undeniable animality of man, there seems no reason why that animality should be more docile for being incarnated in a reasonable being. The form of the adage—*homo homini lupus*—betrays its sense, and in a chapter from his *Criticon,* Balthazar Gracian elaborates a fable in which he shows what the moralist tradition means when it holds that the ferocity of man with respect to his fellow surpasses everything animals are capable of, and that carnivorous animals themselves would recoil in horror from the threat to which he exposes all nature. But this very cruelty implies humanity. It is a fellow creature that he has in his sights, even in the guise of a being from a different species" (Jacques Lacan, "Fonctions de la psychanalyse en criminologie," in *Écrits* [French], 147).

19. Cf. Jacques Lacan, "Le séminaire sur «La Lettre volée»": "it was necessary to illustrate in a concrete way the dominance that we affirm for the signifier over the subject" (*Écrits* [French], 61 [not in English translation—Trans.]); and "we have decided to illustrate for you today . . . that it is the symbolic order which is constitutive for the subject—by demonstrating in a story the decisive orientation *[détermination majeure]* which the subject receives from the itinerary of a signifier" (*Yale French Studies* 48 [1975]: 40).

20. Cf. Jacques Lacan, "Le Facteur de la vérité," in *The Post Card,* trans. Alan Bass (Chicago: University of Chicago Press, 1987).

21. Emmanuel Levinas, "Paix et proximité," in *Emmanuel Lévinas* (Paris: Cahiers de la nuit surveillée, 1984), 345. I cited and commented on this in my *Adieu to Emmanuel Levinas,* trans. Michael Naas and Pascale-Anne Brault (Stanford, Calif.: Stanford University Press, 1999).

22. A study of the value of "fraternity," whose tradition and authority I have attempted to deconstruct (in *Politics of Friendship,* trans. George Collins [London: Verso, 1997]), should also be able to identify the credit given to it by Lacan, and that well beyond the suspicion in which the murderous and patricidal brothers are held according to the logic of *Totem and Taboo.* In various places Lacan in effect dreams of *another fraternity,* for example, in these last words from "Agressivity in Psychoanalysis": "it is our daily task to open up to this being of nothingness the way of his meaning in a discreet fraternity—a task for which we are always too inadequate" (*Écrits,* 29).

23. Jacques Lacan, "The Line and Light," in *The Four Fundamental Concepts of Psychoanalysis: The Seminar of Jacques Lacan, Book XI,* trans. Alan Sheridan (New York: Norton, 1998), 95. See also, especially, 75.

24. Jacques Lacan, "Situation de la psychanalyse et formation du psychanalyste en 1956," in *Écrits* (French), 484.

Sloughing the Human

Steve Baker

One explanation for the continuing attraction of the animal for artists, philosophers, and others is the perception—which may or may not be justified—that the very idea of the animal is in some way aligned with creativity, or in alliance with creativity. What is it to be animal? What does it take, what is sufficient, to suggest or to gesture toward the other-than-human? This is a matter not of extravagance but of sobriety—a matter of judging just what it takes to step aside from the human, to indicate an other, to signal the animal, and thus to enter that privileged "experimental" state of identity-suspension that has so concisely and contentiously been named becoming-animal, *devenir-animal*.[1]

What Does It Take to Be an Animal?

Opportunities to take on the guise of the animal are eagerly grasped. In the 1990s, the artist Jordan Baseman taught himself taxidermy in order to make a number of striking pieces that often use the skins of domestic animals discovered as roadkill outside his studio in east London. The finished pieces occupy an uneasy middle ground somewhere between sculpture and conventional taxidermy; Baseman himself thinks of them as "empty trophies." One such piece, titled *Be Your Dog,* is essentially a headdress made from a scalped pair of Alsatian's ears (Figure 1). It has only been exhibited once, mounted approximately at head height on the wall of

Figure 1. Jordan Baseman, *Be Your Dog,* 1997. Dog's ears, plastic. Photograph copyright Jordan Baseman.

a gallery in Austria. Although never intended to be worn, Baseman found to his surprise that visitors to the gallery eagerly aligned themselves with the piece, their backs to the wall, in order to have themselves photographed appearing to "wear" the ears and to think themselves into this new state of being, just as the title suggests. As the artist acknowledges, "it's about desire, frustrated desire, more than anything else, because there is a strong desire to wear it. It might sicken you, but you do feel compelled to put the damn thing on."[2]

This particular headdress—being made from the skin of a real animal—is no mere representation, but in all other respects it is not so different from the souvenir Mickey Mouse ear sets sold to be worn by visitors to Disneyland, which in other circumstances have served as a sufficient sign of animality (of dressing up as an animal, that is to say) that they have been worn by American animal rights protesters seeking to alert the public to the fate of laboratory mice subjected to cosmetics testing (Figure 2). The frequent adoption of such guises in the cause of animal rights calls for a study in itself, but there too the connection is sometimes made between animal identity and creativity. Brian Luke, for example, specifically views animal liberation "as creative, not restrictive. It extends possibilities for action." The term he proposes for the adoption of these new possibilities is *going feral*—a state in which humans

Figure 2. "Fried to death" protest, circa 1990. Animal Rights Advocates of the Hudson Valley, Beacon, New York.

put themselves into "the position of feral animals, formerly domesticated but now occupying a semiwild state on the boundaries of hierarchical civilization."[3]

Such possibilities, which appear more open-ended in terms of how they see the boundaries of the human and the nonhuman animal, and the scope for some kind of *exchange* across those boundaries, have also been of interest to artists and philosophers. Their various approaches to the question of what it is to be animal tend to complicate the roles of various parts of the performing body in any taking on of animality.

The Hands of Beuys and Heidegger

When, in 1974, Joseph Beuys staged his weeklong performance *Coyote: I Like America and America Likes Me* in the René Block Gallery in New York, the spectacle presented to viewers through the chain-link barrier separating them from the main space of the gallery was that of the artist and a live coyote ("Little John") playing out a mainly improvised encounter as the week progressed (Figure 3). In this confrontation of human and animal, Beuys suggested, "the roles were exchanged immediately." Although initially structured by a cycle of ritualized actions, Beuys was acting out the limits of his own control of the situation, with the coyote figuring for him as "an important cooperator in the production of

Figure 3. Joseph Beuys, *Coyote: I Like America and America Likes Me,* 1974. Photograph copyright DACS 2001.

freedom." The animal enabled the artist to edge closer to that which "the human being cannot understand."[4]

In fact, however, it is the manner in which Beuys established his humanness that is especially revealing. In a space strewn with straw, lengths of felt, ripped copies of the *Wall Street Journal,* and a variety of other materials the artist had brought along, a pair of gloves (which he had painted brown and which were repeatedly thrown to the coyote) are worthy of particular note. Their color represented "the will to sculptural form," and their form was that of his own hands. Beuys explained:

> The brown gloves represent my hands, and the freedom of movement that human beings possess with their hands. They have the freedom to do the widest range of things, to utilise any number of tools and instruments. They can wield a hammer or cut with a knife. They can write or mould forms. Hands are universal, and this is the significance of the human hand. . . . They are not restricted to one specific use like the talons of an eagle or the mole's diggers. So the throwing of the gloves to Little John meant giving him my hands to play with. (Tisdall, *Joseph Beuys,* 28, 29–30)

The artist gives something to the animal, and what he chooses to give is his hands. They carry associations of creativity ("the will to sculptural form") and they enable the animal to play. They are, in a sense, the opposite of Baseman's dog headdress. They are just sufficient to gesture toward the other-than-animal: the human.

This would be of no great interest were it not for the fact that Beuys's position so closely echoes that of the philosopher Martin Heidegger in his 1947 "Letter on Humanism." Heidegger had periodically addressed the relation of humans and other animals, sometimes at great length, since the late 1920s. His initial theses, framed as a means of assessing how it was possible to know or to have access to the experience of the world, ran as follows:

1. The stone is worldless.
2. The animal is poor in world.
3. Man is world-forming.

They were intended as no more than provisional and exploratory tools. Disparaging as the term "poor in world" *(weltarm)* may sound, it was the fact that Heidegger could use it while explicitly acknowledging the great "discriminatory capacity of a falcon's eye" or of "the canine sense of smell"—and while arguing that "amoebae and infusoria" were no less perfect and complete than "elephants or apes"—that led him repeatedly to insist that poverty in world "must not be taken as a hierarchical evaluation."[5]

These writings have been dissected in considerable detail by Jacques Derrida, who by the 1990s had become increasingly concerned with philosophy's (and thus humanity's) responsibilities toward animals. Heidegger's "Letter on Humanism"—which explores the question of the "abyss" separating humans from other animals more briefly and more dogmatically than his earlier writings—contains what Derrida regards as Heidegger's most "seriously dogmatic" sentence: "Apes, for example, have organs that can grasp, but they have no hand."[6]

In a fascinating exploration of exactly what the hand meant to Heidegger (which includes an all too brief reference to "the play and the theatre of hands" in extant photographs of the philosopher), Derrida shows that a number of far from obvious associations clustered around Heidegger's conception of the human hand, marking it out as utterly other than the animal's paws, claws, or talons. For one thing, this hand has a complex relation to thought:

> If there is a thought of the hand or a hand of thought, as Heidegger gives us to think, it is not of the order of conceptual grasping. Rather this thought of the hand belongs to the essence of the *gift*, of a giving that would give, if this is possible, without taking hold of anything. If the hand is also, no one can deny this, an organ for gripping, that . . . is not the hand's essence in the human being. ("*Geschlecht* II," 169, 172–73).

This amounts, Derrida notes, to an "assured opposition of *giving* and *taking*: man's hand *gives and gives itself* . . . like thought or what gives itself to be thought . . . whereas the organ of the ape . . . can only *take hold of, grasp, lay hands on the thing*" (175).

This is indeed an impoverished notion of the animal. Put alongside the earlier thesis that only humans are "world-forming," it leaves the animal gazing across the abyss not only at all that is human, but also at all that is associated with thought, generosity, and creativity. In terms of the widespread cultural fascination with the animal, this seems wrong. Although animals, including the great apes, are still widely regarded and treated as being lower down on some notional phylogenetic hierarchy than are humans, their value to the human imagination has seldom been in doubt.

It is for these reasons that it seems so odd to find Beuys generously (or, more accurately, condescendingly) offering the coyote his own creativity, in the form of the painted brown gloves, when the continuing power and fascination of that whole weeklong exchange between them—already more than a quarter of a century ago—lies in the idea of the artist slowly giving up preconceptions and learning something of what the animal has to offer him.

This tension, this awkwardness, may nevertheless be in keeping with Beuys's role as a performer rather than a philosopher. Philosophy has all too often tried to settle matters (on the question of animals as much as on any other), whereas art has more often seen the scope for unsettling things. Derrida admittedly notes what he calls the "precariousness" of Heidegger's opposition of "the gift and the grip" (176), but it may well be that artists are in a better position to demonstrate and to *act out* that precariousness. And where Derrida states that, for Heidegger, "a hand can never upsurge out of a paw or claws" (178), there is no shortage of art that finds both this and its opposite—paws and claws upsurging out of hands—to be a source of fascination, anxiety, and delight.

Art's Animal Hands

For many contemporary artists, the animal stands in as a new form of being, a creative postmodern being, and it emphatically does have hands.[7] Examples abound. A 1997 video performance by Edwina Ashton, titled *Sheep*, is seen on two adjacent video screens. On the right, a figure dressed as a sheep looks across, as it were, to the other screen, on which an apparently identically dressed figure, in much the same domestic setting, sits at a desk with its script (Figure 4). In a faltering voice, this second sheep recites a series of appalling sheep jokes: "Why do sheep hate pens? Because they can't write"; "Can you stop making that noise with the paper? Why? Because I hate sheep rustlers"; and so on.

Both performers are Ashton herself, but with her voice disguised: "I don't want to be in them," she has said of all her video performances. A long time was spent "trying to get the faces right" on the handmade costumes, to achieve "a sufficient degree of blankness," while nevertheless creating for the animal what she calls a kind of "haphazard" look. Strangely, even on repeated viewings, this characterless sheep is entirely believable. Stuck inside the thing, and telling bad jokes at the expense of the animal identity she has taken on, she physically tugs the features of its makeshift face back and forth. It is the hands, more than anything, that tell of this problematized and uncomfortable identity: when they are not at her face, she is endlessly, agitatedly wringing them throughout the four-minute duration of the piece.

Figure 4. Edwina Ashton, video still from *Sheep,* 1997. Photograph courtesy of the artist.

Aside from Ashton's *Sheep,* it has generally been the hands of primates to which artists have been so keen to attend. The handedness of John Isaacs's 1995 *Untitled (Monkey)* is especially striking (Figure 5). The chimpanzee's hands and "feet" were cast from the hands of the five-year-old son of one of the artist's friends: "The hands are really badly grafted on—there's no attempt to pretend that they're part of the same animal." The realism of the piece, which is more like a waxwork or mannequin than a sculpture, makes this aberrant creation (whose body is both ravaged and delicate) particularly disturbing.

This piece crops up, uncredited but unmistakable, in Will Self's 1997 novel *Great Apes.* The book's central character, the artist Simon Dykes, wakes one morning, after a night of especially heavy recreational drug abuse, to find that he has turned into a chimpanzee, as have all other inhabitants of his previously human world. Toward the end of the novel, at a chimp-packed exhibition opening in the Saatchi Gallery (the place where Isaacs's sculptures had in fact been displayed a year earlier), Dykes comes across a display of "various chimpikins," the strangest of which "was covered with a most inhuman coat of patchy fur, and had hind paws with prehensile digits, one of which it was using to give itself an interminable mainline fix." As Dykes perceptively remarks of these thinly primatomorphized versions of Isaacs's mannequin-like works, "these chimpikins are alluding to some crucial loss of perspective, occasioned by the enforcement of a hard dividing line between chimp and beast."[8]

Art's uncomfortable erasure of such dividing lines is evident in the photographer Robin Schwartz's series of "primate portraits," especially

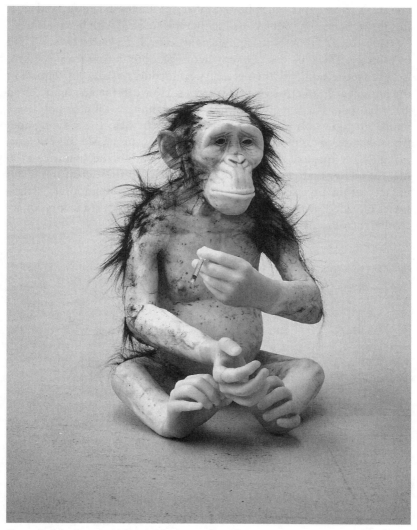

Figure 5. John Isaacs, *Untitled (Monkey)*, 1995. Mixed media. Arts Council Collection: Photography, Hayward Gallery, London. Gift of Charles Saatchi, 1999. Photograph copyright Stephen White. Reprinted with permission of the artist.

the 1988 photograph *Ping* (Figure 6), which shows a female capuchin looking remarkably at ease on a sofa, one arm draped casually across a cushion, and surrounded by cuddly toy animals from which at first glance it is not easy to distinguish the monkey. On further inspection, something about the pose of the animal recalls Barthes's comments on Robert Mapplethorpe's photograph *Young Man with Arm Extended,* about which he wrote: "the photographer has caught the boy's hand . . . at just the right degree of openness," so that it is "offered with benevolence."[9]

Paula Rego's vision of the animal as artist in *Red Monkey Drawing* and in *Monkeys Drawing Each Other* (Figure 7), both dating from 1981, reinforces more explicitly the necessary handedness of any conception of the animal as both creative and generous. How can the ape figure as an artist (as it does in so many postmodern imaginings) if it does not have a hand? The question is by no means entirely rhetorical. The living apes whose handiwork is recorded in Thierry Lenain's survey, *Monkey Painting,* bring Rego's image of the monkey painter (an old theme, in any case) to life. No matter that Lenain insists that the work of these creatures is not in fact "art" in any usual sense of that word. Many contemporary artists, Isaacs included, are keen to distance themselves from just the kind of activities and objects traditionally understood to be art.

Figure 6. Robin Schwartz, *Ping: Capuchin, Female, 5 Years Old,* 1988. Gelatin silver print. Photograph copyright Robin Schwartz, 1997. Reprinted with permission of the photographer.

Figure 7. Paula Rego, *Monkeys Drawing Each Other,* 1981. Acrylic on paper. Photograph courtesy of the artist. Reprinted with permission of Marlborough Fine Art, London.

Lenain's emphasis on the fact that the apes' interest is only in the "pure disruptive play" of active image making, and not at all in "the product of their acts of deliberate disruption," may say more than he realizes about why the distinctly "handed," playful, and nonpossessive ape continues to serve as one rather useful model of the postmodern artist.[10] This is certainly how Hélène Cixous understands the responsibilities of artists: they are "those who create new values . . . inventors and wreckers of concepts and forms, those who change life."[11] In French these are *les désordonnantes,* the sowers of disorder, her neologism significantly incorporating the word *donnant(e)* (generous, open-handed), thus emphasizing the centrality of generosity to this account of creativity.

Imitating the Animal

Any assessment of what it takes to be an animal, or to be taken to be an animal, or to become animal (for this is always an active, acted-out process), cannot dodge the difficult question of imitation. It is Deleuze and Guattari who have made this question so difficult for the postmodern artist, for they rule it out as untenable and uncreative. "No art is imitative, no art can be imitative," they write, and "becoming animal does not consist in playing animal or imitating an animal" (304, 238).

Radical as their account of becoming-animal undoubtedly is (in terms of its exploration of both animality and creativity), a degree of unrecognized fixity underpins this apparently fluid concept. The refusal of imitation is one of the key strategies by which the authors try to clarify what they mean by becoming-animal. They propose: "We fall into a false alternative if we say that you either imitate or you are. What is real is the becoming itself . . . not the supposedly fixed terms through which that becoming passes" (238). Nevertheless, they *warn against* imitation rather than suggest it to be an impossible undertaking. But to be able to imitate an animal (or, indeed, to refuse to do so) already presupposes a knowledge of what that animal *is*. Unlike philosophy, much contemporary art appears to find such knowledge uninteresting.

Whether or not they are done in the spirit of becoming, forms of what are most readily described as imitation seem central to art's exploration of the animal. In being both outlandish and preposterously transparent, however, they make no claims to the "nature" of the imitated animal. These imitations generally act out the instability rather than the fixity of the thing nominally imitated. They suggest playful exchanges between the human and the animal, or between one animal and another, which may allude to borders and distinctions but which are not impeded by them.

In William Wegman's 1970 photograph *Crow,* a stuffed parrot appears to cast the shadow of a crow. In many of Wegman's subsequent photographs of his famous pet Weimaraner, Man Ray, the dog imitates or is dressed as various other kinds of animal: leopard, zebra, bat, dinosaur, and so on. As the artist laconically puts it, "I like things that fluctuate."[12] The dressing up, rather as in Ashton's *Sheep,* is generally a halfhearted and haphazard affair. In *Elephant* (1981), Man Ray is given tusks and a trunk (which appears to be an oversized old stuffed sock), and sits in a domesticized "jungle" setting indicated by a single potted rubber plant. In *Frog/Frog II* (1982), the dog looks down at a frog, which it feebly imitates by wearing Ping-Pong ball eyes and green rubber flippers on its hind legs.

"Imitation" of an animal can be just that easy and approximate. Baseman's *Be Your Dog* is a positive invitation to the viewer to take on dogness merely by imitating one aspect of the animal's appearance. Paula Rego's 1994 *Dog Woman* series begins with a large pastel drawing in which the artist herself is seen "squatting down and snarling"; she suggests that "the physicality of the picture came from my turning myself into an animal in this way."[13] In Lucy Gunning's video *The Horse Impressionists,* four young women take turns to do their best impressions of the sound and movements of horses. Their hands, significantly, are central to these imitations: either held up to indicate the horse's raised forelegs or cupped to the mouth to aid their impressions of the animal's neighing and whinnying. Aware of the preposterousness of these poor imitations, their attempts constantly break down into bursts of laughter.

It is not only artists and their viewers or collaborators who can establish the scope for creative expression in animal imitation, and its inseparability from what Deleuze and Guattari regard as a more thoroughgoing becoming-animal. A brief episode in a home video shows a colleague's young daughter running in circles at some speed around their living room shouting "I'm a bee I'm a bee I'm a bee" at the top of her voice—a compelling and entirely convincing instance of becoming-animal being achieved through conviction and repetition, with no need for dressing up.

In all these instances, it might be said that the thing imitated or gestured toward is not so much an animal as a version of the imitator or gesturer—"l'animal que donc je suis," as Derrida has it.[14] In a postmodern age marked by "a deeply felt loss of faith in our ability to represent the real,"[15] this is perhaps how the animal is now most productively and imaginatively thought in art—as a thing actively to be performed, rather than passively represented.

Such performances appear to necessitate the sloughing of preconceptions and of identities. John Isaacs's animal pieces have been called "anti-subjects,"[16] and Isaacs has himself proposed that for him "the animal plays the role of the nonspecific human," and is therefore necessarily a thing "without an identity." Edwina Ashton, similarly, takes pride in saying of the creatures in her own animal performances, such as *Sheep,* that "you couldn't psychoanalyze those patients, could you?" And although Jordan Baseman himself has no particular interest in the question of psychoanalysis, his manipulations of animal form have been praised for the fact that they operate "without the safety net of psychoanalysis."[17] Jacques Derrida, pursuing his own literary-philosophical variant on these new kinds of beings, puns *animaux* into *animots,* in order to describe an awkward, living word-thing that can only be defined negatively: "Ni une espèce, ni un genre, ni un individu" ("L'Animal," 292). In each of these cases, this is the animal as a thing that can only be thought actively, and that approaches that genuinely experimental state of becoming-animal where things "cease to be subjects to become events" (Deleuze and Guattari, *A Thousand Plateaus,* 262). Any such event is one in which, as Heidegger recognized many years before Deleuze and Guattari, the human devises a means of going along with the animal.

Going Along with the Animal

Flawed as his approach may have been, it should not be forgotten that Heidegger's concern was to understand the animal in its otherness, and to let that otherness be. This understanding was to be achieved, he proposed, through an imaginative transposition of the human into an animal. In this "self-transposition," "the other being is precisely supposed to remain *what* it is and *how* it is. Transposing oneself into this being means . . . being able to go along with the other being while remaining *other* with respect to it." It is a "going-along-with" undertaken for the sake of "directly learning how it is with this being" (*The Fundamental Concepts of Metaphysics,* 202–3). The notion of letting the animal's otherness be has links to those postmodern conceptions of the animal that try to avoid forcibly rendering it meaningful in human terms, thus reducing its otherness to sameness, and its wonder to familiarity.

Two examples suggest how this going-along-with can be acted out as an exchange, a handing-across, which pivots on the work of art itself. Both concern humans in alliance with living animals, "learning how it is" with those beings, as Heidegger puts it. Olly and Suzi, the British artists known for painting predators in their natural habitat at the closest possible quarters—whether it be white sharks underwater off the coast of Cape Town, cheetahs in Namibia (Figure 8), or anacondas in Venezuela—have an unusual working method. The two work simultaneously on each image, "hand over hand," as they put it, and wherever possible they also allow the depicted animals to "interact" with the work and mark it further themselves. This may take the form of bears or elephants leaving prints or urine stains on an image, or of chunks being bitten off by a wolf or a shark. Such interactions are extensively documented "as a performance" by the photographer Greg Williams, who travels with the artists.

It is the paintings themselves, once marked by the animal, that are the crucial document. In a world that has grown largely indifferent to the question of endangered species, these works are described by the artists as "a genuine artifact of the event," and are intended to bring home the truth and immediacy of these animals' precarious existence. For there to be an animal-made mark, the animal has to be present, and actively participate. What is performed through its presence is the animal's reality, and what is challenged is precisely that postmodern "loss of faith in our ability to represent the real" (Bertens, *The Idea of the Postmodern,* 11).

Figure 8. Cheetahs with painting: Olly and Suzi with Greg Williams, Namibia, 1998.
Photograph copyright Growbag. Reprinted with permission of Liza Samos.

A second example concerning the place the living animal may have in
the artist's creativity is drawn from *Monkey Painting,* where Thierry
Lenain recounts the "astonishing collaboration" between the French
painter Tessarolo and a female chimpanzee named Kunda (Figure 9):

> During the sessions in which they both painted, he left the initiative to
> Kunda and then completed her clusters of lines by the addition of figura-
> tive elements. . . . Tessarolo says that at times, Kunda would accept his ad-
> ditions with enthusiasm, at others she would rub them out and wait for
> him to draw something else. Once the pictures were finished they were
> signed by both artists, the painter putting his name on one side and
> Kunda a handprint on the other. (109)

Lenain specifically describes as "postmodern" this art which, "conceived without irony," aims "to give full recognition to the part played by
the animal" (109–11). In works such as those of Olly and Suzi, or of
Kunda and Tessarolo, it is the mark of the hand on the painting as point
of exchange that, for the present, best records the loose creative alliance
of animal and artist. It may not yet be entirely clear what is exchanged
between the human and the animal in these instances, but the politics
and poetics of that exchange call urgently for further exploration.

Figure 9. The French painter Tessarolo working with Kunda, a chimpanzee. Photograph copyright Jacques Münch. Reprinted with permission of Tessarolo.

Notes

1. See Gilles Deleuze and Félix Guattari, *A Thousand Plateaus: Capitalism and Schizophrenia,* trans. Brian Massumi (London: Athlone Press, 1988). Subsequent references are given in the text.

2. Unless otherwise indicated, information about the work of Edwina Ashton, Jordan Baseman, John Isaacs, and Olly and Suzi is drawn from the author's unpublished interviews with these artists, conducted in London between 1998 and 2000. Statements by the artists are also from this source.

3. Brian Luke, "Taming Ourselves or Going Feral?: Toward a Nonpatriarchal Metaethic of Animal Liberation," in *Animals and Women: Feminist Theoretical Explorations,* ed. Carol J. Adams and Josephine Donovan (Durham, N.C., and London: Duke University Press, 1995), 290–91, 313.

4. Beuys is quoted in Caroline Tisdall, *Joseph Beuys: Coyote* (Munich: Schirmer-Mosel, 1980), 28, 26. Subsequent references are given in the text.

5. Martin Heidegger, *The Fundamental Concepts of Metaphysics: World, Finitude, Solitude,* trans. William McNeill and Nicholas Walker (Bloomington: Indiana University Press, 1995), 184, 194. Subsequent references are given in the text.

6. Jacques Derrida, "*Geschlecht* II: Heidegger's Hand," trans. J. P. Leavey, in *Deconstruction and Philosophy: The Texts of Jacques Derrida,* ed. John Sallis (Chicago: University of Chicago Press, 1987), 173. Subsequent references are given in the text.

7. See Steve Baker, *The Postmodern Animal* (London: Reaktion Books, 2000).

8. Will Self, *Great Apes* (London: Bloomsbury, 1997), 341–42.

9. Roland Barthes, *Camera Lucida: Reflections on Photography,* trans. Richard Howard (London: Jonathan Cape, 1982), 59.

10. Thierry Lenain, *Monkey Painting,* trans. C. Beamish (London: Reaktion Books, 1997), 178. Subsequent references are given in the text.

11. Hélène Cixous, "Sorties," in Hélène Cixous and Catherine Clément, *The Newly Born Woman,* trans. Betsy Wing (Manchester: Manchester University Press, 1986), 84.

12. Wegman is quoted in Peter Weiermair, "Photographs: Subversion through the Camera," in *William Wegman: Paintings, Drawings, Photographs, Videotapes,* ed. Martin Kunz (New York: Harry N. Abrams, 1990), 46.

13. Rego is quoted in John McEwen, *Paula Rego,* 2d ed. (London: Phaidon Press, 1997), 212.

14. Jacques Derrida, "L'Animal que donc je suis (à suivre)," in *L'Animal autobiographique: Autours de Jacques Derrida,* ed. Marie-Louise Mallet (Paris: Galilée, 1999), 251–301. Subsequent references are given in the text.

15. Hans Bertens, *The Idea of the Postmodern: A History* (London and New York: Routledge, 1995), 11. Subsequent references are given in the text.

16. Martin Hentschel, "Passage," in *Passage: Neue Kunst in Hamburg E.V.,* exhibition catalog (Hamburg: Kunsthaus, 1998), 6.

17. Jean-Paul Martinon, "On the Edge of the Abyss," in *Jordan Baseman: Blunt Objects,* exhibition catalog (Graz, Austria: Galerie Eugen Lendl, 1997).

Animal Body, Inhuman Face

Alphonso Lingis

Bodies

Sea anemones are animate chrysanthemums made of tentacles. Without sense organs, without a nervous system, they are all skin, with but one orifice that serves as mouth, anus, and vagina. Inside, their skin contains little marshes of algae, ocean plantlets of a species that has come to live only in them. The tentacles of the anemone bring inside the orifice bits of floating nourishment, but the anemone cannot absorb them until they are first broken down by its inner algae garden. When did those algae cease to live in the open ocean and come to live inside sea anemones?

The flowers of Brazil nut trees can be pollinated by only one species of bee. This bee also requires, for its larvae, the pollen of one species of orchid, an orchid that does not grow on Brazil nut trees. When did Brazil nut flowers come to shape themselves so as to admit only that one species of bee? What we know as Brazil nuts are kernels which, on the tree, are enclosed in a very large wooden husk containing hundreds of them. The Brazil nut tree is hardwood, and the husk about its seeds is of wood hard as iron. There is only one beast in Amazonia that has the teeth, and the will, to bore into that husk. It is a medium-sized rodent, and when it bores through the husk, it only eats some of the seeds. The remaining seeds are able to get moisture, and push their roots into the ground. Without that

165

rodent, the nuts would be permanently entombed, and Brazil nut trees would have died out long ago.

There is perhaps no species of life that does not live in symbiosis with another species. When did celled life, with nuclei, come to evolve? Micro-biologist Lynn Margulis established that chloroplasts and mitochondria, the oxygen-processing cellular energy-producers in plants and animals, were originally independent cyanobacteria that came to live inside the cells of plants and animals. Colonies of microbes evolved separately, and then formed the symbiotic systems which are the individual cells, whether of algae or of our bodies.

Human animals live in symbiosis with thousands of species of anaero-bic bacteria, six hundred species in our mouths which neutralize the tox-ins all plants produce to ward off their enemies, four hundred species in our intestines, without which we could not digest and absorb the food we ingest. Some synthesize vitamins, others produce polysaccharides or sug-ars our bodies need. The number of microbes that colonize our bodies exceeds the number of cells in our bodies by up to a hundredfold. Macro-phages in our bloodstream hunt and devour trillions of bacteria and viruses entering our porous bodies continually. They replicate with their own DNA and RNA and not ours. They, and not some Aristotelian form, are true agencies of our individuation as organisms. When did those bac-teria take up lodging in our digestive system, these macrophages take up lodging in our bloodstream?

We also live in symbiosis with rice, wheat, and corn fields, with berry thickets and vegetable patches, and also with the nitrogen-fixing bacteria in the soil that their rootlets enter into symbiosis with in order to grow and feed the stalk, leaves, and seeds or fruit. We also move and feel in symbiosis with other mammals, birds, reptiles, and fish.

A pack of wolves, a cacophonous assemblage of starlings in a maple tree when evening falls, a whole marsh throbbing with frogs, a whole night scintillating with fireflies exert a primal fascination on us. What is fasci-nated in the pack, the gangs of the savannah and the night, the swarming, is the multiplicity in us—the human form and the nonhuman, vertebrate and invertebrate, animal and vegetable, conscious and unconscious movements and intensities in us that are not yoked to some conscious goal or purpose that is or can be justified in some capitalist program for economic growth or some transcendental or theological fantasy of object-constitution or creativity seated in us. Aliens on other planets, galaxies churning out trillions of stars, drops of water showing, under the microscope, billions of squiggling protozoa are mesmerizing. What is mesmerized in us are the inhuman movements and intensities in us, the pulses of solar energy momentarily held and refracted in our crystalline cells, the microorganic movements and intensities in the currents of our inner rivulets and cascades.

Our bodies are coral reefs teeming with polyps, sponges, gorgonians, and free-swimming macrophages continually stirred by monsoon climates of moist air, blood, and biles. Movements do not get launched by an agent against masses of inertia; we move in an environment of air currents, rustling trees, and animate bodies. Our movements are stirred by the coursing of blood, the pulse of the wind, the reedy rhythms of the cicadas in the autumn trees, the whir of passing cars, the bounding of squirrels and the tense, poised pause of deer. The differentials of speed and slowness liberated from our bodies do not block or hold those movements only; our movements compose their differentials, directions, and speeds with those movements in the environment. Our legs plod with elephantine torpor; decked out fashionably, we catwalk; our hands swing with penguin vivacity; our fingers drum with nuthatch insistence; our eyes glide with the wind rustling the flowering prairie.

These movements have not only extension; they surge and ebb in intensity. They are vehement, raging, prying, incandescent, tender, cloying, ardent, lascivious. It is by its irritability, its fear, its rage, its languor, its zest that an octopus in the ocean, a rabbit caught in our headlights, a serpent in the grass, a cat on the couch, a cockatoo in the morning mists, become visible to us.

Our movements become irritable with the insistent whine of a mosquito, fearful before the fury of a hornet whose nest we have disturbed, languid with the purring of a cat, exuberant in the sparkling of the coral fish in the tropical surge.

We assign special importance, in everyday life, to purposive or goal-oriented movement. Certain movements of our bodies are isolated and the circuitry set by conditioning for certain operations in conjunction with the movements and velocities of household utensils, tools, and machines. Of themselves, these movements are not initiatives by which an agent posits and extends its identity. They are nowise the movements by which a conscious mind seeks to maintain and consolidate and stabilize itself; even less integrate itself.

Most movements—things that fall, that roll, that collapse, that shift, that settle, that collide with other things, that set other things in motion—are not goal-oriented. How little of the movements of the bodies of octopuses frolicking over the reef, of guppies fluttering in the slow currents of the Amazon, of black cockatoos fluttering their acrobatics in the vines of the rain forest, of terns of the species *Sterna paradisaea* scrolling up all the latitudes of the planet from Antarctica to the Arctics, of humans, are teleological! How little of these movements are programmed by an advance representation of a goal, a result to be acquired or produced, a final state! All these movements do not get their meaning from an outside referent envisioned from the start, and do not get their direction from an end point, a goal or result. Without theme, climax, or denouement, they extend from the middle, they are spreadings of duration.

In the course of the day, our bodies shift, lean, settle, agitations stir them, most of the movements of our arms and hands are aimless, our eyes glide in their sockets continually buoyed up and rocked by the waves of the sunlight. Even most of the movements to which we assign goals start by just being an urge to move, to get the day going, to get out of the house. We leave our house for a walk in the streets, a stroll along the beach, a saunter through the woods. In the Ryongi Zen Garden in Kyoto, for five hundred years each morning the monk rakes again the sands into waves, his own movements cresting in waves. The campesina in Guatemala occupies her hands with the rhythms and periodicity of her knitting as she sits on the stoop gossiping with her friends; the now old Palestinian who will never leave this refugee camp fingers his prayer beads.

Every purposive movement, when it catches on, loses sight of its teleology and continues as a periodicity with a force that is not the force of the will launching it and launching it once again and then once again; instead it continues as a force of inner intensity. The carpenter climbs up the roof to nail shingles; almost at once his mind lets loose the alleged objective and the rhythm—dum-dum-dum-DUM, dum-dum-dum-DUM—continues his movements as it does the dancer in the disco, and the force he feels in those movements is not the force of his deciding will but the vibrant and vital intensity of his muscles on the grip of his fine, smoothly balanced hammer he likes so much. The rhythm of his hammering composes with the rhythm of the wind currents passing in which he hammers and of the falling leaves and when he pauses he, alone in the neighborhood, registers the nearby tapping of a nuthatch on a treetrunk.

The movements and intensities of our bodies compose with the movements and intensities of toucans and wolves, jellyfish and whales.

The hand of the child that strokes the dolphin is taking on the surges of exuberance that pulse in its smooth body while the dolphin is taking on the human impulses of intimacy forming in close contact with the child's lips and cheeks. The woman who rides a horse lurches with the surges of its impulses, while the horse trots with her prudent programming. The movements of her body are extending differential degrees of speed and retardation, and feeling the thrill of speed and the soothing decompression of retardation. These movements are not productive, they extend neither toward a result nor a development. They are figures of the repetition compulsion; one strokes a calf each night on the farm, one rides a horse through the woods with the utterly noncumulative recurrence of orgasm.

The parents of their first baby feel all sorts of feelings about that baby—astonishment, curiosity, pride, tenderness, the pleasure of caring for a new life, and the resentment the mother feels over the father's unwillingness to share also the tedium and distastefulness of nursing the baby and cleaning its diapers, and also the jealousy the father feels as the woman he so recently chose to devote himself to exclusively as she him now pours most of her affection on the baby. What does the baby feel, aside from hunger and discomfort? Whatever feelings simmer in that opaque and unfocused body are blurred and nebulous. Brought up in a state orphanage, he or she would reach the age to be transferred to the car or tobacco factory assembly line with still opaque, blurred, and nebulous feelings. Brought up in an American high-rise apartment where the parents stay home weeknights watching action movies on television while fondling their gun collection, and go for rides weekends through a landscape of streets, boulevards, underpasses, and highways, seeing only other cars outside the window, the baby would reach sexual maturity with the feelings of Ballard and Vaughan in J. G. Ballard's *Crash*.

Is it not animal emotions that make our feelings intelligible? The specifically human emotions are interlaced with practical, rational, utilitarian calculations which tend to neutralize them—to the point that the human parent no longer knows if she feels something like parental love, finding her time with the baby dosed out between personal and career interests, not knowing how much concern for her child is concern with her own image or her representative. It is when we see the parent bird attacking the cat, the mother elephant carrying her dead calf in grief for three days, that we believe in the reality of maternal love. So much of the human courage we see celebrated is inseparable from peer pressure and the craving for celebrity and for the resultant profit, that it is the bull in the corrida that convinces us of the natural reality of fearlessness.

Is not the force of our emotions that of the other animals? Human infants are tedious at table, picking at their food, playing with it, distracted from it; they pick up voracity from the puppy absorbed with total Zen attentiveness at his dish. They come to feel curiosity with a white mouse poking about the papers and ballpoints on father's desk. Their first heavy toddling shifts into tripping vivacity with the robins hopping across the lawn. They come to feel buoyancy in the midst of the park pigeons shifting so effortlessly from ground to layers of sun-drenched air. They come to feel sullenness from the arthritic old dog the retired cop was walking in the park and that they try to pet. They contract righteousness and indignation from the mother hen suddenly ruffled up and her beak stabbing when they try to cuddle a chick. They pick up feelings of smoldering wrath from the snarling chained dog in the neighbor's yard and try out those feelings by snarling when they are put under restraints or confined. Temper in a human infant dies away of itself; it is from finding reverberating in himself the howling of dogs locked up for the night, the bellowing of tigers, the fury of bluebirds pursuing hawks in the sky, that his and her rage extends to nocturnal, terrestrial, and celestial dimensions.

The curled fingers of an infant ease into tenderness from holding the kitten but not tight, and rumble into contentment from stroking its fur with the pressure and periodicity that are responded to with purring. In contact with the cockatoo who, though he can clutch with a vice-grip around a perch while sleeping, relaxes his claws on the arm of an infant and never bites the ear he affectionately nibbles at, and who extends his neck and spreads his wings to be caressed in all the softness of his down feathers, the infant discovers that her hands are not just retractile hooks for grabbing, but organs to give pleasure. In contact with the puppy mouthing and licking his legs and fingers and face the infant discovers his lips are not just fleshy traps to hold in the food and his tongue not just a lever to shift it into the throat, but organs that give, give pleasure, give the pleasures of being kissed. In feeling the lamb or the baby skunk extending its belly, its thighs, raising its tail for stroking the infant discovers her hands, her thighs, and her belly are organs to give pleasure.

Far from the human libido naturally destining us to a member of our species and of the opposite sex, when anyone who has not had intercourse with the other animals, has not felt the contented cluckings of a hen stroked on the neck and under the wings rumbling through his or her own flesh, has not kissed a calf's mouth raised to his or her own, has not mounted the smooth warm flanks of a horse, has not been aroused by the powdery feathers of cockatoos and the ardent chants of insects in the summer night, gets in the sack with a member of his or her own species, she and he are only consummating tension release, getting their rocks off. When we, in our so pregnant expression, *make* love with someone of our own species, we also make love with the horse and the calf, the kitten and cockatoo, the powdery moths and the lustful crickets.

Orgasm proceeds by decomposition of the competent body, the body upon which have been diagrammed and contracted the efficient operations for functioning in the environment of kitchen utensils, tools, and machines. It begins in denuding oneself. Clothing is not only a defensive carapace against the heat, the cold, the rain, the sleet, and the importunate impulses, curiosity, and advances of others, and protection for our flesh from the grime, dust, and harsh edges of the implements we manipulate and machines we operate. Whenever we go out in the street, or open our door to someone who knocked, we see someone who has first washed off the traces of the night, the anonymity and abandon of the night, from his or her face, who has rearranged the turmoil of his or her hair, who has chosen clothing for his or her departure into the public spaces. He and she dress punk or preppie, worker or executive, inner city or suburban, he dresses up in business suit or dresses down in jeans, she puts on a pearl necklace or a neckchain of Hopi Indian beads. He and she also dress today like he and she did yesterday and last year; she maintains the two-piece crisp look of an active woman with responsibilities, a business executive. He keeps his masculine, outdoors look even when visiting the city or coming to our dinner party; he does not put aside his plaid shirt and jeans for a tie-dyed hippie t-shirt or an Italian designer silk shirt. When we see her, wearing a t-shirt or sweatshirt with Penn State on it, we see someone who is not only dressing in the uniform of a college student, but who has dressed her movements, thoughts, and reactions with those of a college freshman, a dormitory rat, or a sorority sister. We also see in the uniform the uniformity of a series of actions, undertakings, thoughts, opinions, feelings maintained for weeks, months, years, and predictable for the weeks, months, years ahead. We see the time of endurance, and respond to it.

Now he or she undresses before our eyes, and under our embrace. In denuding him and herself, he and she take off the uniform, the categories, the endurance, the reasons, and the functions. Of course in the gym-built musculature we see another kind of clothing, body-armor, uniformization, a body reshaped to fit a model. But in the slight sag of the full or undeveloped breasts, in the smooth expanse of the belly, in the contour of the ass, in the bare expanse of the inside of the upper thighs, we see flesh, carnality, and our eyes already caress it to make contact with what makes it real and tremble with its own sensuality and life. This carnality, this naked flesh is only real in the carnal contact with it, dissolute and wanton.

As our bodies become orgasmic, the posture, held oriented for tasks, collapses, the diagrams for manipulations and operations dissolve from our legs and hands which roll about dismembered, exposed to the touch and tongue of another, moved by another. Our lips loosen, soften, glisten with saliva, lose the train of sentences, our throats issue babble, giggling, moans, sighs. Our sense of ourselves, our self-respect shaped in fulfilling a function in the machinic and social environment, our dignity maintained in multiple confrontations, collaborations, and demands, dissolve; the ego loses its focus as center of evaluations, decisions, and initiatives. Our impulses, our passions, are returned to animal irresponsibility. The sighs and moans of another that pulse through our nervous excitability, the spasms of pleasure and torment in contact with the non-prehensile surfaces of our bodies, our cheeks, our bellies, our thighs, irradiate across the substance of our sensitive and vulnerable nakedness. The lion and stallion mane, the hairy orifices of the body, the hairy bull chest, the hairy monkey armpits, the feline pelt of the mons veneris, the hairy satyr anus exert a vertiginous attraction. We feel feline and wolfish, foxy and bitchy; the purrings of kittens reverberate in our orgasmic strokings, our fingers racing up and down the trunk and limbs of another become squirrelly, our clam vagina opens, our penis, slippery and erect oscillating head of a cobra, snakes its way in. Our muscular and vertebrate bodies transubstantiate into ooze, slime, mammalian sweat, and reptilian secretions, into minute tadpoles and releases of hot moist breath nourishing the floating microorganisms of the night air.

Human sexuality is not just what priggish suburbanites call animal sex, the random and mindless copulation of their domestic dogs; it elaborates all the refinements of eroticism. Lust enlists all the Platonic eros that craves beauty and immortality, the beauty that looks immortal and the immortality of beauty; it elaborates the skills and the arts of seduction, the teasing and provocative usage of language, metaphor and metonymy, synecdoche and irony, the no that is a yes and the yes that is a no, the specific pleasure in appearance, simulacra, and masquerade, the challenge and purely imaginary stakes of games. The consummately feminine look, Baudelaire said, is "that blasé look, that bored look, that vaporous look, that impudent look, that cold look, that look of looking inward, that dominating look, that voluptuous look, that wicked look, that sick look, that catlike look, infantilism, nonchalance and malice compounded."[1]

Courtesans of old Persian gardens, sacred women devoted to all the arts of the Kama Sutra in the temple compounds of old India, sacred women elaborating erotic epics in the temple compounds of the Mayas and Incas in America, Geishas of Japan. A woman not striding in sensible walking shoes, but pirouetting in stork heels, or gliding in water-buffalo sandals; not wearing laundromat-washed t-shirt and jeans, but clad in the silk made by moths and chains of Polynesian shells dangling in the way of her melodic movements. Not muscled arms and bloated, milk-full breasts, but satiny breasts and a belly not destined for pregnancy and stretch marks. An abdomen not emitting the gurglings of digestion and a derrière not smelling of defecations, a woman who survives on celery stalks and champagne, or brown rice and water. One does not see the female, one sees the feminine, obeying nothing but aesthetic laws of her own making. An astral woman who appears in the crowd like a mirage, and who drifts effortlessly through doors to wander in rose gardens and crystal pools the moonbeams create wherever she turns.

Males in the Middle Ages became erotic objects in the ostentatious garb of knights and in tournaments taking place in an enchanted world of sorcerers, stallions, dragons, and rescues, and in the siren songs of out-law gypsies, predators on the organized feudal world. The male erotic objects on the silver screen are eighteenth-century cavalry or naval officers who gamble away fortunes, duel, and dance, and Latino bandidos, or twentieth-century outlaws and high-society con men. The starched white uniforms of naval officers, with their gold epaulets and the hats, capes, and mirror-polished boots of cavalry officers with never the least trace of the muck of the barracks and the gore of the battlefield make them appear as astral men who appear from the outer spaces beyond society like mirages. Nineteenth-century bandidos and twentieth-century outlaws and high-society con men stud their black uniforms with silver and their bloody hands with precious jewels. They prowl in the outer region of sorcery and necromancy, consecrated in that other religion of amulets, talismans, luck, fate, omens, curses, spells, werewolves, and vampires.

But in this the courtesan, sorceress in the rites of eroticism, is in symbiosis with the resplendent quetzal whose extravagantly arrayed glittering plumage serves no utilitarian function; the cavalry officer is in symbiosis with the coral fish whose Escher designs do not outline the functional parts and organs of their bodies and whose fauviste colors are no more camouflage than are his white jodhpurs and scarlet cape. The ceremonies and etiquette with which courtship was elaborated among the courtesans in the court of the Sun King were not more ritualized than the rituals of Emperor penguins in Antarctica; the codes of chivalry in medieval Provence not more idealized than the spring rituals of impalas in the East African savannah; the rites of seduction of Geishas in old Kyoto not more refined than those of black-neck cranes in moonlit marshes.

Humans have from earliest times made themselves erotically alluring, as Immanuel Kant noted, by grafting upon themselves the erotic splendors of the other animals, the glittering plumes of quetzal-birds and the filmy plumes of ostriches, the secret inner splendors of mother-of-pearl oysters, the springtime gleam of fox fur. Until Versailles, perfumes were made not with the nectar of flowers but with the musks of rodents. The dance floors cleared of vegetation and decorated with shells and flowers that birds-of-paradise make for their intoxicated dances, a cock fight exhibits the extravagant and extreme elaborations far beyond reproductive copulation into the eroticism that humans have composed with the other animals.

And today, in our Internet world where everything is reduced to digitally coded messages, images, and simulacra instantaneously transmitted from one human to another, it is in our passions ceremonious delays of eroticism.

Faces

Primates in the savannah, chimpanzees, gorillas, Neanderthals, Cro-Magnons, in packs. Moving with the sun rising on the horizon, with the wind rustling the staves of elephant grass, the movements of their legs and hands composing with the elastic bend and spring of the staves of grass. A flight of a crane draws their heads upward, a rush of wildebeests excites the velocities emanating from them, they dance a punk slamdance with the scavenger hyenas. Hands extended upon the arms, backs, legs, heads of one another, the tensions and flexions of their torsos composing with the tensions and flexions of those arms, backs, legs, heads. They lie on the ground, shifting under the spring of the grass and the stirring of small insects, overhead the branches laden with leaves and berries sway with the gusts of wind. Their fingers clasping the fingers of those leafy branches, berries shifting, holding, falling into their fingers. Their fingers composing with the movements of their lips, their tongues, bringing berries also to the lips and tongues of one another, taking berries from the fingers and lips of one another. Inside their mouths marshes of bacteria, six hundred species shifting in the foaming saliva, pulsate, neutralizing the toxins in those berries. They murmur with the rustling leaves, answer the chatter of monkeys and lemurs and the bellowings of elephants and the cries of parrots and eagles. They hum and murmur and chant with one another as they move. It is in laughter that they both recognize one another as members of the same species, and are attracted to one another. Outbursts of laughter spread among them, making them transparent to one another. They wail and weep together over a dead child, an adult dead of fever. They speak in words, words of blessing over exquisite forest-floor and grandiose cosmic events that delighted them, words of cursing that pursue the evil forces to their own lairs. They have evolved speech, to speak of the things they laugh over, weep over, bless and curse. As the sun descends and the light turns into darkness, their eyelids descend. Lying on the ground, they rest their heads on the bellies, thighs of one another, their legs and hands extending and retracting when the torsos they rest on shift to open bends of intestines for leaves and berries and four hundred species of bacteria to move again. Through the long night the wind stirs, the staves of elephant grass spring up as they shift positions.

In this animal pack, there are forces, intensive movements that are stronger. The antlers of two elk lower, swerve, lock, their feet push, the one buckles and falls. The foot comes down upon the tail of the calf, but the tail swirls and the swift feet of the calf bound away. The feet of one human animal stumble on the cliff face, the hand of the other grasps and pulls him erect. One human, the alpha male leads the pack, drives off the cupidinous junior male, who feints, and another cupidinous son runs off with the alpha female.

Then, in the desert, in the steppes, there arose the despot. He no longer wrestled with the others for the alpha male position, exposing his legs to be kicked under him, exposing his moves to the composition of adversary moves and velocities. He covered the head of his body with a surface, a blank wall, his face. On this blank wall formed signs. The movements and velocities of the pack ran up against this blank wall. When they did so they were sent off, recoded. His signs, his words are directives, imperatives. Action, movements must take their origin in his words.

His directives extend in linear progression: each word follows the last, takes up its sense and extends it to the next word. They extend a line of coherence and cohesion. Of themselves, words are polysignificant, extending rays of allusion in many directions. "Fly" may indicate rhythmic movement through the air, or a departure into the air being ordered, or an escape, a disappearance, or a move in baseball, or a brazen initiative, or an insect. Setting another word after it, and another word after that, progressively eliminates the ambiguity, the polydirectionality, and when the series of words has come to an end, a single line of coherence and cohesion has been laid out. The radiating spread of sounds, tones, and also of movements coming from an animal body, the multiple velocities issuing from that body composing with myriads of surrounding mammals, birds, reptiles, fish, insects, bacteria, have been lined up into one line of inter-referential words, which is one line of meaning. "What did he mean?" becomes an anxiety darkening the laughter and tears, blessings and cursings by which they had come to communicate.

The despot demands an account of themselves of his subjects. They must give an account of what they did yesterday, what they will do today. They must inwardly code what they are now as coherent with, consequent upon, what they did yesterday. They must make what they will do tomorrow be the consequence of what they say today. Their movements must no longer be immediate responses to the rhythms, the melodic velocities they composed with the differentials of velocity and intensity about them, those of the other animals they move and feel in symbiosis with. Their voices no longer resonate, chant, invoke, call forth; they respond to the voice of a law that orders one to move on down the line. They extend before him the blank wall of faces, extended over their heads, surfaces upon which words are inscribed. These surfaces are loci of words, of meanings which become the commanding motor force of their inner coral reefs. They are these blank walls, these surfaces, these faces, nothing but these subjects of discourse, coding, ordering their animal bodies.

On the blank wall, the surface, of his face, there are black holes, dark as the black of the night, in which his pleasure and his displeasure simmer. The words of his subjects facing him, lining up their actions upon him, enter these black holes, where the turmoil of his pleasure and his displeasure turns upon itself, exists for itself. In the black hole on his face turns a spiral of subjectivity, a movement existing for itself, turning on itself, affecting itself.

His authority is these black holes, before which lies the turbulence of a drifting desert, an undulating sea. The crabgrass lines of advances, of radiation, of entanglement in the pack are by his look lined up, directed upon himself, sanctioned or terminated, in the black hole of his look. In these black holes his look orders them.

The black hole of his look is judgment. To be seen by him is to be judged. His arbitration operates by binary oppositions, dichotomies, bipolarities. No. Yes. They will know his pleasure or his displeasure only in more words inscribed on the blank wall of his face.

His words rebound upon his subjects. The lines of movement, of composition with other movements, with which they live and act, they are to line up; the present movement they are to make the consequence of the past movement, coherent with it, the present moment they are to make a pledge for the movement to come. They are to exercise surveillance upon their own movement in his place, subject each movement to judgment, absorb the line extending outward in the black hole of their own look, where it turns in spirals of subjectivity, subjected to judgment, to yes and to no.

The desert world about him becomes a landscape, direct correlate of the landscape of his face. It becomes a blank surface upon which drifting dunes and shifting shadows become significant, material tracings of lines of meaning, a face of the earth facing him, the respondent, the complement and correlate of his own face. In the black holes of its glades and caverns and in the black hole of the night that envelops it, he sees the moods, the passions, the compliance, and the defiance of the landscape corresponding to his subjectivity.

The polis, the geopolitical empire. In every cubicle of the high-rises, the blank screen of the television faces the inmates. The blank screen flickers, traits, lines, wrinkles, within a border long, square, angular: the Prime Minister, the Minister of Defense, the leader of the opposing army, the President of the Chamber of Commerce, the President of Qantas, the star of the national rugby team, the star of the Hollywood superproduction, face millions of inmates in those cubicles. All the radiating, swarming lines of velocities and movements, in the electoral campaign, in the economy, in the stadiums, in the neon-lit night of the city, run up against the blank wall of this face. The traits, lines, wrinkles of the face oscillate. One does not see, divine, touch the nervous circuitry, thin strands of muscles, and the inner rivers coursing billions of bacteria and macrophages in a depth behind this blank wall; the face is all surface, a signboard, on which a succession of words will take form to be heard and read. The words, a ninety-second sound bite, enunciate the meaning that gives coherence, lines up, the radiating movements and velocities of the electoral campaign, the economy, the airline industry, the new line of fashion, the new series of Hollywood action movies. The blank wall of the face is perforated with black holes, in them the eyes turn, sanctioning or censuring, yes, no. The President, the Minister of the Interior, the leader of the opposing army, the president of the multinational corporation, the captain of the Olympics team, the heavy metal star is authoritatively pleased, is authoritatively displeased.

In the corridors, in the streets, the citizens have covered up their bodies to expose blank surfaces—uniforms of business executives and store clerks, nurses and waiters, teachers and students, suburban homeowners and teenage groupies. The legs advance forward and backward, used to move linearly toward a goal fixed by a word. Lest they stray there are words written at highway intersections, on street corners, on doors, along the corridors of shopping malls. If ever these so strictly monitored movements happen, even through no fault of one's own, to so much as brush up against the body of another, one immediately, guiltily says words: Oh, I'm sorry! Oh excuse me! The hands extend to words written on boxes, bottles, cans. The fingers touch letters and words on security alarm pads, on computers, on microwaves, on phonographs, on television sets, on cellular phones. The line of posture in the torso and neck responds to words: attention, the boss is looking, the highway cop is looking at the radar screen, the father, teacher, tour guide is looking over there, the judge, foreman, inspector, borough councilman, coach, star has arrived, the face is appearing on the screen, attention, at ease, attention, at ease.

The citizens do not lean against, rub against, fondle, smell, palpate one another's bodies, feeling the streams and cascades and backwaters within; they look upon the blank wall of the faces, the pure surfaces extended over their heads. They read there the linear traits of meaning. The zigzag, broken radiations of movements and velocities are lined up, past phases taken up and continued in the present, subsequent phases programmed in the present.

A face faces to express meanings. A face is there to express subjective feelings. More than "expresses" there are no meanings without a blank wall on which are inscribed and effaced signs and redundancies. There is no subjectification without a black hole where consciousness, self-consciousness, its passions, its redundancies turn.

A face is a determinate zone of frequency or probability, a field which accepts some expressions and connections and neutralizes others. It is a screen and a framework. To face someone is to envisage a certain range of things there that could be expressed, and to have available a certain range of things one could address to it. One sees what he might say, what he should not have said. One senses the sorts of things one might say, those one might not say. We do not speak the English language, with all the vocabulary available in the dictionary; we speak as "a father must," as an office manager or factory foreman, to the lover we speak a puerilized language; in falling asleep we sink into a oneiric discourse, and abruptly return to a professional language when the telephone rings.

A face is where consciousness and passion exist in the world. They exist in the black holes on the blank wall of the face. In these black holes appear the eyes, the nose, the ears, the mouth. The eyes, the nose, the ears, the mouth subjectivize the outside environment. The movements, fluxes, rhythms, melodies, velocities of continental shelfs, oceans and skies, the other animals, the plants and the viruses are covered over with the blank screen of a landscape, appearing only through meanings, gloom, and pleasures.

To seek out a face is to put a question to it. A question is not a supplication, an entreaty, nor a velleity for knowledge just put out in the air; it is already an order, a command. Beggars, the destitute, students, proletarians, enlisted soldiers, prisoners, patients have no right to question; they can only beg. If they are heard, they will be given scraps to silence them.

The questions command a certain focus of attention, a selection of resources on hand, a certain type of language. The answer lays down a direction, imposes a directive to think further in a certain direction.

Facing one another, we require responsibility. And responsibility requires integrity—that is, not only sincerity, but an integration of the faculties and resources of the speaker. One has to not only respond to the greetings and questions of others, but one has to answer for what one says or said. The others face you as the one present here now who has to answer for things said five minutes ago and yesterday and last year. "But you said . . . But you promised . . ." To speak, to say "I" is not simply to designate oneself as the one now making this utterance; it is to reiterate the same term and attribute to it again utterances and deeds predicated of it before. If one has changed, one has to reinstate what one was as the motive for what one has now become. "Yes I promised to go to India with you this year, but I changed my major and have to study for medical school admissions. . . ."

To find one's identity in facing others is to exist and act under accusation. The temptation to not answer for something that was seen or said or done through one's organism yesterday, to attribute it to another psychic agency, to begin to break up into discontinuous psychic sequences is the very formula for antisocial existence. The schizophrenic is a sociopath. Multiple personality disorder is the ultimate psychosis psychiatry has to deal with, and society sees the sociopath not so much in violence—violence can be, as in policemen or professional boxers, perfectly socialized—but rather in someone who leads a double, or triple, life.

To exist under accusation is to have to provide a coherent verbal justification for every movement that emanates from one's body. One cultivates a memory in which everything is filed in an accessible system; makes what one feels and does today consistent with what one felt and did yesterday, what one was trained to do, what one was brought up to be. Know thyself! The unexamined life is not worth living! What one thinks and says today is a pledge and a commitment, to which tomorrow, next year, next decade is subjugated. The blank wall and black holes of the face of philistine Socrates, one unable to build a house or compose anything but a nursery rhythm out of Aesop's fables, prowls about all the workshops, assembly halls, and studios of the city, accusing, discrediting the carpenter, the leader of men or of women; discrediting even the artist, the poet, the composer if he and she cannot give a verbal account of it motivating each stanza of their compositions with a linear rational justification.

The face extends down the whole length of the body. The hands and fingers no longer probe, punch, caress with the furry caterpillars, the raccoons, and the octopods; held at a distance from contact from any other body, they gesticulate, diagramming meaningful signals and punctuations consistent with the words set forth. The very genitals themselves, exposed in the collapse of posture and skills, the collapse of will, the dissolute decomposition of orgasm, undergoing material transubstantiations solidifying, gelatinizing, liquefying, vaporizing, are under accusation the whole length of their existence: they must mean something, they must carry the dead weight of the meaning, they must express respect for the person, the ego, the identity, the authority of the face, they must confirm the partner in his or her identity, they must serve the population policy of the nation-state and its patron God. Everything animal in the body must be covered up, with clothing which extends the face, the blank surfaces of the business suit and the tailored two-piece suit of the career-woman, with the black holes of its buttons, the blue of deliveryman's and the white of painter's dungarees, the uniforms of air hostesses and politicians' wives and university students, uniforms upon which ordered words are inscribed, where black holes of subjectivity judge and sanction. The surfaces of clothing are facial; they circumscribe zones of frequency or probability, fields which accept some expressions and connections and neutralize others.

But it also happens that the depth of the body breaks through the face, invades it, darkens it with ambiguity and ardor. The expressive lines of the lips and cheeks vacillate, lose the train of the expression, shimmer with the caresses of the sunlight, tremble and begin to rock to the melodies of the insects and rustling trees. Into the smooth contours of the cheeks blank for the inscription of signals, there emerges an exposed and susceptible carnality, where millions of microorganisms swim in churning rivulets and cascades, craving contact with the lips of a calf, the powdery plumage of a cockatoo, the caresses of blades of grass, themselves teeming with minute swarms of living organisms. All the animals within carapaced in the uniforms migrate to the face, sole surface of exposure, to compose with the animals outside.

When our gaze encounters such a face, we see red spots, freckles that stream off in the autumn leaves, eyes one crosses instead of seeing oneself in them, looks our looks surf with. Mane of the centaur-woman bareback riding across the windy prairie, sunlight dancing across the wrinkles of the old woman feeding pigeons in the park, sand dunes of the forehead, cheeks, nose, and lips in Kaneto Shindo's film *Woman of the Dunes,* gelatinous crystals of the eyes in which we see the effulgent light of stars that burned out millions of light-years ago, open mouth upon which we push our tongue upon ecological gardens of six hundred species of microorganisms.

When another greets us, with a voice that trembles with the dance of springtime or threnody of winter, his or her voice invites us to hear the murmur of nature that resounds in it. When someone turns his eyes to us, he or she does not only look in our eyes to order them or find the map of the landscape; his or her eyes seek out first the vivacity and delight of the light in them that summons him and her forth. Does not the gaze of another, which touches us lightly and turns aside, and invokes not the glare of our gaze but the darkness our eyes harbor, refract to us the summons of the impersonal night?

And then when we make contact with the face of another, we make contact with the wounds and wrinkles of the skin, surface of exposure of susceptibility and vulnerability.

The suffering we see may well be a suffering that does not seek to be consoled; Nietzsche warned against imagining that we should alleviate a suffering which another needs and clings to as his or her destiny—the inner torments of Beethoven, the hardships and heartaches of the youth who has gone to join the guerrillas in the mountains, the grief of someone who has to grieve the loss of her child. To be afflicted with his or her suffering requires that we care about the things he or she cares for.

Another's words of greeting open a silence for our words but also for our reticence and our tact before the importance, urgency, and immediacy of the demands of animal packs and of constellations of things. The suffering of the one who faces me, a suffering visible in the bloodless white of her anguished face, may well be not the suffering of her own hunger and thirst, but a suffering for other animals in her care dying of the drought or the peregrines in the poisoned skies, a distress over the crumbling temple and for the nests of seabirds broken by the tidal wave, a grieving for the glaciers melting under skies whose carbon-dioxide layers are trapping the heat of the earth.

Is it only his or her suffering that appeals urgently to us, has importance, and afflicts us immediately? Is there not always joy in the one who faces us, even joy in his suffering—the joy of finding us? Joy is an upsurge that affirms itself unrestrictedly, and affirms the importance and truth of the packs, the gangs of the savannah and the night, the swarming, illuminated by joy. The one who faces us in joy does not only radiate his joy which we find immediately on ourselves; it requires a response. The thumbs-up that the Brazilian street kid—his mouth too voraciously gobbling our leftover spaghetti to smile or say *obrigado*—gives is a gift given us that we must cherish in the return of our smile, a gift that we have no right to refuse. But the joy of the street kid is not only a contentment in the satisfaction of his hunger; it is a joy of being in the streets, in the sun, in the urban jungle so full of excitements, and it is in his laughter pealing over the excitements of the urban jungle and the glory of the sun reigning over the beaches of Rio that gives rise to his hunger and his relishing the goodness of restaurant spaghetti.

Notes

1. Charles Baudelaire, *Œuvres complètes*, ed. Claude Pichois (Paris: Gallimard, 1961), 1256.

At a Slaughterhouse, Some Things Never Die

Charlie LeDuff

It must have been one o'clock. That's when the white man usually comes out of his glass office and stands on the scaffolding above the factory floor. He stood with his palms on the rails, his elbows out. He looked like a tower guard up there or a border patrol agent. He stood with his head cocked.

One o'clock means it is getting near the end of the workday. Quota has to be met and the workload doubles. The conveyor belt always overflows with meat around one o'clock. So the workers double their pace, hacking pork from shoulder bones with a driven single-mindedness. They stare blankly, like mules in wooden blinders, as the butchered slabs pass by.

It is called the picnic line: eighteen workers lined up on both sides of a belt, carving meat from bone. Up to 16 million shoulders a year come down that line here at the Smithfield Packing Co., the largest pork production plant in the world. That works out to about 32,000 a shift, sixty-three a minute, one every seventeen seconds for each worker for eight and a half hours a day. The first time you stare down at that belt you know your body is going to give in way before the machine ever will.

On this day the boss saw something he didn't like. He climbed down and approached the picnic line from behind. He leaned into the ear of a broad-shouldered black man. He had been riding him all day, and the day before. The boss bawled him out good this time, but no one heard what was said. The roar of the machinery was too ferocious for that. Still, everyone knew what was expected. They worked harder.

The white man stood and watched for the next two hours as the blacks worked in their groups and the Mexicans in theirs. He stood there with his head cocked.

At shift change the black man walked away, hosed himself down, and turned in his knives. Then he let go. He threatened to murder the boss. He promised to quit. He said he was losing his mind, which made for good comedy since he was standing near a conveyor chain of severed hogs' heads, their mouths yoked open.

"Who that cracker think he is?" the black man wanted to know. There were enough hogs, he said, "not to worry about no fleck of meat being left on the bone. Keep treating me like a Mexican and I'll beat him."

The boss walked by just then and the black man lowered his head.

Who Gets the Dirty Jobs

The first thing you learn in the hog plant is the value of a sharp knife. The second thing you learn is that you don't want to work with a knife. Finally you learn that not everyone has to work with a knife. Whites, blacks, American Indians, and Mexicans, they all have their separate stations.

The few whites on the payroll tend to be mechanics or supervisors. As for the Indians, a handful are supervisors; others tend to get clean menial jobs like warehouse work. With few exceptions, that leaves the blacks and Mexicans with the dirty jobs at the factory, one of the only places within a fifty-mile radius in this muddy corner of North Carolina where a person might make more than eight dollars an hour.

While Smithfield's profits nearly doubled in the past year, wages have remained flat. So a lot of Americans here have quit and a lot of Mexicans have been hired to take their places. But more than management, the workers see one another as the problem, and they see the competition in skin tones.

The locker rooms are self-segregated and so is the cafeteria. The enmity spills out into the towns. The races generally keep to themselves. Along Interstate 95 there are four tumbledown bars, one for each color: white, black, red, and brown.

Language is also a divider. There are English and Spanish lines at the Social Security office and in the waiting rooms of the county health clinics. This means different groups don't really understand one another and tend to be suspicious of what they do know.

You begin to understand these things the minute you apply for the job.

Blood and Burnout

"Treat the meat like you going to eat it yourself," the hiring manager told the thirty applicants, most of them down on their luck and hungry for work. The Smithfield plant will take just about any man or woman with a pulse and a sparkling urine sample, with few questions asked. This reporter was hired using his own name and acknowledged that he was currently employed, but was not asked where and did not say.

Slaughtering swine is repetitive, brutish work, so grueling that three weeks on the factory floor leave no doubt in your mind about why the turnover is 100 percent. Five thousand quit and five thousand are hired every year. You hear people say, They don't kill pigs in the plant, they kill people. So desperate is the company for workers, its recruiters comb the streets of New York's immigrant communities, personnel staff members say, and word of mouth has reached Mexico and beyond.

The company even procures criminals. Several at the morning orientation were inmates on work release in green uniforms, bused in from the county prison. The new workers were given a safety speech and tax papers, shown a promotional video, and informed that there was enough methane, ammonia, and chlorine at the plant to kill every living thing here in Bladen County. Of the thirty new employees, the black women were assigned to the chitterlings room, where they would scrape feces and worms from intestines. The black men were sent to the butchering floor. Two free white men and the Indian were given jobs making boxes. This reporter declined a box job and ended up with most of the Mexicans, doing knife work, cutting sides of pork into smaller and smaller products.

Standing in the hiring hall that morning, two women chatted in Spanish about their pregnancies. A young black man had heard enough. His small town the next county over was crowded with Mexicans. They just started showing up three years ago—drawn to rural Robeson County by the plant—and never left. They stood in groups on the street corners, and the young black man never knew what they were saying. They took the jobs and did them for less. Some had houses in Mexico, while he lived in a trailer with his mother.

Now here he was, trying for the only job around, and he had to listen to Spanish, had to compete with peasants. The world was going to hell.

"This is America and I want to start hearing some English, now!" he screamed. One of the women told him where to stick his head and listen for the echo. "Then you'll hear some English," she said.

An old white man with a face as pinched and lined as a pot roast com-
plained, "The tacos are worse than the niggers," and the Indian leaned
against the wall and laughed. In the doorway, the prisoners shifted from
foot to foot, watching the spectacle unfold from behind a cloud of cigarette smoke.

The hiring manager came out of his office and broke it up just before
things degenerated into a brawl. Then he handed out the employment
stubs. "I don't want no problems," he warned. He told them to report to
the plant on Monday morning to collect their carving knives.

$7.70 an Hour, Pain All Day

Monday. The mist rose from the swamps and by 4:45 A.M. thousands
of headlamps snaked along the old country roads. Cars carried people
from the backwoods, from the single and doublewide trailers, from the
cinder-block houses and wooden shacks: whites from Lumberton and
Elizabethtown; blacks from Fairmont and Fayetteville; Indians from
Pembroke; the Mexicans from Red Springs and St. Pauls.

They converge at the Smithfield plant, a 973,000-square-foot leviathan
of pipe and steel near the Cape Fear River. The factory towers over the tobacco and cotton fields, surrounded by pine trees and a few of the old
whitewashed plantation houses. Built seven years ago, it is by far the
biggest employer in this region, seventy-five miles west of the Atlantic and
ninety miles south of the booming Research Triangle around Chapel Hill.

The workers filed in, their faces stiffened by sleep and the cold, like
saucers of milk gone hard. They punched the clock at 5 A.M., waiting for
the knives to be handed out, the chlorine freshly applied by the cleaning
crew burning their eyes and throats. Nobody spoke.

The hallway was a river of brown-skinned Mexicans. The six prisoners
who were starting that day looked confused.

"What the hell's going on?" the only white inmate, Billy Harwood,
asked an older black worker named Wade Baker.

"Oh," Mr. Baker said, seeing that the prisoner was talking about the
Mexicans. "I see you been away for a while."

Billy Harwood had been away—nearly seven years, for writing phony
payroll checks from the family pizza business to buy crack. He was Rip Van
Winkle standing there. Everywhere he looked there were Mexicans. What
he didn't know was that one out of three newborns at the nearby Robeson
County health clinic was a Latino; that the county's Roman Catholic
church had a special Sunday Mass for Mexicans said by a Honduran
priest; that the schools needed Spanish speakers to teach English.

With less than a month to go on his sentence, Mr. Harwood took the pork job to save a few dollars. The word in jail was that the job was a cakewalk for a white man. But this wasn't looking like any cakewalk. He wasn't going to get a boxing job like a lot of other whites. Apparently inmates were on the bottom rung, just like Mexicans.

Billy Harwood and the other prisoners were put on the picnic line. Knife work pays $7.70 an hour to start. It is money unimaginable in Mexico, where the average wage is four dollars a day. But the American money comes at a price. The work burns your muscles and dulls your mind. Staring down into the meat for hours strains your neck. After thousands of cuts a day your fingers no longer open freely. Standing in the damp forty-two-degree air causes your knees to lock, your nose to run, your teeth to throb.

The whistle blows at three, you get home by four, pour peroxide on your nicks by five. You take pills for your pains and stand in a hot shower trying to wash it all away. You hurt. And by eight o'clock you're in bed, exhausted, thinking of work.

The convict said he felt cheated. He wasn't supposed to be doing Mexican work. After his second day he was already talking of quitting. "Man, this can't be for real," he said, rubbing his wrists as if they'd been in handcuffs. "This job's for an ass. They treat you like an animal."

He just might have quit after the third day had it not been for Mercedes Fernandez, a Mexican. He took a place next to her by the conveyor belt. She smiled at him, showed him how to make incisions. That was the extent of his on-the-job training. He was peep-eyed, missing a tooth and squat from the starchy prison food, but he acted as if this tiny woman had taken a fancy to him. In truth, she was more fascinated than infatuated, she later confided. In her year at the plant, he was the first white person she had ever worked with.

The other workers noticed her helping the white man, so unusual was it for a Mexican and a white to work shoulder to shoulder, to try to talk or even to make eye contact. As for blacks, she avoided them. She was scared of them. "Blacks don't want to work," Mrs. Fernandez said when the new batch of prisoners came to work on the line. "They're lazy."

Everything about the factory cuts people off from one another. If it's not the language barrier, it's the noise—the hammering of compressors, the screeching of pulleys, the grinding of the lines. You can hardly make your voice heard. To get another's attention on the cut line, you bang the butt of your knife on the steel railings, or you lob a chunk of meat. Mrs.

Fernandez would sometimes throw a piece of shoulder at a friend across the conveyor and wave good morning.

The Kill Floor

The kill floor sets the pace of the work, and for those jobs they pick strong men and pay a top wage, as high as twelve dollars an hour. If the men fail to make quota, plenty of others are willing to try. It is mostly the blacks who work the kill floor, the stone-hearted jobs that pay more and appear out of bounds for all but a few Mexicans. Plant workers gave various reasons for this: The Mexicans are too small; they don't like blood; they don't like heavy lifting; or just plain "We built this country and we ain't going to hand them everything," as one black man put it.

Kill-floor work is hot, quick, and bloody. The hog is herded in from the stockyard, then stunned with an electric gun. It is lifted onto a conveyor belt, dazed but not dead, and passed to a waiting group of men wearing bloodstained smocks and blank faces. They slit the neck, shackle the hind legs, and watch a machine lift the carcass into the air, letting its life flow out in a purple gush, into a steaming collection trough.

The carcass is run through a scalding bath, trolleyed over the factory floor, and then dumped onto a table with all the force of a quarter-ton water balloon. In the misty-red room, men slit along its hind tendons and skewer the beast with hooks. It is again lifted and shot across the room on a pulley and bar, where it hangs with hundreds of others as if in some kind of horrific dry-cleaning shop. It is then pulled through a wall of flames and met on the other side by more black men who, stripped to the waist beneath their smocks, scrape away any straggling bristles.

The place reeks of sweat and scared animal, steam and blood. Nothing is wasted from these beasts, not the plasma, not the glands, not the bones. Everything is used, and the kill men, repeating slaughterhouse lore, say that even the squeal is sold.

The carcasses sit in the freezer overnight and are then rolled out to the cut floor. The cut floor is opposite to the kill floor in nearly every way. The workers are mostly brown—Mexicans—not black; the lighting yellow, not red. The vapor comes from cold breath, not hot water. It is here that the hog is quartered. The pieces are parceled out and sent along the disassembly lines to be cut into ribs, hams, bellies, loins, and chops.

People on the cut lines work with a mindless fury. There is tremendous pressure to keep the conveyor belts moving, to pack orders, to put bacon and ham and sausage on the public's breakfast table. There is no clock, no window, no fragment of the world outside. Everything is pork.

If the line fails to keep pace, the kill men must slow down, backing up the slaughter. The boxing line will have little to do, costing the company payroll hours. The blacks who kill will become angry with the Mexicans who cut, who in turn will become angry with the white superintendents who push them.

Ten Thousand Unwelcome Mexicans

The Mexicans never push back. They cannot. Some have legitimate work papers, but more, like Mercedes Fernandez, do not. Even worse, Mrs. Fernandez was several thousand dollars in debt to the smugglers who had sneaked her and her family into the United States and owed a thousand more for the authentic-looking birth certificate and Social Security card that are needed to get hired. She and her husband, Armando, expected to be in debt for years. They had mouths to feed back home.

The Mexicans are so frightened about being singled out that they do not even tell one another their real names. They have their given names, their work-paper names, and "Hey you," as their American supervisors call them. In the telling of their stories, Mercedes and Armando Fernandez insisted that their real names be used, to protect their identities. It was their work names they did not want used, names bought in a back alley in Barstow, Texas.

Rarely are the newcomers welcomed with open arms. Long before the Mexicans arrived, Robeson County, one of the poorest in North Carolina, was an uneasy racial mix. In the 1990 census, of the one hundred thousand people living in Robeson, nearly 40 percent were Lumbee Indian, 35 percent white, and 25 percent black. Until a dozen years ago the county schools were de facto segregated, and no person of color held any meaningful county job from sheriff to court clerk to judge.

At one point in 1988, two armed Indian men occupied the local newspaper office, taking hostages and demanding that the sheriff's department be investigated for corruption and its treatment of minorities. A prominent Indian lawyer, Julian Pierce, was killed that same year, and the suspect turned up dead in a broom closet before he could be charged. The hierarchy of power was summed up on a plaque that hangs in the courthouse commemorating the dead of World War I. It lists the veterans by color: "white" on top, "Indian" in the middle and "colored" on the bottom.

That hierarchy mirrors the pecking order at the hog plant. The Lumbees—who have fought their way up in the county apparatus and have built their own construction businesses—are fond of saying they are too smart to work in the factory. And the few who do work there seem to end up with the cleaner jobs.

But as reds and blacks began to make progress in the 1990s—for the first time an Indian sheriff was elected, and a black man is now the public defender—the Latinos began arriving. The U.S. Census Bureau estimated that one thousand Latinos were living in Robeson County last year. People only laugh at that number.

"A thousand? Hell, there's more than that in the Wal-Mart on a Saturday afternoon," said Bill Smith, director of county health services. He and other officials guess that there are at least ten thousand Latinos in Robeson, most having arrived in the past three years.

"When they built that factory in Bladen, they promised a trickle-down effect," Mr. Smith said. "But the money ain't trickling down this way. Bladen got the money and Robeson got the social problems."

In Robeson there is the strain on public resources. There is the sub-standard housing. There is the violence. Last year twenty-seven killings were committed in Robeson, mostly in the countryside, giving it a higher murder rate than Detroit or Newark. Three Mexicans were robbed and killed last fall. Latinos have also been the victims of highway stickups.

In the yellow-walled break room at the plant, Mexicans talked among themselves about their three slain men, about the midnight visitors with obscured faces and guns, men who knew that the illegal workers used mattresses rather than banks. Mercedes Fernandez, like many Mexicans, would not venture out at night. "Blacks have a problem," she said. "They live in the past. They are angry about slavery, so instead of working, they steal from us." She and her husband never lingered in the parking lot at shift change. That is when the anger of a long day comes seeping out. Cars get kicked and faces slapped over parking spots or fender benders. The traffic is a serpent. Cars jockey for a spot in line to make the quarter-mile crawl along the plant's one-lane exit road to the highway. Usually no one will let you in. A lot of the scuffling is between black and Mexican.

Black and Bleak

The meat was backing up on the conveyor and spilling onto the floor. The supervisor climbed down off the scaffolding and chewed out a group of black women. Something about skin being left on the meat. There was a new skinner on the job, and the cutting line was expected to take up his slack. The whole line groaned. First looks flew, then people began hurling slurs at one another in Spanish and English, words they could hardly hear over the factory's roar. The black women started waving their knives at the Mexicans. The Mexicans waved theirs back. The blades got close. One Mexican spit at the blacks and was fired.

After watching the knife scene, Wade Baker went home and sagged in his recliner. CNN played. Good news on Wall Street, the television said. Wages remained stable. "Since when is the fact that a man doesn't get paid good news?" he asked the TV. The TV told him that money was everywhere—everywhere but here.

Still lean at fifty-one, Mr. Baker has seen life improve since his youth in the Jim Crow South. You can say things. You can ride in a car with a white woman. You can stay in the motels, eat in the restaurants. The black man got off the white man's field. "Socially, things are much better," Mr. Baker said wearily over the droning television. "But we're going backwards as black people economically. For every one of us doing better, there's two of us doing worse."

His town, Chad Bourne, is a dreary strip of peeling paint and warped porches and houses as run-down as rotting teeth. Young men drift from the cinder-block pool hall to the empty streets and back. In the center of town is a bank, a gas station, a chicken shack, and a motel. As you drive out, the lights get dimmer and the homes older until eventually you're in a flat void of tobacco fields.

Mr. Baker was standing on the main street with his grandson Monte watching the Christmas parade march by when a scruffy man approached. It was Mr. Baker's cousin, and he smelled of kerosene and had dust in his hair as if he lived in a vacant building and warmed himself with a portable heater. He asked for two dollars.

"It's ironic isn't it?" Mr. Baker said as his cousin walked away only eight bits richer. "He was asking me the same thing ten years ago."

A group of Mexicans stood across the street hanging around the gas station watching them.

"People around here always want to blame the system," he said. "And it is true that the system is antiblack and antipoor. It's true that things are run by the whites. But being angry only means you failed in life. Instead of complaining, you got to work twice as hard and make do." He stood quietly with his hands in his pockets watching the parade go by. He watched the Mexicans across the street, laughing in their new clothes. Then he said, almost as an afterthought, "There's a day coming soon where the Mexicans are going to catch hell from the blacks, the way the blacks caught it from the whites."

Wade Baker used to work in the post office, until he lost his job over drugs. When he came out of his haze a few years ago, there wasn't much else for him but the plant. He took the job, he said, "because I don't have a 401K." He took it because he had learned from his mother that you don't stand around with your head down and your hand out waiting for another man to drop you a dime.

Evelyn Baker, bent and gray now, grew up a sharecropper, the grand-daughter of slaves. She was raised up in a tar-paper shack, picked cotton, and hoed tobacco for a white family. She supported her three boys alone by cleaning white people's homes.

In the late sixties something good started happening. There was a labor shortage, just as there is now. The managers at the textile plants started giving machine jobs to black people. Mrs. Baker was forty then. "I started at a dollar and sixty cents an hour, and honey, that was a lot of money then," she said. The work was plentiful through the seventies and eighties, and she was able to save money and add on to her home. By the early nineties the textile factories started moving away, to Mexico. Robeson County has lost about a quarter of its jobs since that time.

Unemployment in Robeson hovers around 8 percent, twice the national average. In neighboring Columbus County it is 10.8 percent. In Bladen County it is 5 percent, and Bladen has the pork factory. Still, Mr. Baker believes that people who want to work can find work. As far as he's concerned, there are too many shiftless young men who ought to be working, even if it's in the pork plant. His son-in-law once worked there, quit, and now hangs around the gas station where other young men sell dope.

The son-in-law came over one day last fall and threatened to cause trouble if the Bakers didn't let him borrow the car. This could have turned messy; the seventy-one-year-old Mrs. Baker keeps a .38 tucked in her bosom.

When Wade Baker got home from the plant and heard from his mother what had happened, he took up his pistol and went down to the corner, looking for his son-in-law. He chased a couple of the young men around the dark dusty lot, waving the gun. "Hold still so I can shoot one of you!" he recalled having bellowed. "That would make the world a better place!"

He scattered the men without firing. Later, sitting in his car with his pistol on the seat and his hands between his knees, he said, staring into the night: "There's got to be more than this. White people drive by and look at this and laugh."

Living It, Hating It

Billy Harwood had been working at the plant 10 days when he was released from the Robeson County Correctional Facility. He stood at the prison gates in his work clothes with his belongings in a plastic bag, waiting. A friend dropped him at the Salvation Army shelter, but he decided it was too much like prison. Full of black people. No leaving after 10 P.M. No smoking indoors. "What you doing here, white boy?" they asked him.

He fumbled with a cigarette outside the shelter. He wanted to quit the plant. The work stinks, he said, "but at least I ain't a nigger. I'll find other work soon. I'm a white man." He had hopes of landing a roofing job through a friend. The way he saw it, white society looks out for itself.

On the cut line he worked slowly and allowed Mercedes Fernandez and the others to pick up his slack. He would cut only the left shoulders; it was easier on his hands. Sometimes it would be three minutes before a left shoulder came down the line. When he did cut, he didn't clean the bone; he left chunks of meat on it.

Mrs. Fernandez was disappointed by her first experience with a white person. After a week she tried to avoid standing by Billy Harwood. She decided it wasn't just the blacks who were lazy, she said. Even so, the supervisor came by one morning, took a look at one of Mr. Harwood's badly cut shoulders, and threw it at Mrs. Fernandez, blaming her. He said obscene things about her family. She didn't understand exactly what he said, but it scared her. She couldn't wipe the tears from her eyes because her gloves were covered with greasy shreds of swine. The other cutters kept their heads down, embarrassed.

Her life was falling apart. She and her husband both worked the cut floor. They never saw their daughter. They were twenty-six but rarely made love anymore. All they wanted was to save enough money to put plumbing in their house in Mexico and start a business there. They come from the town of Tehuacan, in a rural area about 150 miles southeast of Mexico City. His mother owns a bar there and a home but gives nothing to them. Mother must look out for her old age.

"We came here to work so we have a chance to grow old in Mexico," Mrs. Fernandez said one evening while cooking pork and potatoes. Now they were into a smuggler for thousands. Her hands swelled into claws in the evenings and stung while she worked. She felt trapped. But she kept at it for the money, for the $9.60 an hour. The smuggler still had to be paid.

They explained their story this way: The coyote drove her and her family from Barstow a year ago and left them in Robeson. They knew no one.

They did not even know they were in the state of North Carolina. They found shelter in a trailer park that had once been exclusively black but was rapidly filling with Mexicans. There was a lot of drug dealing there and a lot of tension. One evening, Mr. Fernandez said, he asked a black neighbor to move his business inside and the man pulled a pistol on him.

"I hate the blacks," Mr. Fernandez said in Spanish, sitting in the break room not ten feet from Mr. Baker and his black friends. Mr. Harwood was sitting two tables away with the whites and Indians.

After the gun incident, Mr. Fernandez packed up his family and moved out into the country, to a prefabricated number sitting on a brick foundation off in the woods alone. Their only contact with people is through the satellite dish. Except for the coyote. The coyote knows where they live and comes for his money every other month.

Their five-year-old daughter has no playmates in the back country and few at school. That is the way her parents want it. "We don't want her to be American," her mother said.

"We Need a Union"

The steel bars holding a row of hogs gave way as a woman stood below them. Hog after hog fell around her with a sickening thud, knocking her senseless, the connecting bars barely missing her face. As coworkers rushed to help the woman, the supervisor spun his hands in the air, a signal to keep working. Wade Baker saw this and shook his head in disgust. Nothing stops the disassembly lines.

"We need a union," he said later in the break room. It was payday and he stared at his check: $288. He spoke softly to the black workers sitting near him. Everyone is convinced that talk of a union will get you fired. After two years at the factory, Mr. Baker makes slightly more than nine dollars an hour toting meat away from the cut line, slightly less than twenty thousand dollars a year, forty-five cents an hour less than Mrs. Fernandez.

"I don't want to get racial about the Mexicans," he whispered to the black workers. "But they're dragging down the pay. It's pure economics. They say Americans don't want to do the job. That ain't exactly true. We don't want to do it for eight dollars. Pay fifteen dollars and we'll do it."

These men knew that in the late seventies, when the meatpacking industry was centered in northern cities like Chicago and Omaha, people had a union getting them eighteen dollars an hour. But by the mid-eighties, to cut costs, many of the packinghouses had moved to small towns where they could pay a lower, nonunion wage.

The black men sitting around the table also felt sure that the Mexicans pay almost nothing in income tax, claiming eight, nine, even ten exemptions. The men believed that the illegal workers should be rooted out of the factory. "It's all about money," Mr. Baker said.

His co-workers shook their heads. "A plantation with a roof on it," one said.

For their part, many of the Mexicans in Tar Heel fear that a union would place their illegal status under scrutiny and force them out. The United Food and Commercial Workers Union last tried organizing the plant in 1997, but the idea was voted down nearly two to one. One reason Americans refused to vote for the union was because it refuses to take a stand on illegal laborers. Another reason was the intimidation. When workers arrived at the plant the morning of the vote, they were met by Bladen County deputy sheriffs in riot gear. "Nigger Lover" had been scrawled on the union trailer.

Five years ago the workforce at the plant was 50 percent black, 20 percent white and Indian, and 30 percent Latino, according to union statistics. Company officials say those numbers are about the same today. But from inside the plant, the breakdown appears to be more like 60 percent Latino, 30 percent black, 10 percent white and red.

Sherri Buffkin, a white woman and the former director of purchasing who testified before the National Labor Relations Board in an unfair-labor-practice suit brought by the union in 1998, said in an interview that the company assigns workers by race. She also said that management had kept lists of union sympathizers during the '97 election, firing blacks and replacing them with Latinos. "I know because I fired at least fifteen of them myself," she said.

The company denies those accusations. Michael H. Cole, a lawyer for Smithfield who would respond to questions about the company's labor practices only in writing, said that jobs at the Tar Heel plant were awarded through a bidding process and not assigned by race. The company also denies ever having kept lists of union sympathizers or singled out blacks to be fired.

The hog business is important to North Carolina. It is a multibillion-dollar-a-year industry in the state, with nearly two pigs for every one of its 7.5 million people. And Smithfield Foods, a publicly traded company based in Smithfield, Virginia, has become the No. 1 producer and processor of pork in the world. It slaughters more than 20 percent of the nation's swine, more than 19 million animals a year. The company, which has acquired a network of factory farms and slaughterhouses, worries federal agriculture officials and legislators, who see it siphoning business from smaller farmers. And environmentalists contend that Smithfield's operations contaminate local water supplies. (The Environmental Protection Agency fined the company $12.6 million in 1996 after its processing plants in Virginia discharged pollutants into the Pagan River.) The chairman and chief executive, Joseph W. Luter III, declined to be interviewed.

Smithfield's employment practices have not been so closely scrutinized. And so every year, more Mexicans get hired. "An illegal alien isn't going to complain all that much," said Ed Tomlinson, acting supervisor of the Immigration and Naturalization Service bureau in Charlotte.

But the company says it does not knowingly hire illegal aliens. Smithfield's lawyer, Mr. Cole, said all new employees must present papers showing that they can legally work in the United States. "If any employee's documentation appears to be genuine and to belong to the person presenting it," he said in his written response, "Smithfield is required by law to take it at face value."

The naturalization service—which has only eighteen agents in North Carolina—has not investigated Smithfield because no one has filed a complaint, Mr. Tomlinson said. "There are more jobs than people," he said, "and a lot of Americans will do the dirty work for a while and then return to their couches and eat bonbons and watch Oprah."

Not Fit for a Convict

When Billy Harwood was in solitary confinement, he liked a book to get him through. A guard would come around with a cartful. But when the prisoner asked for a new book, the guard, before handing it to him, liked to tear out the last fifty pages. The guard was a real funny guy.

"I got good at making up my own endings," Billy Harwood said during a break. "And my book don't end standing here. I ought to be on that roof any day now." But a few days later, he found out that the white contractor he was counting on already had a full roofing crew. They were Mexicans who were working for less than he was making at the plant.

During his third week cutting hogs, he got a new supervisor—a black woman. Right away she didn't like his work ethic. He went too slow. He cut out to the bathroom too much. "Got a bladder infection?" she asked, standing in his spot when he returned. She forbade him to use the toilet.

He boiled. Mercedes Fernandez kept her head down. She was certain of it, she said: he was the laziest man she had ever met. She stood next to a black man now, a prisoner from the north. They called him K. T. and he was nice to her. He tried Spanish, and he worked hard.

When the paychecks were brought around at lunchtime on Friday, Billy Harwood got paid for five hours less than everyone else, even though everyone punched out on the same clock. The supervisor had docked him.

The prisoners mocked him. "You might be white," K. T. said, "but you came in wearing prison greens and that makes you good as a nigger."

The ending wasn't turning out the way Billy Harwood had written it: no place to live and a job not fit for a donkey. He quit and took the Greyhound back to his parents' trailer in the hills.

When Mrs. Fernandez came to work the next day, a Mexican guy going by the name of Alfredo was standing in Billy Harwood's spot.

Contributors

Steve Baker is reader in contemporary visual culture at the University of Central Lancashire, England. He is the author of *Picturing the Beast* and *The Postmodern Animal.*

Jacques Derrida is directeur d'études, École des Hautes Études en Sciences Sociales, Paris. He is the author of numerous books and articles, including *Specters of Marx, Of Grammatology,* and *The Gift of Death.*

Ursula K. Heise is associate professor of English and comparative literature at Columbia University. She is the author of *Chronoschisms: Time, Narrative, and Postmodernism* and is currently working on a book on ecocriticism.

Charlie LeDuff is a staff writer and investigative reporter for the *New York Times.*

Alphonso Lingis is professor of philosophy at Pennsylvania State University. He has written widely on philosophy and ethics and has published, among other works, *Foreign Bodies, Sensation: Intelligibility in Sensibility,* and *Dangerous Emotions.*

Paul Patton is associate professor of general philosophy at the University of Sydney. He has translated and written on the work of several French poststructuralist philosophers, including Michel Foucault, Gilles Deleuze, and Jean Baudrillard. He is the editor of *Nietzsche, Feminism, and Political Theory* and *Deleuze: A Critical Reader,* and the author of *Deleuze and the Political.*

Judith Roof is professor of English at Michigan State University. She has written widely on gender, sexuality, and critical theory, and is the author of *Reproductions of Reproduction: Imaging Symbolic Change, Come As You Are: Narrative and Sexuality,* and *A Lure of Knowledge.*

David Wills is professor of English and chair of Language, Literatures, and Cultures at the University at Albany, SUNY. He has written widely on literary theory, film theory, and comparative literature, and his published works include *Self De(con)struct: Writing and the Surrealist Text, Screen Play: Derrida and Film Theory* (with Peter Brunette), *Deconstruction and the Visual Arts: Art, Media, Architecture* (edited with Peter Brunette), *Prosthesis,* and a translation of Jacques Derrida's *The Gift of Death.*

Cary Wolfe is professor of English at the University at Albany, SUNY. His books include *Critical Environments: Postmodern Theory and the Pragmatics of the "Outside"* (Minnesota, 1998) and *Observing Complexity: Systems Theory and Postmodernity* (edited with William Rasch; Minnesota, 2000). His latest book is *Animal Rites: American Culture, the Discourse of Species, and Posthumanism.*

Index